# Finding Pieces of the Puzzle

# Finding Pieces of the Puzzle

*A Fresh Look at the Christian Story*

RONALD A. N. KYDD

WIPF & STOCK · Eugene, Oregon

FINDING PIECES OF THE PUZZLE
A Fresh Look at the Christian Story

Wipf & Stock
An Imprint of Wipf and Stock Publishers
199 W. 8th Ave., Suite 3
Eugene, OR 97401

www.wipfandstock.com

ISBN 13:978-1-60608-567-7

Manufactured in the U.S.A.

*For Roseanne*

# Contents

# Credit List for Images and Maps

Where no source is indicated for an image or a map, the material was located in the public domain.

**World Map**—with permission of Michael N. Dawson (UC Merced)

**Hadrian's Wall**— Ronald Kydd

**Map of Roman Empire 117 AD**

**Map illustrating divisions of the Church**— NASA Satellite image

**Map of the Silk Roads**— NASA Satellite image

**Antonio Emanuele ne Vunda**— with permission of Roberto Piperno and Basilica de Santa Maria Maggiore, Rome

**Maximilian I**

**Desiderius Erasmus**

**Holy Trinity, Long Melford**—Ronald Kydd

**Argula von Grumbach**

**Ziegenbalg Monument**— with permission of Joel Johnson

**Jerusalem Church**— with permission of Janaki Srinivasan

**Ziegenbalg's Grave**— with permission of Joel Johnson

**Paul Cuffe**— with permission of Library of the Religious Society of Friends in Britain

**Friends' Meeting House, Westport, MA**— Ronald Kydd

**Paul Cuffe's Grave**— Ronald Kydd

**Hudson and Maria Taylor**

**The "Lammermuir Party"**

**The Cambridge Seven**

**The Ministry Team at the Azusa St. Mission**—with permission of Flower Pentecostal Heritage Center

**William and Jennie Seymour**—with permission of Flower Pentecostal Heritage Center

# Preface

IN SEPTEMBER 1970 I began the first course I ever taught on the History of the Christian Church. I cringe when I think about some of those first classes, but the students were tolerant. For the last forty years I have criss-crossed through this material in various Bible Colleges, Universities, Seminaries, and less formal settings. Since 2004 the work I have done as Research Professor of Church History at Tyndale Seminary, Toronto has been in a particularly stimulating environment. The allure of the material has become more and more intense. During the years in classrooms, I have developed an approach to the subject which students consistently say they find helpful. Consequently, when my wife, Dr. Roseanne Kydd, encouraged me to get something into writing which demonstrates my view of the Christian Story, I began to listen. Shortly after that my dean, Dr. Janet Clark, said much the same thing. When two clear-headed, powerful women agree on something, I try to pay attention. Five years later, *Finding Pieces* is the result.

In addition to Roseanne and Janet, there are many to whom I wish to express gratitude. First, Mrs. Margaret Yarwood has been helping me buy books for more than ten years now. I now have many key texts on the shelf beside me which would have required a trip to a library previously. Some I could not have found in Canada. Second, Dr. Earl Davey is now Vice-President, Academic at Canadian Mennonite University. In 2008, while Provost at Tyndale University College and Seminary, Dr. Davey provided funding which made it possible for me to work in the archives of Franckesche Stiftungen in Halle/Saale, Germany. Third, Tyndale's Faculty Research Committee twice extended grants to me. The first made it possible for me to attend a conference in Salzburg, Austria in 2009 on the Church of the East and then continue to London, England to work in the archives of the School of Oriental and African Studies. The second grant underwrote a return trip to SOAS in 2010.

Several have read parts of the manuscript and offered expert criticism for which I am grateful. They include Dr. Christoph Baumer, Founding President of The Society for the Exploration of EurAsia, Hergiswil, Switzerland; Prof. George Egerton, Emeritus, Department of History, University of British Columbia; Prof. Donald Goertz, Chair of the Department of Theology and Church History, Tyndale Seminary; and our son, The Rev. Matthew G. Kydd, Priest, Parish of Oxford, Diocese of Ontario. They strengthened specific section in their areas of expertise and pointed in new enriching directions.

A number of people provided important assistance. Our daughter-in-law, Sarah Kydd, located most of the pictures used in the book, adapting maps to my fussy specifications. Our son, David Kydd, carried out several internet searches for me and also read sections of the book, making valuable suggestions. Our daughter, Emilie Kydd, offered some well-placed legal advice, and Ian Kydd, our son, gave unflagging encouragement to me throughout the project.

It is Roseanne, however, who must receive most of the plaudits. She endured innumerable discussions as the project took shape and empathized as I struggled through the writing. Then she read the whole manuscript at least twice. Her trained editorial eye and her Ph.D. in musicology which focused on the language of music criticism helped her to root out many weaknesses in my text. But I didn't always take the advice of my excellent readers. I take responsibility for any errors or omissions.

# Introduction

Bessie Wood knew it was winter. The twenty something was standing in the snow in the middle of nowhere on the northern Prairies. She had come from the comforts of her home farther south because she believed God had called her. It was back in the mid-1920s. She and her colleague, Madge Black, were Pentecostal "lady workers." This new revival movement made a practice of sending women into hard places to plant churches. When I asked Bessie why they did that, she snapped back, "Because women are tougher than men!"

Bessie and Madge's story is remarkable—two young women set down in the expanse of snow, the only resident pastors for miles around to care for a homesteading rural community. No salaries, no transportation, living on care packages from their parents, surviving for part of the winter in the Orange Lodge which had no insulation and no heater, only a wood cook stove, and with a snake in the wall which once slithered out to join them. They did their pastoral calls together and on foot, particularly careful on their visit to a recently-widowed farmer. People such as these are essential to the Christian story which has routinely overlooked them.

Here is another book on the story of Christianity. How can one possibly justify it? There have been thousands upon thousands written already, and countless other thousands of monographs, articles, and essays that focussed on bits and pieces, and they continue to pour off the presses. I am impressed by the work of my colleagues. For example, there is the *Handbook of Church History* edited by Hubert Jedin and John Dolan and published in the 1960s and 70s. Originally written in German by experts in various periods and running to ten weighty volumes, it is an exceptionally helpful work. Earle E. Cairns' *Christianity through the*

*Centuries* has been in print since 1954. It has been used as a textbook in many places around the world, and has sold as many as 200,000 copies.

The understanding of Church history is being carried deeper and deeper through ever sharper questions being directed to a continuously broadening and expanding deposit of sources of every conceivable kind. The "mine sites" are being exploited ingeniously. The vividness and clarity of the answers which are emerging are occasionally breath-taking. Christoph Baumer's *The Church of the East: An Illustrated History of Assyrian Christianity* is outstanding as are Samuel Moffett's two volumes on Christianty in Asia, the seven volumes of *A People's History of Christianity*, edited by Denis R. Janz, and Diarmaid McCulloch's recently-published eleven hundred page book, *Christianity: The First Three Thousand Years.*

The passion for the past grew among Europeans and their children who scattered around the globe. Jewish, Greek, and Christian influences taught them to take previous centuries seriously. Like their compatriots, the Christians of "the West," with exceptions, have been intrigued by what their ancestors and they themselves have done and were doing. They gathered eagerly around their figurative campfires to tell each other their stories. The stories tended to be of the bold and the brave, the high-powered men who strode through jungles or into the councils of the Church or across the Alps, or who stood undaunted before hostile powers to bear witness to their faith. Granted there was the occasional cobbler or Matilda or Elizabeth whose conduct captured attention.

Over the last century those of us who revel in the past ran into a number of seemingly unrelated but powerful trends. There were organizations and ideologies that pushed the 'working class' forward. These were the people who wore blue collars and earned their livings by the sweat of their brows. The upheavals of the economic crises of the 1930s coupled with climatic disaster in parts of the world heightened the starkness of the challenges they faced. Then around the middle of that century a new wave of feminism struck the historical guild along with the rest of western culture. We had to acknowledge that the statistically dominant female component of the human family was virtually absent from our reporting. The pictures we sketched would continue to be inaccurate and distorted unless they were thoroughly revised. Finally, as the century wore on economic realities and international trade, along with the innumerable applications of technology, shrank the globe. "Globalization" became the shibboleth of the world leaders who assembled at Davos, Switzerland.[1] Wherever we lived, we had to concede that people not so different from ourselves lived on the other side of the blue planet and we were their neighbours. It was a bit of a shock.

All of the above, plus a myriad of other influences, have sent those interested in the Christian past, along with many of the human family, back to the sources. Holding the focus on those examining the Christian story, we can observe that the results of their research have been truly enlightening. But there is a problem: fewer and fewer care what happened in the dust-laden past. Technological development hurtles forward at an ever accelerating pace. Social networks and cool devices tumble over each other at a feverish pitch desperate to dominate enraptured markets. With everything driving on fast-forward, who has time to think about the past!

Many of us have felt a growing ahistoricism, but it was Pulitzer Prize-winning American historian Gordon Wood who put some numbers on the table: "From 1970–71 to 1985–86, years when there was a boom in student enrollments, the number of history degrees granted by all American colleges and universities declined almost by two-thirds, from 44,663 to 16,413. A drop in membership of the American Historical Association in the 1970s and 1980s was itself a sign of this weakening interest in history."[2] Wood attributed much of the drop-off in interest to the approach many historians themselves were taking to their work. He saw them turning away from narrative writing toward tightly-restricted, highly-technical social and cultural issues directed to other members of the trade rather than to a wider readership. The big, beautiful books that do appear face a significant problem: how do you get people to open the covers?

I am trying to respond to that problem. I am not writing primarily for members of the "guild." I want to bring human beings from the past and the present together. One can conceptualize history in many ways. At a very basic level, history is the examination of human behaviour. It is about "poor players who fret and strut their hours upon the stage," but, with due respect to the Bard (Shakespeare), they do not then just

1. The World Economic Forum was founded in 1971 and meets annually in Davos. Participants include top business leaders, international political leaders, along with selected intellectuals and journalists. Their goal is to produce a better world.

2. Wood, *Purpose of the Past*, 3.

vanish. In large and small ways, they influence each other and those who come after them.

Regardless of how well-intentioned, no volume can look at every human being who ever lived or every event that ever took place. We have to choose our subjects. Every history book is selective, and this one is, too. No doubt some will feel annoyed with my choices and ommissions. In broad strokes, I am writing a narrative account which focuses on Christianity—the whole of Christianity. If anything sounds like folly, that does, but let me clarify my approach further. I have selected twelve events, twelve dates, and each one is the center-piece of a chapter. A variety of criteria have suggested the dates I have chosen: historical importance, gender of participants, geographical location, race of participants, the nature of the action, and the fact that some have just been overlooked, pieces of the puzzle that slipped under the table and got lost. Admittedly, the selection is somewhat eccentric.

You will find that four chapters deal with material from what we in the trade call the *New Testament* and *Patristic* periods, roughly before about 650 AD. We will go to Jerusalem, Carthage, Nicaea, and Xi'an, China. Two chapters are *Medieval,* the eight hundred years immediately following 650. Baghdad and Clermont, France will be the venues. Two of the events come from the *Sixteenth-Century,* but one is situated outside the West. The locations will be Mbanza, then Kongo, now Angola, and Ingolstadt, Germany. The last four chapters center around events

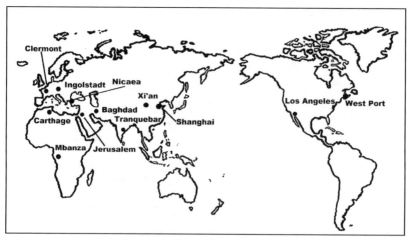

Locations featured in this book

from the next *four centuries*. We will visit Tranquebar, India; Westport, Massachusetts; Shanghai, China, and Los Angeles, Califoronia.

My distribution of energy and space certainly is different from most of the general works on Church History that I read. In addition to the criteria above, it represents my own interests and the sources I have been able to pursue on both sides of the Atlantic. The collections of letters and documents I examined were intriguing. I happen to write my letters often by email in the twenty-first century, but that does not mean that my century is the most important or even the most interesting. To choose one example, seventeenth and eighteenth century Europe, the time of the Industrial Revolutions had an incalulable impact on humanity in general and the Church in particular that has lasted to the present. Their long hand musings with quill and paper can open the door to fascinating times.

My choice of people and events also reflects the difficulties we experience when we try to organize Christian history into periods. We do it so as not to have to deal with the bulk of two millennia of human experience all at once. Roughly speaking, after the New Testament, the chronological divisions we have commonly used are something like "patristics, medieval, reformation, modern, and contemporary." However, various historians put the boundaries in different places. Occasionally it can feel arbitrary, and, it must be added, these eras almost invariably rest primarily on the experiences of Europeans. When non-western parts of the world are taken into consideration, the historical frames become questionable and occasionally completely irrelevant.[3] What does "medieval" mean to a South Asian?

How does my narrative account take shape? The events and dates I have chosen are embedded in a continuous unfolding of the story of Christianity from the beginning to the present. The narrative contextualizes the events and along the way draws attention to the usual canon of personalities and stories which have appeared in histories of Christianity. This has, of course, the tendancy to reduce the significance of the usual array of periods and personalities we have grown accustomed to in Church history and to create a difference balance of emphasis. For example, I am giving more attenton to the period before 1500 than it usually receives.

3. Regarding the dividing of history into periods see Phillps, "Problems of Periodisation Reconsidered," 363–77.

In particular, my approach highlights individual personalities. Each of the events I examine places one individual, and sometimes two, in the spotlight. This brings you, reader, into contact with flesh-and-blood people, women and men you can identify with, and of course, let me say again, that is the essence of history—people struggling with life. The reading of this history is intended to introduce you to historical individuals. This is an attempt to bring the text to life, and it is here where the influence of what has been called social history[4] is most evident. Some of the individuals we will meet were among those who lived out on the margins of their societies and who were largely overlooked. Some were women. On the other hand, some of the others I highlight were safely perched on the social and political peaks of their world, and we will try to get to know them a little better from perhaps a less "textbook" perspective.

I am working with a dominant image—a jigsaw puzzle. One begins by emptying the pieces out of the box on a table and then turning them all face up. I like to do the outside edges of the puzzle first. That establishes the perimeter. Then bit by bit the pieces begin to fit together to build the picture. Sometimes pieces go missing. They fall on the floor or disappear under somebody's coffee cup, or sometimes they just get overlooked for a long time because of how the fit escapes our lens. Occasionally the missing piece is quite imporant—the eye of Frodo Baggins—but sometimes it is not—one of his friend Sam Gamgee's toe nails. It does not matter. Important or not, if you do not find it, you are left dissatisfied with the puzzle. You need all the pieces if you are really going to catch the full impact of the picture the puzzle presents.

Clearly, the image breaks down when you apply it to the Church. One will never have all the pieces, at least not here on earth. But we can already see most of the picture; that is, we know a great deal of the story of the Church. What I am aiming to add are parts of the story that are not familiar to most people, that is, pieces of the puzzle which have been lost or overlooked. So, many of the people we will be focusing on are those who are not widely-known.

I want to be clear about the structure of each chapter. There are three parts to each of them. I will identify them as *Setting*, *Event*, and *Developments*. At the center of each chapter is an event and the person or people who were primarily involved in it. I will be approaching these in as much detail as possible. It is in these parts of the chapters that I did

4. Magnússon, "The Singularization of History," 701–35.

the most biographical research. These are something like Facebook pro-files, but of the dead.The narrative leading up to and then away from the key events will be very different. I will be painting in sweeping strokes, covering hundreds of years in just a few pages by skipping over many details. The figures we have come to love or hate in the usual historical presentations will show up here too, but we will not be spending much time with them. Some may find that troubling.

Furthermore, I am cultivating a global perspective in this study in attempting to avoid privileging western perspectives. The central stories I tell come from many parts of the world, ranging from Jerusalem to Bavaria to Baghdad to Los Angeles. The ongoing narrative reaches even more widely—from Iceland to the Caribbean, from Mongolia to Quebec. We are looking at people who were important or insignificant, but all are projected against the larger background of the world. This global focus starts with the Early Church and will be maintained throughout.

I am also interested in the intercultural experiences of Christians. The idea of mission has been characteristic of Christianity from its be-ginning. Living under the mandate to carry forward the message of Jesus Christ, Christians have reached into the cultures surrounding them in a wide variety of ways. Over and over again with great sensitivity, they have broken through those barriers which separate people groups. The specific stories I highlight and the general narrative of the book draw attention to the challenges inherent in doing this, whether it be Patrick in Ireland or Plütschau in India.

Many have become aware that we have to stretch the way we look at the Christian past. For example, in his recently published *The Changing Shape of Church History,* Justo L. González argued strongly that those who write Church history have got to reach beyond Europe and Europeans. He insisted upon making our treatment of the Christian story "polycentric,"[5] and this call is urgent.[6] The alternative is to perpetu-ate á delusion. Most of the Christian history is still done in the "West." Happily, that is definitely changing. The ongoing western bias is in some way related to the fact that most of the research funding comes from the west. This study resists that tunnel vision.

Sweeping changes in communication and travel have had the ef-fect of collapsing distances. People above the Arctic Circle watch "CSI:

---

5. Gonzáles, *Changing Shape of Church History*, 15.

6. He has also added chapters to his popular text, *The Story of Christianity.*

Miami," and the East in its millions is immigrating to the West, meanwhile the West is increasingly travelling to the East either on business or as tourists. It has become clear to me that the story of Christianity in the non-west has to take its place as an integral part of a whole story we can all tell. There are more historians than ever working on the non-west, but the fruit of their toil has to be integrated into that vast and deepening store of information we have about the Church in the west. We need as complete a picture as possible of the whole story of the whole of Christianity

There are two important reasons why this must happen. First, religion is not declining in importance anywhere on the globe.[7] In fact, its signficiance is growing everywhere. Ruling elites, policy makers, the people who gather at Davos, must take religion with absolute seriousness or their projections will be cripplingly flawed. As I write Egyptians have taken to the streets by the million to challenge their government. Religion will play an important role in the way these events play out.

Second, Christianity is the largest religious family in the world, and it is found throughout the world. This makes it doubly important that the fullest possible understanding of Christianity be available to the greatest number of people as the globe tries to deal with the twenty-first century and its challenges. The responsibility on the shoulders of the historian of Christianity has never been more pressing. Ultimately, we are not talking about personal satisfaction or the approval of one's colleagues. We are talking about life on the planet.

There is an even larger question I have not addressed yet: what kind of a story or puzzle is this? I believe the story of Christianity is the central part of God's working out His love for humanity and His will for the universe. It is God's story, but it is God's story as God relates to His world. To us it is a puzzle. We are called to faith.

I close with a word about the format of dating. I will use the traditional designations of BC and AD. BCE and CE was a generous gesture, but it is still western with an imperialistic flavour. It suggests that the "common" era only came into existence with the birth of Christ and the addition of another religion. Does that mean that before the birth of Christ there was only one religion and not a common era? In fact, there were many religions then. The designation Common Era could be applied equally well to the whole of recorded human history. If one is going

---

7. See p. 241–42 below for relevant discussion and statistics.

to divide time around Christ, as BCE and CE does, it is less confusing to use BC and AD.

# 1

## *Released in Jerusalem*

## *49 AD*

### INTRODUCTION

THE STORY OF THOSE people called Christians is what occupies us here. I have characterized history as the examination of human behaviour, and here we begin a long series of events arising out of decisions large and small which Christians made. The account which unfolds is truly remarkable. It starts with a band of shivering people from what could be called an "under class," and it reveals that in around 250 years this little group had grown into one of the dominant social forces to be found anywhere on earth. What will emerge as this study unfolds is how Christians strode and struggled from their rag-tag origins to be found ultimately in every corner of the globe. In the twenty-first century they belong to the faith group that enjoys the loyalty of many more people than any of the religious alternatives, numbering about 2,292,454,000, or approximately one third of the human family. It is a challenging, amazing story.

One of the most important moments in this development occurred in 48 or 49 AD. It is often called the Council of Jerusalem. The label injects more formality into the occasion than was actually there, but its importance can hardly be over-emphasized. At the most basic level, what the meeting did was define Christianity as a movement with a global mandate. It was a time of release—release from ethnic, cultural, and geographic boundaries. It freed Christians to continue what they

had already begun—go everywhere and anywhere to proclaim the good news of Jesus Christ. Most of what we know about the gathering we find in the *Book of Acts*, chapter fifteen, in the Bible.

Furthermore, most of what took place in relation to the Council of

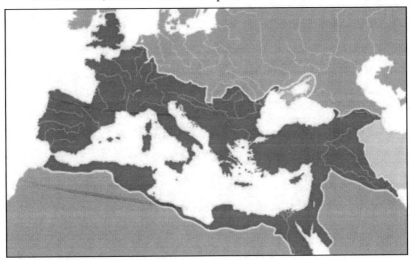

The Roman Empire 117 AD

Jerusalem happened in a particular political context: the Roman Empire. By the time in question that empire stretched from the northern parts of what is now England, south along the Rhine and west to the Atlantic, then east to the Black Sea following the Danube. From there it reached south to approximately the Atlas Mountains at the top of Africa, inland from the Mediterranean Sea, making that body of water a "Roman Lake." The eastern boundaries of Roman power are a little more difficult to describe. Sweeping east the empire included Egypt, what we now call the Holy Land, and then north to take in the whole of what is now Turkey. One of the less stable frontiers of the empire ran down the eastern end of Turkey and past Syria. That border shifted east and west depending on changes in political configurations in the area, but we might take the Euphrates River as the boundary.

As particularly troublesome as that eastern area of the empire was, Rome kept trying to subdue it, to extend the *pax romana*,[1] or Roman peace. The idea of tranquillity brought by Rome's legions is a bit optimistic, but there was a kind of peace imposed by Rome at times and in places within the empire. It rested on the Eternal City's remarkable

1. This is an expression coined in the eighteenth century.

success in developing a daunting military machine. You get a deep sense of the tremendous power of Rome, for instance, when you stand beside the ruins of Hadrian's Wall with its towers and forts in the north of

Hadrian's Wall

England. There it is thousands of miles of Rome, thrown up in a relatively short period of time early in the second century AD sealing off annoying tribes, Picts and Scots, to the north. The short sword of the Roman legionaire enforced order. The closer you lived to the various frontiers, especially in the east, the less likely it was that you could enjoy peace and the more likely you were to experience instability, even horror. On the other hand, if you lived in the imperial hub, Rome, you lived in comparative peace, apart from palace coups and assassinations, and you could satisfy your taste for blood by watching gladiators brutalize each other. And the epicenter was the Emperor, the political and symbolic unifying presence brooding over everything. However, there was another center, a "center of the World" nonetheless, that even emperors had to cope with—Jerusalem.

The significance of Jerusalem was recognized by Greek geographers and even by Rome. When Augustus' indispensible right-hand-man, Marcus Agrippa, created his world map, Jerusalem lay very close to the center. Wolfgang Reinhardt concluded his meticulous study of the population of Jerusalem in the first century AD acknowledging that that number could not be calculated precisely, but saying that "a figure of 60,000 is a conceivable lower limit, though it is more probably that the figure was up to 100–120,000 inhabitants in the forties."[2] Then three times a year that population would have jumped dramatically as pilgrims flocked into Jerusalem for the celebration of festivals. Fiensy suggested that the number coming to these festivals ranged between 125,000 to over 300,000 each,[3] and Reinhardt reached a similar figure, calculating that about 1,000,000 people came annually.[4]

Over many centuries, Jews had left on their own or been wrenched away from Jerusalem violently to settle in many parts of the world. This was the Jewish Diaspora, and it stretched toward all points on the compass. From all directions, said Richard Bauckham, Jerusalem "was the centre to which they travelled on pilgrimage if possible, to which they sent their Temple tax contributions, to which some even returned to settle, and to which, they prayed and expected, the whole Diaspora would be regathered by God in the messianic age."[5] This ebb and flow of masses of worshippers must have reassured the residents of Jerusalem over and over again that they were living at the heart of the world. Its streets were dotted with community centers purpose-built to accommodate pilgrims. It was bicultural marked by Jerusalemites speaking both Greek and Aramaic with the wealthy displaying their "Greekness" ostentatiously in architecture and art.[6]

## SETTING

Having acknowledged the broader context in which these events unfolded, I am going to focus on the specific setting out of which the Council of Jerusalem arose. It happened, of course, during the first generation of Christian experience. We are almost totally dependent on the New Testament for information about that generation. There are a few hints elsewhere, and within the New Testament, the *Book of Acts* plays a major

---

2. Reinhardt, "Population Size of Jerusalem," 263. He had poured over twenty-four other estimates of the population of the city, eleven calculations of the area within Jerusalem's wall at the time, and conducted a study of likely concurent population density. Fiensey concurred with Reinhardt's conclusion (Fiensy, "Composition of the Jerusalem Church," 214.)

3. Fiensy, "Composition of the Jerusalem Church," 233.

4. Reinhardt, "Population Size of Jerusalem," 262.

5. Bauckham, "James and the Jerusalem Church," 418.

6. Fiensy, "Composition of the Jerusalem Church," 231.

role. As a generalisation we can say that the people shown to us in the early chapters of Luke's account come across as a dynamic group. Their experience of God through Christ appears to have eclipsed everything else in their lives. They were convinced that they had seen God in the flesh in Christ; they had felt God's power in what they had experienced of the Holy Spirit. The stories that Jesus' closest followers could tell them of what he had said and done were being circulated orally and perhaps even in writing. They were hanging on them, memorizing and meditating on the details.

Four themes can be identified in Luke's portrayal of the early years of those who gathered around the message of Jesus. First, Luke presented these people as commissioned and empowered by the risen Christ. One telling of the story is found in Luke 24:45–49,[7] but the passage I want to emphasize is Acts 1:8: "But you will receive power when the Holy Spirit has come upon you; and you will be my witnesses in Jerusalem, in all Judea and Samaria, and to the ends of the earth." Laying aside the idea of empowerment for the moment, this mandate has two particular features. In the first instance, it focuses on a person—Jesus Christ. Christ spoke of those who received the command as "my witnesses." The task with the highest priority for Christians was to make Christ known. Acting on what they had seen, heard, and experienced of Christ, they would use whatever legitimate means available to introduce others to him. Further, their authority to act was rooted in their relationship to this person and in his command.

Their mandate also introduced a program, which in a word is mission. There was a geographical expansiveness in what Christ's followers were told. They were to go to the ends of the earth. I wonder how clearly they grasped the challenges embedded in that. It would mean crossing unimagined cultural and linguistic boundaries, a task more difficult even than crossing political borders.

Taking these two features together, we are talking about "translation." The idea here is Andrew Walls'.[8] He used the process of translating one language into another to help us understand what the first generation of Christians (along with all later generations as well) were up against. In Christ God had become human, and he had spoken and acted in a particular place (Palestine) and in a particular time-frame (early first

---

7  See also Matt 28:19–20.

8.  Walls, *Missionary Movement in Christian History*, 26–30.

century AD). Divinity had been "translated" into humanity. Of course God remained divine; a language being translated into another does not disappear in the process either. Furthermore, when you translate a language you can never reproduce in the new language precisely what was said in the first one. There is always that "remainder" that cannot be captured. Along with the cental meanings of words there are these peripheral impressions they carry along with them that you can never quite tuck into a new language.

In Jesus Christ we get the fullest possible expression of who and what God is, limited not by any weakness in God, but by humanity's inherant inability to comprehend God completely. Furthermore, most Christians believe that the clearest presentation of what God was doing through his Son, Jesus Christ, is to be found in the Bible. This has meant that every time Christians have moved across linguistic and cultural boundaries they have felt the need to translate the Bible, and they have done it, over and over again. But that is not the end of the story. Cultures and languages are not set in concrete. They keep changing. So to keep up, Christians have had to continue reviewing and revising the translations. But that is only part of what it means for Christians to translate their message.

Acts 1:8 also talks about power and associates it with the Holy Spirit. This should be seen as a promise that the Holy Spirit will be among Christians. Part of Luke's account of the first Christian Pentecost is Jesus' "pouring out" the Holy Spirit on his followers. (Acts 2:33) The Spirit would be with Christians to do extraordinary things in them and through them. Christians have counted on this through the centuries. But it also means more than this. It means that the Holy Spirit empowers Christians to become like Jesus.[9] Here is transformation at an extraordinary level. The kind of lifestyle laid out in Matt 5–7, in 1 Cor 13, in Phil 2, among other passages, can become a reality in the lives of individual Christians because the Holy Spirit is with them to help them. So, in a sense, just as we can see the life of God in Jesus we can also see the divine life through the presence of the Holy Spirit in the followers of Christ. Ordinary people start to look, act, think, and speak like Christ. This is a

---

9. There is a cluster of New Testament passages which point in this direction: John 14:26; 15:26–27; 16:12–14; Rom 8:29; Eph 4:11–12; 1 Cor 3:16, 6:19; 2 Tim 1:14; Gal 5:22–23. Rowan Williams discussed this in *On Christian Theology*, 115–27.

profoundly important part of the "translation" of Christianity. It is translation involving both texts and lives.

And it seems to have begun very quickly. Early in *Acts* we hear of thousands responding to what the apostles said (2:41 and 4:4),[10] but others are spoken of in ways implying that they were coming in smaller numbers (5:14 and 6:1). They were almost certainly all Jews, and many may have been pilgrims present for the feast of *Shavout*, or Weeks, or Pentecost. A rapidly developing concept in the minds of these followers of Jesus Christ was to see themselves as a newly restored and reconstituted Israel.[11] As pilgrims made their ways home it is likely that some were the first to carry out of Israel the message of the new Messiah and his new People.[12] Later others would have taken the same familiar routes to carry out the commission they had been given.[13]

As a second theme, Luke provided a picture of community development among these early believers. As the book of Acts unfolds, and especially the earlier chapters, we watch what we now think of as the "Church" emerge. There is the initial growth displayed in Acts 2 with massive numbers coming to faith and all of them devoting "themselves to the apostles' teaching and fellowship, to the breaking of bread and the prayers" (Acts 2:42). Everyone we can identify in this first group of Christ followers was Jewish.[14] However, events started to make it apparent that there was something different about them—an astonishing healing, trouble with the authorities, jail overnight, threats. "And after they [Peter and John] were released, they went to their friends and reported what the chief priests and the elders had said to them. When they heard it, they raised their voices together to God" (Acts 4:23–24) and prayed. Peter and John were back among their friends, and something was happening to them all whether they sensed it or not. This was still a Jewish group, but it was becoming quite clear that they shared common ideas and experiences that were setting them apart from the wider community.

---

10. Reinhardt argued that the numbers are entirely credible ("Composition of the Jerusalem Church," 263 and 265).

11. McKnight, "Parting within the Way," 97.

12. Bauckham, "James and the Jerusalem Church," 422 and 426.

13. Bauckham, *Jude and the Relatives of Jesus*, 70.

14. See Acts 3:1.

A remarkable round of activities developed. These early followers of Jesus and their converts kept going to the temple like good Jews, but their daily lives were punctuated by extraordinary happenings, "wonders and signs," and they frequently shared meals, like Jesus and the Twelve had done before his execution. They also were passionately concerned about each other. They shared resources liberally so that Luke could say, "There was not a needy person among them," (Acts 4:34). Furthermore, they learned a sobering lesson about honesty and transparency through the perplexing, puzzling affair of Ananias and Sapphira (Acts 5:1–11). This group was causing a stir. Outsiders did not know what to make of it. On one hand, people were wary of them and held back, but on the other, they were strangely drawn toward them.

In weaving his account, Luke occasionally turned to a third and considerably darker theme—persecution. I have already referred to the first dramatic run in with the authorities; Peter and John had been picked up and jailed for the night in an attempt to keep them from talking about Jesus. Acts 6:1–8:3 shows that the violence soon rose to a much higher level. One of the leaders of the Christian community, Stephen, was seized by a mob and stoned to death. He became the first of a long line of Christian martyrs which stretches right up until the present. The flashpoint was the preaching of Christ. To many who heard Stephen, it felt like an outright attack on their local belief systems, and it threatened religious and social structures as well. People were worried about the impact this new message would have on their communities and families. The response to this threat was swift and effective. It also set a pattern for much of the persecution that has followed from the first to the twenty-first century. These attacks on Christians over time have certainly been official policy by one or other government, but they have more often been the actions of angry groups of people—mobs.

The last of Luke's themes I will mention is outreach to non-Jewish people. A number of passages make mention of this—Acts 8:4, 9:31, 10:1–48, and 11:19–21. There was a kind of informality here. This was not a tightly coordinated program of evangelization. For the most part, people were just looking for safe places away from persecution, and incidentally they witnessed to their faith wherever they found themselves. However, here we come across one of the first of those "translations" I mentioned earlier. In the first Christian community in Palestine Jesus was often referred to as the "Messiah" ("Christ," in Greek). As more and more non-Jews came to faith, and as the message moved farther and farther from Jerusalem, another title started to appear as well— "Lord," lifted out of the Greek translation of the Old Testament. It was used to make the point that God the Father had transferred his name to his exalted son, Jesus. Among Greek-speaking, non-Jewish groups of Christians "the Lord Jesus" became the routine way of referring to the one whom they followed.[15] This meant growth for the Christian community, of course, but it also presented the followers of Jesus with a truly major question—could non-Jewish believers be integrated among Christian Jews?

## EVENT

As we look back at events, it was this talking about Christ with non-Jews which precipitated the crisis and led to the Jerusalem Council. For those involved, as significant as they knew the issue was, they could not have guessed at the massive ramifications of their actions. Luke's record of the conversion of non-Jews was happening most dramatically around Antioch and then in points to the north (Acts 11:19–30; 13:1–14:28).[16] Some Jews insisted that this had to happen through their own religious beliefs and practices: "Then certain individuals came down from Judea and were teaching the brothers, 'Unless you are circumcised according to the custom of Moses, you cannot be saved'" (Acts 15:1). We have come to refer to people who thought like this as "Judaizers." The disagreement over how to treat these "outsiders" who came to faith heated up rapidly and led to significant disruption among Christians in Antioch (Gal. 2:12) and presumably elsewhere.[17] A gathering in Jerusalem became the venue at which the problem would be addressed.

The key player in the discussions was James, the brother of the Lord. The shadows of Peter and Paul, which have engulfed him for centuries have been lifting over the last twenty years, and we are getting to know him.[18] The James I am talking about was the younger brother of Jesus,

15  See Hengel, *Acts and the History of Earliest Christianity*, 105–106.

16.  I note in passing that Christianity started in Asia, the western part, but Asia nonetheless, and everything Luke was describing here was on that same continent. This will become significant later.

17.  In the light of Gen 22:18 and Isa 55:5–7, among other passages, this need not have been a surprise, but those readings are not parts of the recorded discussion.

18.  See Matti Myllykoski, "James the Just in History and Tradition," 79 and Painter,

our Lord, most probably born to Mary and Joseph.[19] Bruce Chilton, joint-editor of one of the recent collections of papers on James, reviewed the range of sometimes conflicting opinions on James and then said,

> James the Just was, in the time between Jesus'resurrection and his own death, the most prominent and widely respected leader in Christendom. His theology, and its corollaries of emotion and practice, were grounded in the Scriptures of Israel and in the conviction that his brother, risen from the dead and installed in divine glory, offered both Israel and the nations the prospect of justice when he arrived to judge the earth (Jas.5:7–8).[20]

The word "christendom" sounds a bit out of place, but his point is clear, and it certainly challenges assumptions about the relative importance of some of the outstanding figures of the first few decades of Christianity. His sentiments were echoed by Scot McKnight: "James was indeed a significant figure, a (perhaps the) dominant leader of the Jerusalem church and the spokesman for the earliest form of Jerusalem-based Christian Judiasm."[21] McKnight also noted that for at least two decades after the resurrection James carried enough weight to be appealed to by Paul in Corinth to strengthen a case of his own.[22]

According to Bauckham, Luke's comment about Peter in Acts 12:17 is significant: "Then he [Peter] left and went to another place." This was Luke's way, Bauckham suggested, of saying that Peter stepped out of the role he had filled as leader of both the community of Christians in Jerusalem and of missionary outreach. Peter did not disappear, but in Luke's narrative he was replaced by Paul in missions and James in Jerusalem.[23] Then, given the central place that Jerusalem occupied in the whole Jewish world, it is not surprising that the Christian community there played a comparable role in the growing Jewish Christian world—and James fit perfectly. Richard Bauckham:

> As permanent head of the mother church, he [James] continued to symbolize the centre while other apostles now represented

---

"Who Was James?" 61. However, it must be noted that W. H. C. Frend at least was acknowledging James's significance in the 1960s—Frend, *Martyrdom and Persecution*, 170.

19. Painter, "Who Was James?" 57

20. Bruce Chilton, "Epilogue," 185.

21. McKnight, "Parting within the Way," 99.

22. McKnight, "Parting within the Way," 100.

23. Bauckham, "James and the Jerusalem Church," 436.

the movement of the gospel out from the centre. James in the period of his supremacy in Jerusalem was no local leader, but the personal embodiement of the Jerusalem church's constitutional and eschatological centrality in relation to the whole developing Christian movement, Jewish and Gentile.[24]

In another place Bauckham suggested James came close to being a "monarchical bishop" in Jerusalem[25]—one with a great deal of power.

Scot McKnight and Richard Bauckham have both commented on the relationship between James and his older brother, Jesus. McKnight was prepared to say that "it was James, the brother of Jesus, who carried on the vision of Jesus in its most consistent form,"[26] seeing "Israel as did Jesus: the new community around Jesus is the eschatological, restored Israel."[27] Bauckham perferred to talk about James' "creative indebtedness"[28] to Jesus and to trace similarities in their moral teachings.[29] Both scholars also compared James as he appeared in Luke's narrative in *Acts* with the James behind the *Epistle of James*, and both found remarkable similarity. Bauckham went on record saying that he could see no serious reason why *The Epistle of James* cannot be what is says it is, an encyclical from James in Jerusalem to Jewish Christians of the Diaspora.[30]

James was executed under Herod Agrippa in 62 AD.[31] Shortly thereafter the Romans laid seige to Jerusalem and took it, destroying the Temple in 70. This catastrophy would have greatly reduced the number of Jews travelling to Jerusalem whether Christian or not. The end of the Bar Kokhba revolt in 135 would have resulted in Palestinian Christianity losing most of its influence.[32] However, James's eminence survived well

---

24. Bauckham, "James and the Jerusalem Church," 450.

25. Bauckham, *Jude and the Relatives of Jesus*, 74.

26. McKnight, "Parting within the Way," 98.

27. McKnight, "Parting within the Way," 113.

28. Bauckham, "James and Jesus," 101.

29. Bauckham, "James and Jesus," 116 and 124–29.

30. Bauckham, "James and Jesus," 106. Peter Davids left the door open for that possibility (Davids, "Palestinian Traditions," 34).

31. Possibly for being a *maddiah*, a deceiver of the people who leads them away from God. (Bauckham, "For What Offence Was James Put to Death?" 232).

32. Bauckham, *Jude and the Relatives of Jesus*, 93.

into the second century as demonstrated by the range of very diverse groups that appealed to him.[33]

These people and events completed the setting for the Council of Jerusalem. One group of participants included those from Antioch, led by Paul and Barnabas, who took an inclusive position. They wanted to find a way to be able to welcome the Gentiles in. The Judaizers were on the opposite side of the issue. The apostles and elders led by James, the brother of the Lord, were somewhere in the middle. It is not clear if the meeting lasted hours, days, or weeks. There seems to have been plenty of discussion (Acts 15:7), including what were probably lengthy comments from Peter (Acts 15:7–11) and Paul and Barnabas (Acts 15:12). They all talked about their ministries among non-Jews. In the cases of all of them, the results had been dramatic. There had been miracles and there had been many who came to faith. The stage was set for a resolution to the problem, and everyone must have been hoping that it would not take too long to find. It came from James. Acting in full authority, he said "I have reached the decision that we should not trouble those Gentiles who are turning to God" (Acts 15:15).

In the first part of the solution he offered, James shifted the focus of the discussion from action, in this case evangelization, to the foundation of the action, theology, and in this case that meant the way we think about the end of time, eschatology. James wanted the group to focus on what God might be doing through them instead of what they, themselves, were doing. The question implied in James's intervention was not "How should we handle Gentile converts"? but rather, "When God completes his purposes and brings time to a close, who will make up the people of God"? The Old Testament passage he cited is Amos 9:11 and 12: "On that day I will raise up the booth of David that is fallen, and repair its breaches, and raise up its ruins, and rebuild it as in the days of old; in order that they may possess the remnant of Edom and all the nations who are called by my name, says the LORD who does this."

McKnight granted that the interpretation of the text "can be reasonably assigned to James,"[34] and Richard Bauckham moved far beyond that, offering a superb treatment of James' argument. Noting how James framed the Amos passages by alluding to other prophetic material in the Old Testament, he emphasized that James wanted to demonstrate that

33. Painter, "Who Was James?" 61.
34. McKnight, "Parting within a Way," 102.

Gentiles did not have to become Jews in order to be included in God's eschatological people. There were two critical points in the interpretation. First, the Messianic Temple ("booth"-v.11) must be understood as the Christian community. Second, the phrase "over whom my name has been invoked" ("who are called by my name" in the translation I have used) should be seen as it often appears in the Old Testament to indicate a people with whom God has a covenant relationship, that is, who are people who belong to God. Understood in this sense, Amos 9:11–12 "states that the nations *qua* (as they are in themselves) Gentiles belong to YHWH" (God). Precisely as 'all the nations' they are included in the covenant relationship (God's name has been invoked over them)."[35] The Gentiles could not enter the old Temple without becoming Jews, but they can enter the New Temple (the Christian community) as just what they are, Gentiles.

The second part of James's proposal was equally important. It is Acts 15:20—"We should write to them to abstain only from things polluted by idols and from fornication and from whatever has been strangled and from blood." Bauckham pointed out these prohibitions are exactly the commandments applied to non-Jews living among Jews, "resident aliens," in Lev 17 and 18.[36] These non-Jews who were becoming Christians would be welcomed in the New Temple, that is, in the restored Israel, and they would be expected to abide by these prohibitions. James' decree both upheld the Law of Moses—the Jewish Christians would keep it as they already were, and specifies for non-Jewish Christians what freedom from the Law means for them. They would not have to become Jews, but they would be expected to keep the prohibitions the Law laid on resident aliens.

Bauckham closed his discussion of the decree by saying, "All the evidence suggests that the apostolic decree was generally accepted by Jewish Christians as authoritatively defining the relation of the Gentile believers to the Law of Moses."[37] This resolution made the Council of Jerusalem an event of crucial significance in the whole story of Christianity.

---

35. Bauckham, "James and the Jerusalem Church," 457–58.

36. Bauckham, "James and the Jerusalem Church," 459.

37. Bauckham, "James and the Jerusalem Church," 470.

## DEVELOPMENTS

This event was a release for Christianity. It would not be restricted exclusively to a particular ethnicity. Consider the following: Jesus was Jewish. All the originative moments of the new faith occurred in Israel. The sacred books of the Hebrew people provided the framework within which these new religious claims had to be interpreted. In the light of all that, it was understandable if people assumed that there were very real ethnic, cultural, geographic, and religious boundaries to the worship of this young Messiah who lived, died, and rose from the dead in the midst of Israel. But it was not to be. The Council of Jerusalem took all those kinds of brakes off the movement that was growing up around the resurrected Jesus Christ, and it spread.

The expansion of Christianity was partly strategic and partly incidental. In the *Book of Acts* there were the Pauls and Silases, the Barnabases and Marks who chose to leave families and friends explicitly to evangelize and bring others to the faith. As they appear in *Acts,* they were anointed and led by the Holy Spirit, feeling privileged and compelled to proclaim the good news wherever God willed, and Luke presented them as they took a north-west route into the Greek and Latin worlds. Those who went to the east would have found a way open for them. Having reviewed developments east of Jerusalem in the centuries prior to the appearance of Christianity Amir Harrak said, "The Near East, from Palestine to Babylonia and from Upper Syria to Jerusalem, was a compact region, monolingual, and mostly unified culturally. This being the case, the missionaries who undertook the Christianization of Upper Syria and Mesopotamia had simply to take normal trade routes to disseminate their religious beliefs."[38] So there were favorable conditions, and not only for missionaries who were eager to evangelize.

Some of the others who left Jerusalem in the early days of Christianity did so because things got too hot. They were refugees. The antagonism that grew up in Jerusalem around them and toward them propelled out a wave of people looking for safety (Acts 8:1–40 and 11:19) some time around 40 AD. Then about twenty years later the insurgency related to the Roman occupation of the area increased with the violence ending in the destruction of Jerusalem in 70 AD. In the run up to that calamity, many more Christians looked for shelter

38. Harrak, "Trade Routes and the Christianization of the Near East," 51.

elsewhere. However, we do have to remember that, as far as the sources can show, Christians were not facing red-hot persecution constantly. In fact, there seems to have been a period lasting from before 40 AD until after 60 AD when conditions were comparatively calm, and life went on with a tolerable level of normalcy.

That meant, first, that Diasporan Jews could continue to come and go to and from Jerusalem. As the Christian community in Jerusalem became more numerous, better structured, and more certain of itself it is possible that an increasing number of the Jewish pilgrims encountered the idea of a New Israel centered around Jesus Christ while they were in Jerusalem. Converts may have increased and then taken the message home with them.

Second, in a period of acceptable calm it would have been "business as usual." What that means is merchants continued to exploit the web of routes that criss-crossed the area. Harrak argued that it is very likely that merchants following those routes played a significant role in planting Christianity across the Near East, perhaps being the ones who opened up new lands for their faith. Harrak noted that Jews in the area did precisely that and then said, "The Christian neighbours of the Babylonian Jewry merely did the same. Thus, if trade routes were carriers of religions through the ages, it is not a far-fetched scenario that Christianity too spread out in greater Mesopotamia and beyond through trade routes."[39]

Well then, what did this preaching of the faith actually look like? I only wish we could know. Apart from what we find in the New Testament, the details elude us. Luke lets us follow Peter and then Paul and their associates, and we have the canonical epistles and the canonical gospels. However, outside of that fairly narrow historical frame, for decades the progress of Christianity was in the shadows. Then when the lights do come on, that is, when there actually are sources that we can examine, they shine on only a very small proportion of Christians who carried their faith with them. In other words, we just do not have many sources which let us see what Christians were doing and thinking in the early decades. In spite of all that, there are some comments we can make.

As should be clear already, initially the outreach was primarily Jewish. As an example, we can look at Rome. Some of the Jewish pilgrims in Jerusalem on the first Christian Day of Pentecost were from Rome (Acts 2:10). Then later, when Paul wrote his letter to Christians in

39. Harrak, "Trade Routes and the Christianization of the Near East," 57.

Rome, a significant number of them were Jewish. It is conceivable that some who embraced Jesus as messiah as recorded in Acts 2 went home to Rome and shared their new-found faith with family and friends. And remember those who fled Jerusalem had in face of troubles? They probably did what refugees throughout the centuries have done—scurry to relatives in safer places who could help them.

It must also be said that the first pulses of Christian dispersion were almost totally uncoordinated. Acts 8:4 puts it powerfully: "Now those who were scattered went from place to place, proclaiming the word." It was something like wind blowing dry leaves rather than a chief of staff planning a military campaign with subordinates. People went where there was a lower degree of danger so that they and their families might find a little bit of security. As they went they talked about Jesus. In the midst of turmoil and dislocation there were countless acts of "translation" as the word about the Christ spread.

It is worth thinking a little further about the actual experience of these early Christians. As they went, they had very few resources which would help them with their faith. Birger Gerhardsson has argued that as Jews they were part of a literate society insofar as they had been trained to memorize texts.[40] This may be true, but it is also true that the only texts those among the early waves leaving Jerusalem had were in their minds. Old Testament manuscripts were too expensive, and what would become the four accepted gospels existed only in gradually emerging oral or written collections of sayings and acts. For their part, the epistles were in the process of being written and winning their way to status as scripture at the same time. Those departing Jerusalem early believed in God; in Jesus as God's son; in salvation available through the life, death, and resurrection of Jesus; in baptism and a sacred meal, and in the restoration of a New Israel. There were probably other ideas commonly held, but not too many, and they would not have been marked by much precision.

As these early Christians finally made their ways to relative security, they were faced with many new challenges, pretty basic things like language and culture. For however long they stopped, they were the "foreigners," or some less kind epithet, their reception varying from place to place and time to time. Eventually some explanation of themselves and

---

40. For example, see Gerhardsson, *Memory and Manuscript*, 79–84 published first in 1961. See also his "Secret Transmission," 1–18.

their presence would have been necessary. In many cases, the conversations had to be carried on in a partially understood trade language, perhaps Syriac or Sogdian, or in some other language in which they were just beginning to learn their way. Of course, the languages were embedded in cultures, and the newcomers might have found them deeply puzzling, too. Sooner or later the conversations turned to theology. After all it was their new beliefs that had led to the need to leave home in the first place. They then discovered that the trade language, or the partially known local tongue they were trying to use, did not handle the abstract explanation of whom the "Lord Jesus" was very well. This discovery opened up an even greater challenge.

From our perspective this flegling group had less than afirm grip on anything approaching a system of beliefs. Nor did they have resources to help them. There were no sacred texts at hand in most cases, and there were no helpful study guides. They found themselves becoming theologians with virtually none of the preparation now assumed necessary. On top of that, for many of these wanderers it was impossible to communicate with anyone who was more grounded in the faith than they were. It was a long way back to Jerusalem. This meant that there was inevitably some floundering as they tried to explain themselves and the ideas, doctrines, that had brought them to wherever they were. The stage was set for some pretty unusual explanations of Christianity.

It is almost certain that if a few of these followers of Jesus stayed together for some time in whatever place, they realized there was a need to establish methods of social interaction among themselves. Groups of humans begin to sense who the leaders and who the followers are. In other words, organization appeared. The first patterns to emerge were likely the tried and true, the familiar ones. As Jews, they called their leaders "elders." If there was Greek influence present, others may have opted for "episcopos," or "bishop" in English. Eventually three offices became fairly common, bishops, elders, and deacons, but they certainly appeared at different times in different places.

Accordingly, social organization was added to some expression or expressions of what they believed which in turn rested on sacred words, teachings, and memories that they held in their hands or in their heads. And that was all connected to Jerusalem and its surroundings, "home" for the Jews, but a bit of a mystery to Gentile converts. This collective memory involved not only concepts but also standards of behaviour which may have tended to isolate them socially. If this clustering offered relief in their own language, culture, beliefs, and memories, it no doubt also set them apart, highlighting their differences from the communities in which they were now living.

## CONCLUSION

The picture I have sketched is, of course, largely tentative, even speculative. There are virtually no sources which throw any light on the actual experience of many, if any, of these early Christians as they searched for places to live in peace and preached the gospel along the way. What we have are, on one hand, the documents of the New Testament. They give us some light on some Christians in some places at various times, but they most certainly do not take us everywhere Christians were and they do not help us beyond the mid-nineties at the latest. On the other hand, when we move into the second century, we find a growing body of solid historical sources which give us some information about what Christians were experiencing and what they were were doing and believing. In other words, in the second century, here and there, the lights start to come on. In the portrayal I have given above, I am reaching forward and then reading back into the shadows, trying to picture what might have led to the kinds of developments we see when we actually have sources to build on.

Those involved at the time might have had only the vaguest feeling that what they were going through was a release. For some of them at least it probably meant profound and frightening change. They were a movement. Some social psychologists have described a movement as a group of people gathered around central ideas and experiences which they are sure will make their lives better. Movements are polycephalous (have many leaders), segmented (are made up of many different clusters), and reticulate (united in a loose network). That describes the first generation of Christian believers fairly well. Added to that, the power of the Father released through Jesus Christ and the Holy Spirit made them dynamic.

2

# Martyrdom in North Africa

## *203 AD*

### *INTRODUCTION*

T HE RANGE OF EMOTIONS Christians felt as they left Jerusalem in the
thirty or so years after Jesus had departed must have been extraordinarily wide—sorrow, frustration, relief, isolation, maybe even excitement. Some had decided to make their escape when Saul (later Paul)
launched the attack which Luke recorded in Acts 8 and others, twenty
years later, when it became obvious that Rome was going to lay siege to
the city at any moment.

Others in between these two times of danger were scurrying away
eagerly. They had come as pilgrims to worship at the old Temple, but
now they could not wait to tell family and friends that they had become
part of the New Temple since they had accepted the young rabbi, Jesus,
who had risen from the dead as their Messiah. In that twenty or so years
of relative calm, others had gone and come back and gone again as either
evangelists preaching a message or as merchants hocking their wares—or
as both at the same time. Still others likely just left because they thought
it was a good time go somewhere else and put down roots.

All of them were facing a demanding level of novelty in practically
every area of their lives, and of course some coped with that better than
others. The farther they travelled from Jerusalem, the more difficult it
was to maintain contact with people back there. Those who had no plans
to return must have felt this keenly. There is no way of knowing exactly

how many did leave, precisely where they went, or how they handled the challenge. The sources are silent. Many of the ones who were fleeing persecution or war were likely members of intergenerational family units. Where possible, they headed to someone who could take them in and shelter them—usually kith and kin. However, they still had to travel strange roads among suspicious strangers in order to get there, and then to varying degrees they had to face cultural and linguistic difficulties just to eke out livings. The merchants and the missionaries quite likely had calculated the risks, but there is no doubt that they, too, met circumstances which stretched them.

That is what life looked like for many Christians in the later part of the first century and well into the second. The focus of this chapter is the turmoil and uncertainty that was the context of their faithful witness. I am using an event which occurred in Carthage in the Roman province of North Africa to convey a sense of the challenges they faced. We will take the three steps you will see in each chapter of this book. First, the focus will be really wide looking at the setting in which the event took place. Then it will narrow to the event and the people involved. Last, the focus will open again with an examination of developments which unfolded subsequent to this event.

## SETTING

The boundaries of our discussion will be the Roman Empire set out in the first chapter. Remember the *pax romana* and the sheer dominance of the Roman Empire and its legions? The Emperors were the key figures. Typically, these men were intensely ambitious, highly entrepreneurial risk-takers whose egos would fill an amphitheatre, and they were ruthless. Some exhibited significant mental and social pathologies, but there was at least one philosopher among them, Marcus Aurelius. Mind you he could be ruthless, too.

The Emperors were the political, cultural, and religious center of the Empire. They were the guarantors of a legacy that stretched back to the founding of Rome in 753 BC by Romulus and Remus, and they were expected to guard it jealously. Loyalty to them was demonstrated by an occasional sacrifice to the emperor's *genius*, a kind of guardian spirit which Romans believed were with people from birth. That could be no more than a pinch of incense tossed on an altar. A collision was inevitable—somewhere the absolute head of state and the Absolute Lord (Jesus Christ) would meet.

For awhile, Christians were able to 'fly under the radar' because people thought they were Jewish. On the basis of local and regional arrangements, Jews had been able to negotiate exemptions from Roman religious observations which conflicted with their own. In Roman eyes, the Jews were a readily-identifiable ethnic group with a significant level of cultural homogeneity and with a passion to preserve tradition. Romans could identify with some of that, perhaps sparking a touch of sympathy. However, Christians soon started to slip out from under this umbrella with people noticing differences between them and what they thought the Jews were. Christians appeared to be multi-racial; they were disturbingly closed, even secretive; and people began to suspect that they were getting organized

Real trouble came in the shape of would-be-musician and actor, Emperor Nero. Around 60 AD it was rumored that he ordered some houses burned to make way for a palace he wanted to build. The fire reduced much of Rome to ashes. Trying to avoid a backlash, he blamed it on the Christians whose large numbers made them a ready target. These Christians, including the apostles Peter and Paul, were viciously murdered. What was the trumped up charge? W. H. C. Frend's masterful study showed that it is tricky to determine that. The people of Rome thought the Christians were guilty of *odium generis humani*—turning your back on other human beings.[1] It is more likely that Nero just sent in the police on grounds that Christians belonged to some kind of superstitious secret society.[2] His persecution quickly became deeply embedded in the story of the Church, serving to create the impression that there was something criminal about Christianity.

There might also have been trouble in the 90s AD when some have thought that Emperor Domitian acted against members of the Roman upper classes who had become Christians. Certainly, tension between the Absolute Lord and the absolute head of state was building, and it erupted around 110. In correspondence between Pliny (the governor of a Roman province in what is now northern Turkey) and the emperor of the day, Trajan, a discussion was carried on regarding what to do with people who confess to being Christians. The result was something like

1. Frend, *Martyrdom and Persecution*, 162.
2. Frend, *Martyrdom and Persecution*, 166.

imperial policy: do not hunt Christians; prosecute only on legally valid evidence; if people convicted of being Christians refuse to disown their faith, execute them.

Other persecutions in which Christians were tortured and died followed. They probably occurred in many places, but those in Asia Minor, Rome itself, and Lyons and Vienne (south-eastern France) serve as examples. They were local, they involved lynch parties, they caught the attention of Roman officials, and they were brutal. Some Christians crumbled and denied their faith, but for others, remaining true was the ultimate counter-cultural act. Christ owned them, not the emperor, even if it meant fire and blood. The stage was set.

## THE EVENT

Six young people—four men and two women. We know very little about the men, but the women have clearly-developed personalities. One is Felicitas, a pregnant slave. There are no clues about the father of her child—a husband? Maybe, but more than likely the man who owned her. The other, Vibia Perpetua, the star of the story, is a twenty-two year old with character.

Perpetua came from a family of five—mother, father, herself, and two brothers, one of whom had died. She is credited with writing the document that tells her story, so her family must have been willing to make sure she received some education. Along with that, her father was capable of interrupting legal proceedings and speaking eloquently, giving some indication that he enjoyed considerable status. Perpetua was breastfeeding an infant son. This adds pathos and confusion particularly because the child's father is never mentioned.

As the narrative opened, five of the six in the group of young people were arrested solely on the suspicion of being Christians. The authorities must have been very worried about Christianity. In some undefined sense, they were seen as "terrorists" who threatened their society. And why just them? There were other Christians who were not picked up. Did somebody rat on them or was it just random violence on the part of some Roman official? The arrest immediately touched off passion.

Perpetua's father broke into the scene. He was horrified at what was happening to his daughter—understandably, and he tried to persuade her to get out of it, to disown any connection with that Christian bunch. Here we get a glimpse of her character. She pointed to a vase or a pot nearby and asked him, "Can it be called by another name?" When he muttered "No," she continued, "I am a Christian, and neither can I be called by any other name." The word "Christian" almost drove him crazy, but he got a hold of himself and left.

Somehow Perpetua was baptized—by whom? how? She was in a hole of a dungeon, crowded, hot, dark, and worst of all, she did not know where her baby was. In the midst of that, we get the first glimmer of her spirituality. She said she was "inspired by the Spirit" not to ask for any favors, but to endure. She experienced God speaking directly to her. We will hear more of this later, but help eventually came from another source.

Two leaders of her church, deacons, were able to offer concrete assistance. At some personal risk, they talked to the jailers and bribed them. Perpetua and her friends were moved to a better part of the prison and given some privacy. Best of all, her baby was brought to her and she was able to care for him. Her mother and brother were also able to visit her, and that brought both comfort and agony. Together they were able to make plans for her son, but her mother and brother were torn by fear and sorrow as badly as her father was, and that in turn drove a spike through Perpetua's heart. However, she had her child and conditions were better. In fact, she could say, "My prison had suddenly become a palace, so that I wanted to be there rather than anywhere else."

She felt herself to be on intimate terms with God, and prompted by her brother, she asked God to show her how things were going to turn out for her. She got her information through an extremely vivid vision. This suggests she was living in a spiritual world that was intense, immediate, almost concrete. God was "right there," all around her, saturating her. People have seen this as evidence that she belonged to an early Christian prophetic movement called Montanism. It is more likely that the whole Christian community of North Africa throughout the first half of the third century was very familiar with this kind of experience.[3]

3. Very little is known about the Christian community in Carthage in the first half of the third century outside of Perpetua's story, the writings of a contemporary of hers and possibly her editor, Tertullian, and the literary remains of the famous mid-third century bishop, Cyprian. Tertullian certainly valued the kind of experiences Perpetua talked about. However, much more important is the experience of Cyprian. He, himself, placed great weight on the visions he had and in addition to that, contemporaries of his addressed him as a prophet.

Pressure on Perpetua built as her father returned. Beside himself he cried, "Daughter, have pity on my grey head—have pity on me your father!" As well as his abhorrence of what awaited his daughter, the issue of shame was present. They belonged to a well-placed family in a relatively homogenous culture. There was shame in someone turning her back on the 'old ways' to join a bizarre 'cult.' "Give up your pride!" he screamed, "You will destroy all of us! None of us will ever be able to speak freely again if anything happens to you," and he meant it. Yet out of love he fell before her, kissing her hands. She did not yield. He left, and worse followed.

The prisoners were summoned before the governor, but Perpetua's father reappeared, her son in arms. He pulled her off the steps to the altar and begged her to "Perform the sacrifice—have pity on your baby!" Just a pinch of incense—that would do it. The governor added his voice to her father's, trying to persuade her to take this tiny step which would relieve everybody. He was just a functionary obediently carrying out an unpleasant job. He did not want to kill this girl. But, no. Under questioning, she eagerly confessed that she was a Christian, and, along with the others, she was sentenced to die by being exposed to wild animals. Surprisingly, they went back to their prison rejoicing.

Now something happened that only a nursing mother can really understand.

> My baby had got used to being nursed at the breast and to staying with me in prison. So I sent the deacon Pomponius straight away to my father to ask for the baby. But father refused to give him over. But as God willed, the baby had no further desire for the breast, nor did I suffer any inflammation; and so I was relieved of any anxiety for my child and of any discomfort in my breasts.[4]

Events pile on top of events. Perpetua's father came again in great agony and Perpetua had a rush of more dramatic visions. In one she was permitted to understand her persecution at great depth. Her mortal combat would not be with a Roman magistrate or an emperor, but with the devil, himself. Her opponent was a fierce, dark-skinned Egyptian; the conflict was overseen by a trainer who fantastically towered above even the amphitheatre; the prize awaiting her was a green branch with golden apples, and, strangest of all, when her handsome, young assis-

---

4. *Martyrdom of Saint Perpetua and Felicitas*, p. 115.

tants prepared her for the bout, she discovered she was a man. The fight started, and after an astonishing performance, she won. Bathed in the adulation of her assistants and the crowd, she received the branch and started the victorious walk toward the Gate of Life. She closed the account of her experiences by saying that when she 'awoke' from the vision she knew she would be victorious in her upcoming battle.

The editor now related another vision. This one was recorded by Saturus, one of the male prisoners. He saw himself and Perpetua after their deaths in the amphitheatre and said to her, "This is what the Lord promised us. We have received his promise." They were in heaven. The scene which unfolded is replete with angels and chanting choirs, and they were welcomed by God. They were swept with rapture and joy, seeing many of their martyred friends. They also got to help sort out a misunderstanding between their old bishop and an elder.

The other young woman, Felicitas, now entered the story. She was in prison, going through the same process, but she was almost eight months pregnant. As a pregnant woman, she would be spared execution until after the birth. She would miss dying with her friends, and that caused her great distress. They all prayed that God would undertake. "They poured forth a prayer to the Lord in one torrent of common grief." She immediately went into labour and gave birth to a baby girl whom she surrendered to the care of a Christian woman who would raise her.

They were granted a "free meal" customarily given to condemned criminals or gladiators who would shortly enter the arena. A mob gathered to watch them eat, but they turned the meal into a "love feast," a celebration with fellowship and rejoicing. They also turned it into a moment for witness, reaching to those standing amazed at their courage.

We get a further sense of Perpetua's pluck. She prodded a guard who had treated them miserably, pointing out that they are special prisoners, "seeing that we belong to the emperor (Geta); we are to fight on his very birthday."[5] The guard realized it would be a good idea to have them looking as good as possible for the occasion and started to treat them better. Later as they reached the gates of the arena attendants tried to force them to parade into the arena in the robes of pagan priests and priestesses. Perpetua would have none of it. She protested, "We came to this of our own free will, that our freedom should not be violated. We agreed to pledge our lives provided that we would do no such thing. You

---

5. *Martyrdom of Saint Perpetua and Felicitas*, p. 125.

agreed with us to do this."[6] She was a Roman appealing to a Roman on Roman procedure, and she won. They were permitted to enter as they were dressed.

This amphitheatre has received careful archaeological study.[7] It is an intimate little place with the seats as near as possible to the action offering excellent sightlines for all. Those people sitting there were not just spectators—they were participating actors in a life and death drama, and did they ever play their part.

The Christians stepped out onto the sand, and they preached! The men turned to the crowd and to the governor, himself, and warned them of the judgment and condemnation that awaited them from God's hand. The enraged mob screamed for blood, and the Christians had to run a kind of gauntlet, being flogged by gladiators.

Then it was on to the wild animals. The men were mauled, but survived. With exquisite irony a mad heifer was reserved for the two young women. They were stripped naked and ordered into the arena in nets. "Even the crowd is horrified when it sees that one is a delicate young girl and the other is a woman fresh from childbirth with the milk still dripping from her breasts."[8] The soldiers took them out and clothed them in tunics before bringing them back to the heifer where they are thrown, gored, trampled. Then something happened which must have silenced the mob.

Perpetua rolled over and sat up. She tugged her tattered garment around her to regain her modesty, and she—asked for a pin to fix her disheveled hair! This was her moment of triumph; she must not appear to be mourning. She climbed off the sand and made her way to where Felicitas lay in a bloody heap. She helped her to her feet, and propping each other up, they turned to face whatever else was coming.

But the blood lust of the mob was satisfied for the moment, and the women were led out. Then to the amazement of those who heard, Perpetua started as though she had been asleep and asked when she was going to face the animal. She had to be shown her wounds and her torn dress before she would believe it had already happened.

6. *Martyrdom of Saint Perpetua and Felicitas*, p. 127.

7. On your computer type "Carthage Amphitheatre" and/or find it on Google Maps©. Look for Carthage in Tunisia on the north coast of Africa.

8. *Martyrdom of Saint Perpetua and Felicitas*, p. 129.

The end was near. The mob demanded to see their deaths. The condemned rose and assembled where they would die, bruised, broken, bleeding, one unconscious from blood loss. They shared their hope and their love with kisses of peace. It was probably the short, little Roman *gladius* which then came into play. It was a sword whose design and use had been perfected through countless campaigns. Now it is turned on tortured, quiet, calm Christians. Silently, one by one they fall at the hand of an awe-struck, young gladiator. He came to the last—

> Perpetua, however, had yet to taste more pain. She screamed as she was struck on the bone; then she took the trembling hand of the young gladiator and guided it to her throat. It was as though so great a woman, feared as she was by the unclean spirit, could not be dispatched unless she herself were willing.[9]

The mob sat in silence as the pool of red grew in the sand.

It is quite a story. It portrays a step of ultimate counter-culturalism. The Absolute Lord, Jesus Christ, meets the absolute state, personified in the emperor of the day, Geta. It was war between the Kingdom of God and the kingdom of this world. The battle was in Perpetua's heart. The 'front' was her skin. There was no doubt in her mind about who would win. With the short slash she expected to feel, she would find herself worshiping around the very throne of God with those who now lay in the sand beside her.

## DEVELOPMENTS

To catch the significance of this spell-binding event as strongly as we should we need to step back for a moment. The first and most important feature of the context is the kind of thing that was going on in the hearts of these young people. These were not theologians, these were not leaders of their groups of believers, these were not landowners, these were not scholars. They were kids who had met God through Christ in the power of the Holy Spirit. It probably never occurred to them to put it together that way, but that's who they were. They were the saints of Heb. 12 of whom the world was not worthy. And as such, they represented the vast majority of Christians who were scattered around the Mediterranean basin and beyond in all directions. We will never know the names of this host of people, but they were there and their

9. *Martyrdom of Saint Perpetua and Felicitas*, p. 131.

experiences of new life in Christ shaped everything that would happen in the Church. Shaped everything.

The leaders, the bishops, priests, deacons, and theologians I will talk about, served this anonymous, multidimentionally-diverse mass. They got their agendas from these people. Commentaries on the Bible were written to help those whom they led. Leaders explained the faith to those whom assembled with them. They took cues from these people in the worship for which they all gathered. No one person or class controlled the Church. All who gathered out of some degree or quality of faith contributed to making the Church what it became. So what was happening? Everything. The balls were all in the air, and as they juggled, leaders and people alike kept finding more balls up there—more challenges.

When we look back at them, we see that Christians found themselves at a period in time when many, many important issues were screaming for attention. It is not clear if the complexity of their situation had sunk in or if concerns were just grappled with as they arose, and those concerns would have come up out of different circumstances at different times in different places. Furthermore, Christians did not have the luxury of choosing to work on one issue for several months while everything else was on hold. Practically nothing was decided, nothing was fixed. Everything had to be dealt with at the same time on the fly.

Leaders and people alike had to find a way of living in the midst of the political powers around them. It became critical to get a firm sense of whom they were and how they would be governed. The question of sexuality demanded attention as did what the respective roles of men and women in the organization would be. Decisions had to be make about what would be in their sacred literature, and what was to be done during their times of worship just had to given careful thought. These were some of the questions that demanded answers. And I have not even mentioned one of their biggest concerns—what do we believe? I am just going to bracket that one out and deal with it later, something they could not have thought of doing.

Relating to the political powers was one pressing problem. By this time Christians were living under the rule of Romans, Parthians, and assorted other tribes and dynasties. In some places they were experiencing the influence of the surrounding culture strongly, and, to use a sociological buzz word, their organization, the Church, was institutionalizing. As so many other minority groups throughout history, Christians were trying to reduce tension between themselves and everything around them. Like most of the others who have done this, members of these Christian groups were likely unaware of what was happening. They were just trying to make life more liveable.

Looking specifically at conditions within the Roman Empire, we note on one hand that the empire was imposing its values by force. There were the persecutions. What Nero, Domitian and the other emperors did and what the young people we have just looked at went through illustrate that. On the other hand, there were Christians who were deciding that some of Rome's values were pretty attractive. In other words, the Church, as early as the late first century and in the very midst of extremely hostile times, was starting to find ways of reducing tension, looking for ways to fit in a bit. This was going on even as it resisted pressure from the outside. This was paradox in spades.

There is some reason to believe that Christians as a group, at least in places, were moving up the socio-economic ladder. Writing about 150, the converted philosopher, Justin said, "Those who are well-off and are willing to give" donate money to the leaders of the group who distribute the offering to those in need.[10] One is not surprised to hear a reference to the needy, but the fact that some could be identified as "those who are well off" is noteworthy.

Justin, whom I just quoted, was one of a new category of Christians—an "apologist," one who interpreted, or defended, or gave an explanation of something. He aimed his two apologies for Christianity at the very top of the Roman society. Among others, Athenagoras, Tatian, and Tertullian were doing the same thing. They were all profoundly committed Christians, and they all knew the Greco-Roman world thoroughly. They spoke to the relatively thin stratum of decision makers and *literati* at the top of that world, and their very existence testifies to the fact that Christianity was on the rise socially and economically.

There were other Christians as powerful as them who were prepared to go at least as far as the apologists were. Clement of Alexandria, who lived about the same time as Tertullian, was one of these. You find a shift in mood as you read his works. Writing in north Egypt around 200 AD, he was on the offensive. Using his rich education in mythology, philosophy, and literature to build a case for the superiority of the Word of God, Jesus Christ, he wrote in very high quality Greek. Along the way

10. Minns and Parvis, *Justin*, 261.

he cheekily lampooned Greek religion and culture mercilessly. Aiming his salvos at the upper classes, he clearly expected to be read.

Another, Callistus became an aggressive Bishop of Rome early in the third century. Shocking for the time, he was prepared to bring back into church fellowship those who had committed sin after baptism. But where he stepped across the line as far as Roman custom was concerned appears to have been in marriage practice. There were prohibitions in Rome of transclass marriages. Disregarding that, Callistus permitted aristocratic women and "inferior" men, even slaves, to come together, and he endorsed their unions as marriages even though they were illegal in the eyes of the state.

Christians were still vulnerable to violence in many forms, but as a group things were changing. Numbers were increasing, members were to be found in the upper eschalons of various communities, and some were acquiring considerable wealth. Their cadre of leaders included some very articulate, powerful people. These Christians were sharply discriminating about the Greco-Roman culture of which they were parts, but they were also learning how to use the economy, the educational opportunities, and even some social institutions to their own advantage. In the midst of the uniqueness that persisted in the struggle to understand themselves, they were adapting to the world around them in various ways and various places.

Nonetheless, tensions between them and their non-Christian milieu were still there. To the East, beyond the Euphrates, Christians had been able to settle and grow without the kind of harassment that broke upon them sporadically in the West. That changed for awhile starting about 225 AD, and they suffered under the weight of official disapproval.[11] The first official attempt at the containment of Christians in the west erupted about twenty-five years later under the emperor Decius and his successor Valerian.

There was more than a whiff of imperial paranoia in this. Christians were everywhere. They were increasingly cohesive, and they were still disturbingly closed to casual outsiders. On top of that, there was too much swagger about some of them. Perhaps those tough-minded critics we have looked at may have been ruffling some feathers. These Christians had to be brought to heel.

---

11. Baum and Winkler, *The Church of the East: A Concise History*, 8.

Emperor Decius and then Valerian went after the leaders and the sacred books. They also imposed a policy requiring all citizens to have a certificate showing that they had sacrificed to the imperial genius and the traditional gods of Rome. The emperors did not break the Church, but they did create difficult times. After a period of relative peace across the empire, the smell of burning incense and the glint of swords came as a terrible shock. Some stood true and died or were tortured in prison. Many others cowered, denying their faith. Others bought certificates from friendly officials ready to be bribed. It made church life particularly challenging for awhile as people who had bought safety stood to worship beside others who had been tortured, the 'confessors,' or beside the families of those who had paid the ultimate price of loyalty to Christ.

The next big issue to be reviewed is the matter of self identity. In the late second century, the "catholic" church appeared. This was not a name that anyone sat down and chose. What appears to have happened was that as people moved around, or heard from other places, they became aware of a set of ideas that was emerging in different areas. The content of this set of ideas was being called the *regula fidei*, the rule of faith. It was not very clearly defined, but it is likely that its substructure had been inherited from Judaism from which a basic understanding of God had been taken over. Added to and modifying this was belief in Jesus as the divine Son of God who was crucified but raised from the dead to bring God and humanity back together. They embraced the idea of a holy book, a rite of baptism, and the practice of the eucharist, or Lord's supper. These convictions were likely expressed in different ways in different places, and it is possible they had other ideas included among them in various locales. There was diversity from village to village, but they may have become aware of a range of acceptable diversity. And then, here and there were ideas that were shockingly different, the kind that kept leaders awake at night.

On the other hand, the ideas many leaders could feel comfortable with, those beliefs that could be found in many places, came to be thought of as 'universal.' The Greek word for universal was "catholic." So the beliefs that were common in many different places were "catholic" ideas, and the people who believed them were "catholics." The network to which these people belonged came to be seen as the "catholic church"— the network or fellowship of Christian believers whom you could meet in many, many places.

Along with the awareness of a Catholic Church (note the capital letters now), internal structures began to emerge. By the early third century, the episcopacy was established in most communities of believers. Episcopacy is the name for a form of church government in which ultimate authority resides in bishops. The idea has roots in the New Testament, but was first promoted most strongly by Ignatius, Bishop of Antioch, early in the second century. He argued passionately for a church structure in which the bishop was at the top with two other "orders" beneath him, the presbyters (elders) and the deacons.

However, this pattern was not the norm everywhere in the first half of the second century. There is even a hint that the Christian community in Rome was led by a group of elders into the middle of the second century as opposed to just one bishop. At the same time there may have been one who was dominant among those elders. Nevertheless, it is clear that by the third quarter of that century the pattern of bishops, elders, and deacons was becoming the norm. Irenaeus of Lyons, whom I mentioned earlier, was sure that the orderly succession of bishops was a key in asserting that the ideas found in that *regula fidei* were the ideas that Jesus taught. He believed they were passed from our Lord to the apostles, and from them to those who were appointed by them to lead particular groups of Christians, and from them to their successors, and so on. Irenaeus even provided lists of bishops for the more important churches around the Mediterranean.

Bishops, then, had become a common feature of Christian communities, and people talked routinely about a 'catholic' church. As we move through the third century another structural development becomes obvious. For centuries Rome had dominated western Europe politically. The Christian community in Rome began to make claims to religious precedence, too. Through a rough and tumble series of events, the idea caught on, and as we pass mid-century the Catholic Church, at least in its Latin and western form, was well on its way to being the 'Roman' Catholic Church.

Christians were improvising as they went along with very little to call on for guidance. They had been a movement earlier and in some respects they still were into the middle of the third century, but they were 'maturing'—a euphemism for tightening up, developing institutional procedures and controls. But we must never forget, underneath and behind it all were the people intimately involved in all these developments.

Behind these structural issues, there was a myriad of other questions simply demanding attention from Christians. One of them had to do with sexuality and the body. Christians of the time were taking hold of all kinds of ideas about sex, more liberal in Rome and more conservative in North Africa, but most conservative in the east.

Among many at the eastern end of the Mediterranean and beyond, sexual intercourse in any context, marriage or otherwise, was unacceptable. Tatian, generally viewed as acceptable doctrinally on other points, was one who held this view, and so was Marcion whose ideas about God were so far from the norm that he became known as a 'heretic.' Others were the little, unknown folks who provided markets and audiences for that strange genre of literature now known as the *New Testament Apocrypha*.[12] Some who held this extreme position were tagged with the name 'Encratites,' meaning people who practice extreme self-denial. They probably made up a much larger part of the Christians from Syria and Egypt and eastward than is usually realized.[13]

In fact, some Christian leaders insisted on monitoring much more of Christian life than just sexuality. Clement of Alexandria would have liked to exercise control over clothing and shoes worn by both women and men, and even over hair styles and shaving practices. His contemporary, Tertullian, was prepared to offer a list showing which occupations were acceptable for Christians and which were not, with the primary issue being the association of particular trades and professions with idolatry.

And then there were women. Male leaders were at pains to regulate them, too.[14] The irony, of course, is that the intensity of the male arguments shows that there must have been women, perhaps many of them, in prominent roles in groups of Christians in the early third century. For example, there was a woman in Tertullian's church who seems to have seen visions fairly often during worship. However, she was not permit-

12. See the introductory material in *New Testament Apocrypha* in two volumes, revised edition edited by Wilhelm Schneemelcher and also Richard Bauckham, "Apocryphal and Pseudepigraphical Literature," 68–73.

13. See Brown, *The Body and Society: Men, Women and Sexual Renunciation in Early Christianity.*

14. See the study by Karen Jo Torjesen, *When Women Were Priests: Women's Leadership in the Early Church and the Scandal of Their Subordination in the Rise of Christianity.*

ted to share them in the service. She had to wait until the meeting had broken up and then tell the male leadership what she has seen.[15]

The standard procedure at the time was to see active women as doctrinally wayward. That is what Firmilian, a correspondent of Cyprian of Carthage, thought. It was also a major part of the criticism leveled against that most misunderstood prophetic movement known as Montanism. Two of the three original leaders of this groups which appeared in what is now Turkey were women.[16] Nor should Thecla be overlooked. This powerful and beautiful young woman appears in the apocryphal *Acts of Paul and Thecla.* As part of her highly dramatic story, she baptizes herself and then later is commissioned by the Apostle Paul to go and preach the Gospel. Of course this 'tale' comes from the apocryphal material which is legitimately viewed as being out on the margins of Christianity, but that is where powerful women seem to be finding themselves by this time.

This was a tremendously important period for Christianity. Not only was all of the above taking place, but Christians were also identifying their scripture. They had not come out of the first century empty handed. They had brought what they were beginning to view as the 'Old Testament.' They carried books which contained the carefully memorized and preserved words that Jesus had spoken along with accounts of his actions. They had other books bearing the names of leaders from the first generation of Jesus' followers whose memories they cherished. All of these were making their ways towards an authoritative list, a canon.

At the same time Christians were developing patterns of worship. The sources do not make tracing that development easy, but it was under way. Sunday, 'the Lord's Day,' had been chosen as their primary day of meeting. They may have borrowed some ideas from Judaism, but exactly what shape that may have taken is difficult to determine. Reading sacred writings, preaching, participating in the Lord's Supper, all of those practices were important. Along with that, the spontaneous manifestation of the spiritual gifts was still to be found in Christian worship.

In all of these issues with which Christians were grappling, the religious experiences of all of them were playing a key role. Christians were conscious of meeting the Father, through the Son, in the power of the

15. Tertullian, *A Trestise on the Soul*, Ch. 9.

16. See Trevett, *Montanism: Gender, Authority and the NewProphecy* and Tabbernee, *Montanist Inscriptions and Testimonia: Epigraphic Sources Illustrating the History of Montanism.*

Holy Spirit. It was a dynamic time. This sensitivity to God helped them hear the voice of God as scripture was read. In fact, because they heard it so clearly in some of the material which was circulating, they were prompted to read that material again and again while they laid other writings aside. In a sense, it was a case of texts choosing readers rather than readers choosing texts. These believers knew that God was with them all the time and especially present when they gathered to worship. This immediacy stimulated words, postures, and practices. They were not laying down their lives for an abstract concept. These people were surrendering to a living reality.

## CONCLUSION

There can be no doubt that there was a breadth of diversity among those who named the name of Christ, stretching as they did from the North Atlantic to the deserts and steppes of Central Asia. Their ideas about God ranged along that spectrum of acceptable diversity; they worshipped in different languages and different forms; within limits, their mores of suitable Christian behavior varied, but their day-to-day experience with the communities around them could still crash down into a life-and-death struggle without warning. Jesus is Lord—of that they were clear.

# 3

## *Orthodox and Powerful*

## *325 AD*

### INTRODUCTION

Two words which could be used to describe Christianity thus far are "pluriformity" and "marginal." Paul Bradshaw used the first to describe Christian worship in the first few centuries—it came in many forms. The same thing can be said about practically everything else Christian: spiritual experience, the manner of talking about beliefs, suitable clothing, which books should be in the Bible, jobs that were appropriate, and what should be done about marriage. The second word indicates that Christians were out on the edges of society wherever they lived.

All of this was about to change. Certainly Christians were consciously trying to make things better on all levels, but they could not in their wildest dreams have imagined the way events were going to unfold. What a classic case of making the best decisions you can in the light that you know while not knowing what you do not know. As always the future held a big surprise.

Specifically, we will be watching a remarkable blending of the sacred and the profane, of Christianity and political power. The consequences are with us yet. Christianity will shift from the shadows of the western world to center stage and in the process, launch an optimistic attempt to ensure that all Christians will be on the same page doctrinally. And a key player will wear imperial purple. By the way, nothing like this ever happened in the East—in Asia, the land east of Jerusalem. But more, much more, of that later.

## SETTING

Conditions under which Christians initially left Jerusalem were bound to impact the way in which they talked about their beliefs. Remember— there were no sources apart from sayings and accounts that had been memorized and personal religious experience; very little possibility of maintaining contact with home or with others who went in different directions; in many cases relatively low levels of literacy and education; uncertainty about what was to be viewed as Scripture; anxiety caused by danger and unfamiliar surroundings; having to explain themselves and their beliefs to people whose language and culture were strange to them. Given all of this, it would not have been surprising if what these people believed got more than a bit scrambled.

And it certainly did. The histories of theology make this abundantly clear. The garden of Christian thought was alive with exotic and extraordinary plants. One of the groups, the Nazoreans, was made up of "born Jews who observed the Law out of tradition, but believed in Christ."[1] Their observation of the Law meant they practiced circumcision, worshipped on the Sabbaath, and perhaps avoided pork.[2] Boyarin thought that they functioned "much as the mythical 'trickster' figures in many religions."[3] in their blending of features from different cultures. Non-Jewish Christian groups were at least as interesting. The Docetists believed that Christ's body was a kind of phantom. Marcion dropped the whole Old Testament and all of the New except for the Gospel of Luke and ten of Paul's epistles, aggressively edited incidentally. Starting from a Jewish-Greek base, different groups that we now call Gnostic merged a range of ideas from unrelated philosophies and religions, teaching that secret knowledge could awaken a spark smouldering in a person and lead to salvation.

This is just an inadequate sketch comprising a fraction of the ideas that were floating around, but it gives a bit of an impression of what people were facing. Many, probably all of them actually, were trying to

1. Kinzig, "'Non-Separation,'" 33.
2. Kinzig, "'Non-Separation,'" 32.
3. Boyarin, "Rethinking Jewish Christianity," 23.

hold onto the teaching of the apostles as they understood it. Irenaeus, in south-central France around 180 AD, and Tertullian, North Africa just after 200, come to mind. The former emphasized the "rule of faith," a kind of early creed of essential beliefs; and the latter, in the midst of a fruitful and colorful career, talked about God as one substance in three persons using the word "trinity," a concept which is still current.

The Alexandrian, Origen (185–251), was famous among his contemporaries as one who defended and explained the Truth. He received invitations from far and wide to serve as a kind of theological trouble shooter. He was the first Christian systematic theologian, the first person to try and make sure he had the best text of the Old and New Testaments possible, the first to exploit the idea of commentaries on biblical books, and the first to provide guidance about cultivating the spiritual life. That is an impressive list of "firsts" for one person to chalk up. However, he was also a creative, innovative thinker. He was prolific in floating ideas—like trial balloons—which were angrily pricked about three hundred years after his death. Faced with a teeming thought world, he and the others sought ways of talking about Christian faith which would be faithful to what Jesus Christ and the apostles taught and lived, but new challenges emerged.

Early in the fourth century, Donatism, another variation of Christian themes, burst on the scene in North Africa. During a persecution some people had turned copies of the scriptures over to the Roman authories to be destroyed. Those who did this were call *traditores*, traitors. Donatus and others thought that if anyone had done that he had made himself ineligible to become a bishop, and they protested strongly when a *traditor* was elected to the office. They believed that anything this person did, administer the sacraments, preach—anything—could not possibly have any spiritual value.

Theology here got mixed up with racial and cultural issues. The Donatists tended to be from the indigenous population of North Africa, Berbers. The other side tended to be Latin speakers from Roman families which had settled on the southern shore of the Mediterranean for longer or shorter periods of time and ran the area. The conflict became violent, and in response about 315 the troops were sent in to suppress the Donatists. However, they were pulled out after five years because the popular insurrection was too strong to contain. In fact, the Donatists survived until the seventh century. The Emperor Constantine was deeply involved in this, and we are on the way to the Council of Nicaea (325 AD).

*EVENT*

In the run up to the Council of Nicaea, we need to become acquainted with Emperor Diocletian. He served as Roman Emperor from 284 to 306 AD. One of the great challenges every emperor faced was maintaining the loyalty of generals who served under him while at the same time trying to rule a sprawling empire. It was not uncommon for a victorious general in some far flung corner to decide that he would make a better leader of the world than the incumbent. At that point it was a matter of mobilizing his legions to march on Rome and overthrow the emperor. The cost in blood shed and mayhem is obvious.

Diocletian's idea was the "Tetrarchy," or rule by four. He divided the empire into an East and West section and placed an Augustus over each half. He took the East. He then divided each half in half again keeping one section for each Augustus, and appointed east and west Caesars who would manage the remaining two sections, each under the leadership of the respective Augustus. Diocletian was the senior authority, and each of the others owed his power to him. The system ran smoothly, at least most of the time.

One of the other problems Diocletian faced was the Christian Church. It was a movement—polycephalous, segmented, and reticulate. It was everywhere in the empire, and far beyond. In fact, it was growing, and it had acquired a kind of a swagger. Diocletian decided to destroy it. He issued increasingly vicious edicts aimed at wiping out Christianity. In the east, the orders were carried out effectively and many died, but in the west very little happened. The Augustus there was Constantius, and there seem to have been Christians in his family.

One of his children was Constantine. He was born c. 274 and he was raised to wield power. In the 290s he compaigned with distinction in a war the Romans fought against Persia in the east side of the empire, and then he spent the next few years at Diocletian's court, also in the east. Passed over in the selection of a caesar in 305, he headed for Britain and spent a year with Constantius, his father, teaching those impertinent Scots a lesson. When Constantius died on July 25, 306, Constantine insisted that his father had raised him to the rank of Augustus, and he claimed authority over Britain, Gaul, and Spain. The dominant Augustus, Galarius, recognized him only as a Caesar. Constantine took it and bided his time. As Timothy Barnes said, "Implacably ambitious, Constantine was determined to become sole ruler of a united Roman Empire."[4] What was going on in his mind? He had a lust for power—the man was a politician after all—but was he also thinking about the Christians?

The first person who stood in Constantine's way, whatever his overall plans were, was his fellow caesar, Maxentius. Moving deliberately—he took years in fact—Constantine led his troops across France, consolidating his position as he went. He led his army over the alps and through north Italy. Then came what seems to have been a pivotal moment in his life. On the march, he and his troops saw a cross of light in the sky accompanied by the words "In this conquer." The next night Christ appeared to Constantine in a vision bringing the same sign and instructing Constantine to make standards for the army that looked like the cross in the vision.[5] On October 28, 312 AD his forces met Maxentius's in the Battle of the Milvian Bridge just north of Rome, and he was gloriously victorious. There's a mural in the Vatican showing Maxentius and his steed sinking beneath the waters of the Tiber while Constantine sits astride his mount and gazes at him, probably feeling rather smug. This was the defining moment in Constantine's rise to power.

The previous year Constantine and the Augustus of the East, Licinius, had issued an edict from Milan granting toleration to Christians. Licinius seems to have been humoring Constantine to keep him at bay because up to then he had been brutal in his attack on Christians, and he continued his assault even after the edict. Another edict was proclaimed in 313, also from Milan, in effect granting freedom of conscience throughout the empire. The previous year Constantine had taken control of the whole western half of the empire, and he now trained his cross hairs on the east. Successfully disposing of Licinius and others, he gathered the whole empire into his hands in 324 AD. The eastern frontier of the empire was the most volatile, so Constantine decided to locate there. Renaming a town on the Bosphorus "Constantinople," he created a new Rome with wide promenades, marvelous arches, wonderful buildings. Nothing was overlooked. There had to be magnificence suitable to his grandeur. A new era in Roman history opened. This was the beginning of what became known as the "Byzantine Empire." It was called that because Constantine had built his city on the village of Byzantium. The

4. *Constantine and Eusebius,* 29. I am relying heavily on Barnes here.
5. Barnes, 43.

Byzantine Empire lasted until 1453, but at this point it was still officially the Roman Empire.

Constantine demonstrated a keen interest in the Christian Church. What the motivation was is debatable. On one hand, some time before the Battle of the Mulvian Bridge he may have embraced his mother's faith. He had brought the persecution of Christians to an end and now he wanted to be a blessing to the Church. On the other hand, like Diocletian he knew that the Church pervaded his empire and reached beyond it. It was increasingly organized, it preached peace, and it was ecstatic at having the sword lifted from its neck. The empire was a sprawling, multicultural, hard to govern mass, and Constantine needed all the help he could get to keep it together. If he could keep the Church on his side and happy, he might find he had an important ally in maintaining peace and order. He chose a "hands on" policy towards the Church.

His mother became the most famous pilgrim to the "Holy Land." She discovered the actual cross on which Jesus had been crucified and the nails that had fixed him there.[6] She also found the place of the crucifixion, the grave that Jesus left empty, and the manger/stable/cave in which he was born. Constantine ordered that fabulous copies of the whole Bible should be prepared, and it is possible that several of them still exist. He made large sums of money available for key church buildings. The architectural style of choice was the Roman basilica. It offered open space where large numbers of people could gather and it featured a central dias which focused attention on the most important person in the building. The structure which the emperors loved spoke of majesty and cosmic power, traits many bishops found strangely attractive.

It was Constantine who in 314 AD at a meeting of bishops held in Arles on the south coast of France ordered legionnaires into North Africa to shut down the Donatists. He was trying to maintain peace in the Church and in an important part of his empire at the same time. In 318 he formally elevated bishops to a position comparable to judges in the empire's civil service. This gave them authority they never dreamed of having and helped smooth out the administrative procedures of the empire.

There were considerable perks that went with the office. Bishops could now sit on a throne, wear a crown or mitre and a gold ring, be greeted by chanting choirs as they entered their basilicas, have their portraits hung in offices, be served by people with veiled hands, and have

6 According to Sozomen, "Ecclesiastical History," 258–59.

others who approached them first prostrate themselves before them and then kiss their feet.[7] This was a long, long, long way from those earlier brother bishops who had their heads clicked off or who died doing slave labor in salt mines. What a difference a Christian emperor made. The impact of these events continues to ripple in our world.

How can one really come to understand a man like Constantine who carried great responsibility and who held unimaginable power? Why is he even in this study? He is certainly not one of the little people, one of the pieces that has been overlooked. He is here because he is the first of a particular breed of the people who are called Christian—a politician. There have been many of them since. It is noteworthy that this first one was one who came to wield absolute power. How does that go together with Jesus of Nazareth? Did Constantine ever think about that? He was creating a role as he went along. He had no models, and quite possibly very few who would dare offer negative opinions of his performance. As a kind of a windfall, he gives us an opportunity of ponder questions about the blending of the kingdoms of this world with the Kingdom of God, questions that are relevant not only to him but to everyone since who has dared to try it. In Constantine we meet claims to deep religious experiences, excessive largesse to the Church, and the expenditure of considerable time on the affairs of the Church. One would like to hope that in the heart under that moulded leather breastplate there was something authentic, something sincerely Christian that can be recognized as such. But there is so much that is contrary—the violence, the naked manipulation, the insatiable ambition. Pictures have been crafted of Constantine that are critical to the point of cynicism. Can one identify in Constantine a true faith that sometimes wavered or fell short of his own standards, or of ours? Can we live with a fully human person who is both an imperfect Christian and a shocking political figure? When trying to evaluate Constantine how can one not take into consideration the pecularity of living a life that was focused from birth on weilding absolute power? How would sincere Christianity appear in a man brought up to live like that?

Then onto the stage came Arius, and Constantine had to get involved again. In the western world we like to think that what you believe is your own business. Do not bother other people, and no one will bother you. In early fourth century Alexandria nothing could have been

---

7. Klauser, *Short History of Western Liturgy*, 32–37.

further from this "live and let live" philosophy. There and then theological disagreements could precipitate riots and often did.

A respected elder of the Christian community there, Arius, began to teach that Jesus Christ, the Son of God, was not an eternal being, but had been created by the Father. His bishop, Alexander, could not tolerate this, and strongly continued to affirm that the Son was, in fact, as eternal as the Father. This boiled up into a major theological row. Both sides wrote leaders in other cities soliciting support and both sloganized. "There was when he was not," cried Arius to which Alexander replied, "There was not when he was not." The argument certainly divided the Alexandrian Christian community, but it threatened to result in a much broader rift among Christians. The whole eastern end of the Mediterranean was polarizing behind either Arius or Alexander. Theological argument was destabilizing cities and regions.

There was another issue stirring up controversy, too. That was the date on which Christians would celebrate the resurrection of Christ. We call the festival "Easter." There were two options which were current almost from the beginning. One was to do it on the same day as the Jewish feast called the Passover, the 14th of the month Nissan, which was the date of the first full moon following the spring Equinox. Jesus' trial and crucifixion had taken place in conjunction with that. The other was to commenorate it on the Sunday following Nissan 14, which was the day when Jesus rose from the dead. The first practice meant that Easter might come up on any day of the week following the spring Equinox, while the second stipulated that it should always be on a Sunday, the first Sunday following the first full moon after the spring Equinox. Both practices claimed apostolic support, and it was an argument begging a solution. The Emperor decided to intervene: "Let's get the bishops together and settle this thing!"

There were precedents for getting the ecclesiastical heavy hitters together. The first meeting of this kind had been held almost two hundred years earlier. Constantine himself had pulled bishops together back in 314 in Arles, and played an active role at that meeting. This man was an archetypical activist. However, there were some new wrinkles this time.

One was the geographical reach of the invitations. Constantine wanted to leave the impression that every bishop in the inhabited world had been invited. The Greek word for "inhabited world" was "oikoumené". This where the name "ecumenical council" comes from. This must have been a propaganda exercise. I am sure he knew he did not have every possible bishop on his list.

The other innovation was the role Constantine played. Claiming that he was acting under the direct command of God, he called the meeting on his own. Here is a person who had not even been baptized yet calling together all the bishops in the inhabited world. Quite a picture. Added to this was the fact that where necessary the bishops travelled at imperial expense, with the entire cost of the meeting being underwritten by the emperor. Constantine's motivation was likely multi-layered.

First, Constantine was very concerned that this meeting take place. The theological questions may have been in his mind, but so were the social and political implications of not resolving these issues. Secondly, it is remarkable that more than 300 bishops responded to the call. Most of them would have been able to remember when they or their predecessors had been hunted by imperial forces with torture and death awaiting them. Now the man in purple seemed to be courting them. The reverse was staggering.

Eusebius the historian gives us an account of the meeting. Constantine treated the bishops with something like deference and respect. He sat to one side, but close enough to participate in the theological discussion and to call out encouragement and praise as the bishops spoke. A purple robe affirming theologians! Eusebius gushed with delight. Constantine may even have introduced into the fray the word which was apparently the key to solving the doctrinal problem, although he likely had a little expert assistance. It should be noted that there is some dispute regarding how important the word actually was.[8] The word was *homoousios*, roughly translated "the same nature." The idea was to state that the Son was of the same nature, or substance, as the Father. In other words, they were equal. Arius and his followers were seen to be wrong in saying that the Son was a created being. The council inclined toward Alexander and the twenty-four year old deacon, Athanasius, who was working alongside him. Constantine recommended acceptance, and when a count was made all but three of the bishops present went along with him. This guaranteed that the result was God's will. On the date of Easter celebrations, the assembled bishops backed the practice of holding them on the first Sunday follow-

8. Lewis, "Athanasius' Initial Defense of the Term ‘Ομοούσιος: Rereading the *De Decretis*," 337–59.

ing the first full moon following the spring equinox. The Church has maintained both these decisions from that day to this.

Probably not surprisingly, Constantine had gotten his way on both issues. Whatever he really thought theologially, he certainly had much to gain politically. Maintaining order in this far-flung empire was not an easy task. If in fact he had the bishops on his side, his hand would be considerably strengthened, and as the council ended it certainly looked as though they were in his pocket.

As for the bishops, they were in uncharted waters. For the first time the Church, the "whole" Church, had a carefully-worked out position on a particular and very important point of doctrine with which a very large number of them had explicitly agreed. In addition to that, their decision had the full backing of the entire weight of the Roman empire. They now had a ruler, a measuring device, by which they could determine the straightness, the correctness, of what anyone happened to think about the relationship between the Father and the Son. "Measuring device," "ruler" was approximately what the word "orthodoxy" meant. There had never been a widely-held, officially-approved standard of orthodoxy on anything before. Now there was. Many of them liked it, and the idea of orthodoxy stuck. It was framed in the carefully-balanced, finely-nuanced document that came to be known as the "Nicene Creed." It served as a kind of theological gyroscope to insure that Christian thought was level and heading in the right direction. The significance of the idea is acknowledged up to the present. Nicaea 325 was where orthodoxy was spawned.

There was another side to this on which the bishops' experience was unprecedented. They were now bound to the empire. The emperor had called the meeting, paid the expenses, participated in the discussions, introduced the key word, urged its acceptance, and stamped his seal on their decision. Never had Christian bishops been so intimately intertwined with political power. What they and their successors would soon learn was imperial closeness came with strings. Here was a blending of the sacred and the profane. Of course it was not that simple. After all, Constantine was doing everything that he, at that moment, could possibly do, as he saw it, to show that he was a Christian who respected his "Fathers in God," (the bishops) and that he wanted to help them in any way he could. What's wrong with that?

As the council drew to a close, Arius and a couple of others were exiled. Everybody else packed his bags and climbed into the wagon for home. However, once people returned home something important happened. Many, perhaps as much as one third of those who had signed on, withdrew their support. Apparently, they felt they had acted under duress, and that had made their agreement invalid. So what had really been going on? Maybe the chariots sent to help biships get to the council were actually commissioned to ensure that Constantine had the largest assembly of Church leaders possible. In other words, perhaps he actually had the bishops rounded up. Perhaps bishops agreed to the proposed positions because they were not sure they would get home if they did not. And possibly some only began to sniff a coercive undercurrent to the meeting as the days unfolded. I wonder if there were others who guessed that something was up and conveniently chose to visit far reaches of their dioceses about the time their taxis showed up. What is very, very clear is that what did not come out of the council was a warm, overarching sense of uniformity.

## DEVELOPMENTS

The Council of Nicaea definitely was a key moment for the Christian Church. It has played out through the rest of the Christian story in some striking ways. First, it established the idea of creating creeds. A creed is an unique phenomenon. In this era it was the whole Church which was at work, at least that seems to have been the goal of the major players. They wanted the important issue of the day to be addressed by representatives of all Christians. These representatives were bishops. Did they know where all Christians bishops were? Unlikely. Did they get invitations to everyone in the areas of the world they knew about? Probably not. But effort seems to have been made to cast the net as wide as possible.

The issues at stake were fundamental. The council was convinced that God had acted in Jesus Christ to provide salvation for humanity—everybody. They were trying to find ways to express this idea in the clearest, most accurate way possible. To us what they produced can sound strained, stuffy, over-done, even weird, but we must not forget they were setting the bar high, trying to do the best job possible. They were paying absolute attention to Scripture, struggling to get their picture of God's revelation of himself as sharply into focus as they could.[9]

From that time on, people have thought that councils, conferences, or synods of leading members of the various Christian groups are important, and there have been countless numbers of them. Back then bishops met over and over again in one place or another, and theological issues were debated passionately. As I mentioned before, these were times in which there was great interest in the doctrine of the Church. One bishop complained that he could not even go and get a hair cut without ending up in a theological wrangle. Prior to 450 AD two more councils were held which were regarded as having the same kind of authority as the one at Nicaea did. They were "ecumenical" councils. The first was held in Constantinople in 381. It reaffirmed the findings of Nicaea, declared that the Holy Spirit was equal to the Father and the Son, and insisted on the full humanity of Christ.

The second was the Council of Ephesus in 431. I pause over this one just a little longer because of the significance it took on later. It was tumultuous in its proceedings and irregular in its findings. It affirmed that Jesus Christ existed with two natures united in one person, and it condemned the leader of the church in Constantinople, Nestorius, for having taught that Christ not only had two natures, but was two persons. Behind all that there was an astonishing degree of rivalry among churches, on one hand, and emperial politics, on the other. It was not a pretty picture. In fact, Nestorius did not teach the ideas he was charged with, but that did not prevent his being charged as a heretic. Through a series of events a very large part of all Christians who have ever lived east of Palestine have been tarred with the same brush from that day to this. They have been called "Nestorians," to indicate that they are "heretics." Many are attempting to correct that now, and the best discussion of the whole issue I have come across, which includes a look at the ideas about Christ that are at the center of it, is by Sebastian Brock.[10]

Around Nicaea Christians were finding themselves sucked into a whirlpool of action, and by no means were they helpless, innocent bystanders. The interest emperors had in the Church rapidly deepened.

---

9. Some work being done by Lewis Ayres and others is putting a discussion of Nicaea and the creedal process in general back on the table and at a new depth. See Ayres, "Nicaea and Its Legacy: An Introduction," 141–44.

10. "The 'Nestorian' Church: A Lamentable Misnomer," 23–35.

By 325 AD most people of influence had come to see Christians as integral and significant parts of the empire, and that meant their Church had to be managed. When Constantine died in 337, his plan to turn his domain over to his three sons went into effect. They were Constantine II, Constans, and Constantius II. The first two died fairly soon leaving the whole empire to Constantius, and he governed until his death in 361. Interestingly enough, he was a committed Arian. In other words, he backed the theologians who lost at Nicaea. That looks a little strange, but then we have to remember that when his father, Constantine, was finally baptized on his deathbed the bishop who performed the rite was also an Arian. Had Constantine begun to have other thoughts about what orthodoxy was? Perhaps. Maybe he had just grown weary of theology.

What it meant on the ground is noteworthy. The Arian bishops began to be installed in the really big, significant churches while the theologians who had "won" at Nicaea started to experience some difficulty. For example, Athanasius, who had been one of the victorious heroes at that council, became the Bishop of Alexandria, only to find himself having tremendous trouble with Constantius. Of course it was Constantius who thought he was having trouble with Athanasius. At any rate Constantius saw to it that Athanasius spent about fifteen of his forty-five years as Bishop of Alexandria far away from his home town in exile.

When Constantius died, he was succeeded by the brief reign of Julian, who tried to reverse what had been happening during the last fifty years and swing the whole empire back to paganism. He had received Christian influence while growing up, but he pivoted a 180 degrees. He is not called "Julian the Apostate" for nothing. But he failed. In fact, modern politicians in the west are doing a better job of repaganizing their countries than he did. He was followed by Jovian, a Nicene believer, and then Valens, who was an Arian. In 379, Theodosius I seized power. He supported the Nicene Creed. Determined to "set things right," he acted on his own to call the bishops of his area together for a council (Constantinople, 381). The Bishop of Rome did not even know it was happening. Theodosius also moved aggressively against heresy and paganism, making the Catholic Church the official religion of the state.[11]

The picture that emerges is one in which Christians who lived anywhere in the Roman Empire, especially those who dwelt around the Mediterranean Sea, were deeply involved in the life of the empire

---

11. Codex Theodosianus, XVI.1.2, 150.

and the empire was fully a part of theirs. If you as a Christian had lived through the persecution of Diocletian when life was at best precarious, or had heard your grandparents talk about their survival, you could perhaps be excused if you thought you had reached paradise under the the new conditions Constantine had set in motion. It was now okay to be a Christian. In fact, for many it was politically and socially desirable. It was a way up.

But we cannot oversimplify things. Social and spiritual reorientations involving huge numbers of people and spreading over vast areas do not happen overnight. They take a long time and are very complicated. The popular view of the Apostle Paul's sudden conversion on the road to Damascus is the exception, not the norm. There is no question but that many people drifted into an identity with the Church. One of the burning issues then for leading Christians was "What do we do with all these people"? It is unlikely that there was a church-wide educational program for children and adults or a newcomers class for converts. What would have been the results from this loosely-structured arrangement? One of the results was likely that those who were really interested in the spiritual life could usually find the guidance they wanted. However, those who were less highly motivated simply missed the boat on Christian formation. Their tendency would be to "add on" the more accessible aspects of Christianity, rituals for example, to whatever religious assumptions they brought with them. Perhaps they caught some of the ideas of the new faith, but at many times and places, this led to expressions of Christianity that Jesus Christ, himself, would have had difficulty recognizing. The sources from the time show that at least some theologians from around this time, Augustine of Hippo for example, understood all this and were troubled by it.

These developments could take particularly nasty turns. Without the benefit of a firm grounding in the Christian faith, people tended to learn how to live the way they always had, and still do, by soaking up the values of the societies around them. Whatever worked for the elites of their worlds would work for them, too, or so they thought. It could be argued that at times and places this resulted in a brutalization of the Church. Some of the behaviour that surfaces from the sources is blood-chilling. Historians like Sozomenus, Socrates, and Theodotus recorded some of this, and it can be down right embarassing for Christians.

Around the middle of the fourth century, a man named Paul was the Bishop of Constantinople. He was a defender of the Nicene faith, and a favorite with the people, but Emperor Constantius wanted rid of him. Acting on imperial orders, an official kidnapped Paul in a public bath and immediately sent him into exile. He then prepared to install an Arian on the bishop's throne. Getting wind of this, crowds of people rushed to the cathedral. When the emperor's candidate arrived, his armed escort found they were unable to push their way through the crowd. Thinking the people were actively opposing them, they led the would-be bishop down the aisle and into the sanctuary by hacking a path through the throng with their weapons. Blood ran in the church while hands were laid on and prayers were said elevating this man to sacred office. One historians recorded that 3,150 people died.[12]

Scenes like this began to appear often enough in the late fourth and early fifth centuries to make one raise questions. What was going on here? Does the wedding of Christianity and social and political power always have to have negative consequences for the faith? Was there true faith anywhere among Greek and Latin, that is, western, Christians?

The answer is yes. Historians then, as now, tend to focus on the power brokers, and among them there were some wonderful Christians. I mention only one, Basil the Great, the Bishop of Caesarea in what is now Turkey. Power did not always, and does not always, mean corruption. We must not forget that the mighty at any given time and place, those who have been easy for historians to find, have always been just a small part of the total human family living and active. It is the case that the rest were living in the shadows, and it is difficult to find out about their lives given the existing resources available to us. We have to avoid romanticizing them. Looking at the Christians in the period we are dealing with, some were office-holders in churches and many were just ordinary folks. There is no doubt that a significant number of them were fairly indifferent Christians and had little understanding of what it meant to be a Christian. Their behavior could be scandalous and embarrassing. On the other hand, it is also certain that there were many who were living the Christian life authentically, carrying out the vision of leaders like Basil, or just quietly and undramatically reflecting the life of Christ in their daily devotion and behavior among family, friends, and neighbors.

12. Socrates, *Ecclesiastical History*, 43.

Some of these nameless ones—other pieces of the puzzle?—started showing up in strange places, for example, the desert. Maybe the offensive behavior of some of their so-called fellow Christians had repelled them. Or perhaps it was an inner hunger for God which compelled them to abandon the world. It is hard to determine what started it or even where it started, but people began to leave populated areas to pursue the spiritual life in solitude. A trickle which became a flood of Christians heading for the wilderness may have began in Egypt or in Syria, or in both places about the same time, late third century.[13] The most famous early example is Antony the Great in Egypt. He became "the Great" in part because of Athanasius, Bishop of Alexandria and defender of the decisions of Nicaea. This thorn in the sides of Arian emperors wrote a page-turner of a biography of Antony featuring all-out, hand-to-hand battles with demons in all shapes and sizes, mind-numbing accounts of self-starvation, endless intercessory prayer, and flawless orthodoxy in a life utterly dedicated to God.[14] It had the effect of making Antony the poster boy of the monastic movement. We have some letters of Antony, and the Antony of the biography is recognizable in the Antony of the letters, but Athanasius' Antony is *the* Antony.[15] Maybe Antony was just being modest in what he wrote, or maybe Athanasius was making him a little more heroic because it was good for the cause of orthodoxy.

Be that as it may, Antony became the model of a new kind of Christian, the hermit. This was a person who turned his, or her (because there were women who did this, too) back on the ordinary lives people were living at the time. They headed out into the deserts south of Alexandria in Egypt and east of Antioch in Syria so that they could wait on God with fewer destractions. What they discovered, of course, was that they went with themselves, and when they got there, there were all the tensions, temptations, and frustrations that they had dragged along with them. Now they had to deal with them directly under sun and frost with sand being whipped into their faces by the wind.

---

13. It has been suggested that it drew its inspiration from Mani (c.216–76), who became impressed with the life of self-denial when he saw it in India and then brought it back to Syria and worked it into the religion that he founded there. See Vööbus, "Origins of Monasticism in Mesopotamia," 34–37.

14. Athanasius, *Life of Antony.*

15. Rubenson, *Letters of St. Antony.*

To our minds, a few of them did some really bizarre things— ate only grass or exposed themselves to the elements by wearing no clothes.[16] Others did not go quite that far, but did exhibit some far-out eccentricities. One was Simeon, the Stylite, so-called because he spent the last thirty or so years of his life on a platform at the top of a sixty-foot column.[17] He prayed most of the time he was up there, but he also counselled people who flocked to see him. He became famous as a spiritual giant, sought out by the lowest and the most powerful in the empire alike.

Around the same time Simeon was up on his pillar, Pachomius in southern Egypt launched another style of monastic living. This featured groups of men or women living together under the control of an *abba* or *amma*, an abbot or abbess. The style became very popular in Egypt with thousands of men and women moving into well-structured and organized communities dotting the desert. Group monasticism, or cenobitism, became the norm in Europe and elsewhere in later years.[18]

## CONCLUSION

We have moved through the epoch-making Council of Nicaea and entered the fifth century, a time marked by more fluid lines and much greater complexity. Following Nicaea, Christians had a standard of orthodoxy, but many were challenging it. Freed from imperial persecution, they sometimes treated each other with violence; some trod the halls of highest power, while many sought solitude in the desert. The Church had moved into uncharted waters. In fact, the implications of the intertwining of Christianity with political power will probably perplex us forever. The ghost of Constantine continues to haunt the political process. The doctrine of church and state separation has not succeeded in dispelling his wandering spirit.

---

16. Vööbus, "Origin of Monasticism in Mesopotamia," 31–32.

17. See Hadjar, *Church of St. Simeon the Stylite.*

18. There was a third type of monasticism, too, called *laura*, in which small groups of men lived alone, but near each other in connection with an abbot. They would meet together once or twice a week.

4

*The Emperor and the Monk*

*635 AD*

## INTRODUCTION

AT THIS POINT IN the story we make a major shift in focus. Up to now the discussion has been centered on the Mediterranean basin with Rome, itself, receiving much attention. In this respect, like most other people who have written about Christianity, I have been influenced by a pattern which developed very early. There is a particular orientation in the biblical Book of Acts. The story starts in Jerusalem, swings north and west around the upper eastern corner of the Mediterranean, and ends in Rome. Then when Eusebius of Caesarea sat down to write the first history the Christian Church in the late third century, he followed the same north-then-west flow. Among other concerns, both authors seem to have wanted to reassure Rome that there was no danger to the empire in Christianity. Of course, we know that the relationship between Christians and Rome turned out to be a rocky one for a long time.

This directional flow, along with the west's achievements and the sense of its own importance, has established a tendency. Over the centuries, those of us who have taught and written about the history of the Church have started from Jerusalem, logically enough, then stayed with the north-westerly trajectory. We have made our way to western Europe and then, as Europeans, followed ourselves around the globe. Less attention has been given to the south and the east, even to eastern Europe. From here on I am stepping out of that trajectory.

For the rest of the story, we stretch into a wider world, but regrettably not all of it. Like all historians, I am compelled to be selective, which means there will be many, many parts of the story left untouched, and I blush when I think of what I am sliding past. In this chapter in particular, I will look at an event which highlights the eastern, even Asian, nature of early Christianity. But first we have to provide some links with adventures we have already explored.

## SETTING

As a general rule, nothing happens in human experience which is not connected in some way with what has gone on before, so it is no surprise that the focus in this chapter has precedents in many places. However, let us be aware that there are three hundred years between the event we are moving to and the last one we examined. This vast array of human experience points to the need to frame these centuries in such a way as to illuminate the flow of Christian experience. I will take two steps. The first and longer one will involve tracing the development of the world Church—that is right—the Church of the whole world as we find it around 600 AD. The second and shorter one will offer comments on some of the theology from the same period.

### Step One

In teasing out this sketch of the Church I am working with a map which extends from the Atlantic Ocean in the west to the Pacific Ocean in the east. I'm going to divide this space with two lines running roughly north and south. The first north-south line will follow along the east coast of

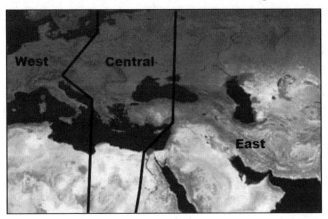

Italy, extending north and south. The second north-south line will start running east along the north coast of Africa then turn north to follow the eastern shore of the Mediterranean, cross Turkey then continue north. West of the first line is the Western Church. Between the lines is the Central Church, and east of the second line is the Eastern Church.

*Western Church*

Unfortunately, before we can begin to make sense of the Church in western Europe between c. 400 and c. 600 there is another phenomenon that calls for scrutiny. That was a massive movement of Germanic and Slavic and, perhaps even Turkic peoples, from the north and the east into the Roman Empire. The Germans have a wonderful word for it—*Völkerwanderung*, the movement of peoples. Less poetically, it has also been called the "Barbarian Invasions," but this was not a series of strategically-planned military actions. These are perhaps more accurately thought of as migrations with violence. Mind you, if you were on the receiving end of this "invasion," the nomenclature would not have made much difference. In fact, these people moving west and south could be thought of as forerunners of those who are currently trying to migrate to Europe and the United States in order to escape the dire conditions of their homelands.

The boundaries of the Roman Empire had been defined for centuries. They were Hadrian's Wall barring the Scots from north England, the Rhine River running south, the Danube River flowing east, the Tigris or Euphrates Rivers in the east, and the Atlas Mountains inland from the south coast of the Mediterranean. These were not exact borders, especially the one in the east, but people living at the time would have had fairly clear ideas of whether they were in or out of the Empire. For many, Rome was the hub and the center of power with a population which fluctuated, but which could be placed at around 800,000, declining as time went by.

By c. 370 pressure had begun to build from the north and the east. Some were peering into the Roman Empire and longing for the lives which others were enjoying there. In 376 a massive wave of Visigoths poured over the Danube with catastrophic results for Rome. Conditions in the empire became increasingly confused as tribal groups made their way in with some of the newcomers taking over responsible positions. The early fifth century brought a torrent of "barbarians" across the north-east frontier that seemed to go on forever. Some say the Rhine froze solid December 31, 406 and provided a highway. Unfortunately, literary sources which could shed light on these events are virtually non-existent. The people involved were almost completely illiterate. Archaeology provides some assistance. It can trace burial practices from north to south over a period of about two hundred years, starting c. 400 AD. This was a totally unstructured series of full-blown mass migrations. We have no idea of numbers, but whole tribes were involved. They were not armies of male warriors. These were large and small groups of women, men, and children with dogs, cows, pigs, chickens, and whatever other domestic animals they had. Carts, sleds, or other contrivances were loaded with whatever belongings they had. And they tended to move very slowly, perhaps a few miles a year. Again, these were not carefully-organized movements following well-mapped-out routes. Desperate people were crossing the river and struggling toward better lives, they hoped, wherever they might find them. Many tribal groups were represented—Saxons, Angles, Jutes, Vandals, Visigoths, Ostrogoths, and Huns, to name a few. They constituted a human tsunami surging south-west, and the Empire found them unstoppable.

How unstoppable? The Visigoths under Alaric overflowed Rome in 410 AD and sacked it thoroughly. That sent shock waves throughout the western world. Everyone knew Rome was the "eternal city." Yet Rome had been pillaged. How could this be? Even as far away as Bethlehem, St. Jerome heard about it and wrang his hands in grief. Astonishingly, these Goths were Christians, but heretics, Arians. They had been evangelized in the 370s by an Arian missionary.

Meanwhile the Vandals crossed France by c. 406 and passed through Spain into North Africa in 425, leaving devastation in their wake. This was the original "vandalism." The Saxons, Angles, and Jutes crossed the North Sea into England in the early 400s, then Attila and the Huns pushed south through Italy sacking Rome in 453. Two years later the Vandals, who had made their way across North Africa to Carthage, got into boats and came at Rome from the other direction. Imagine them running amok in the Imperial city with its fine art and architecture. What must it have been like to have been living in Rome?

Why did all this happen then? In fact, there are no explanations which are totally adequate. The sources are simply not good enough. Famine might have been behind some of it or pressure from tribes even farther to the east. The Juan-juan, or Avars, in Central Asia seem to have been on the move west at about this time. There has even been the suggestion that around this time coastal lands along the north shore of Germany sank, causing wide-scale flooding with the accompanying loss of agricultural land, critical to the food supply.

The consequences? Devastation throughout the western end of the Roman Empire. Universal despair. The total collapse of carefully constructed infastructure—road systems and aquaducts. Stone buildings were no longer maintained. Beautiful private and public buildings just crumbled, creating the ruins we admire throughout western Europe. People pitched tents inside the shells of once magnificent residences. Formal education came to an end. Complete lack of stability meant that groups could not stay together long enough to teach or learn anything beyond the rudiments of life. Wealth had to be portable or you could easily lose all you had. So gold was turned into the exquisite jewelry which comes from this period. People buried what treasure they had assuming they would return to reclaim it. Many never made it back, but the hoards they buried have shown up from time to time.

The one institution which survived more or less intact was the Church. Sons from old and prominent families found their ways into leadership. Then in the vacuum caused by the loss of all political structure they were drawn into positions of responsibility in large or small communities. The Church, in fact, found itself more deeply woven than ever into the social fabric in western Europe.

But the chaos did not end with the close of the fifth century. In 546–7 the Ostrogoths under Totila emptied Rome totally in forty days. When it became possible to return, no more than 25,000 people did—25,000 in a city which during its glory days accommodated up to 1,000,000. Inhabitants sank farther and farther away from the old city walls, watching the glories of Rome become ruins while wild animals roamed in forests springing up where villas, circuses, and theatres used to be. Utter devastation.

With that as background, we return to our discussion of the western Church. In Britain Christianity had been originally established somewhere around 150 AD. Archaeology points in that direction. It became the religion of landowners and their villas, but it did not remain unchallenged. W. H. C. Frend called on literary and archaeological remains to show that it ran into serious trouble in the fourth century. He points to a "barbarian conspiracy" in 336–7 AD. It seems to have involved invasions from the east, the west, and the north during which the Angles, Saxons, Jutes, Picts, and Scots entered some kind of an alliance with local slaves to push back against Christians. It constituted a revival of Romano-Celtic paganism and threw the Church off a trajectory of growth. [1]

The picture of difficult times for Christianity in Britain was sharpened by work done on grave sites in the north-east of what is now England. It shows that Christianity which was there earlier came under pressure from a wave of paganism that struck the area in the mid-fifth century. In a burial ground just south of Bamburg Castle along the east central coast of England, fifth century, non-Christian Saxons broke into earlier graves when they were laying their own dead to rest. The posture of the skeletal remains and the absence of objects placed in the grave to help the occupant travel to the after life makes the earlier graves identifiable as Christian.

The Venerable Bede sketched the hazardous existence that Christianity led in Britain as tides of pre-or non-Christian peoples ebbed and flowed around it. The faith had to be established again in the seventh century. In 635 after Christian King Oswald demolished the latest pagan army, he contacted the monastic community on Iona asking for help. St. Aidan eventually came to assume the responsibilities of bishop.

Iona was an outpost of the Celtic Church of Ireland, so romanticized in our world. The Celts were the "barbarians" of an earlier day. In the late first century BC, they dominated Europe from Turkey to the British Isles. They were a tribal society which was comparatively democratic and egalitarian. Rulers could be removed by their subjects, and women played much more prominent roles than in other societies of the time. However, they failed to be able to centralize power to protect themselves. In the face of Roman might and other tribes, they were pushed into the north-west of France and the west of the Atlantic isles.

Around 400 AD Celts began to feel the influence of Christianity as the eastern monastic traditions spread through France, into western Britain, and then across the Irish Sea. It was on its way to being established in Ireland when St. Patrick (c.389-c.461) returned as bishop in 432 to the island on which he had been enslaved and launched a very effective ministry. The church that evolved in the Emerald Isle was tribal and monastically-based. Abbots tended to hold office as bishops and abesses

---

1. Frend, "Pagans, Christians, and 'the Barbarian Conspiracy,'" 121–31.

were very important. Perhaps influenced by its links to the east, it was a rigorously ascetic church featuring long fasts and vigils through the night, sometimes while standing in the frigid waters of the Atlantic Ocean. The Celts developed the concept of private confession to a priest who then pronounced the forgiveness of sin which God had extended. Eventually this idea was taken over by the whole Roman Catholic Church.

The Celtic Church was also animated by missionary passion. In 563 AD St. Columba (c. 520–97) left Ireland and settled on the island of Iona where he established what became a famous monastary and used it as a base of missionary operations along the west coast of Scotland. Then in c.590 St. Columbanus (d.c.615), monk of Bangor Abbey, set his face east. With a burning desire to evangelize he travelled across Britain and onto the European continent to preach and establish monasteries in France, Switzerland, and Italy, itself. And there was St. Aidan, already mentioned, who answered the call to "come over and help us" from King Oswald and reestablished the Christianity in the north-east of Britain, with his ministry as bishop centered on the Holy Island of Lindisfarn just off the east coast. This turning away from home and wandering in ministry was a part of the Celtic self-denying spirituality.

The Church in France, then called Gaul, also makes an intriguing story. It was established early, met great difficulty, but grew in strength as the persecution in Lyons (177 AD) and the Council of Arles (314 AD) show. But it was almost swamped by the Germanic incursions from across the Rhine. Yet the Church survived to offer a kind of stabilizing influence at a time of great disorder. It eventually found a political ally in the person of Clovis, a Merovingian who became King of the Salian Franks in 481 AD. Through a series of events, he sought baptism in c. 496, and as his political power grew in what is now France so did the stature of the Catholic Church. The conversion of the populace was a long, slow process. The relics of saints[2] and shrines that were associated with them played important roles in supplanting paganism. Some have said that these were significant in strengthening the French church. They dispersed "the Sacred," helping the people as a whole to gain some idea that God was not to be found only in the Middle East.

---

2. P. Séjourné identified three categories of relics: (1) corporal relics (remains of bodies); (2) real relics (objects saints used while on earth); (3) representative relics (tombs of saints, objects that had touched tombs of saints)—"Reliques," col. 2313. For a fuller discussion, see Kydd, *Healing through the Centuries*, 115–40.

Meanwhile, the staggering, crumbling city of Rome was limping on with its glorious Christian tradition suffering along with it. During his long reign Emperor Justinian I (r.527–65) in Constantinople tried to pull the Roman Empire around the Mediterranean back together again. He had a measure of success, but it did not lead to much benefit for Rome. The city needed a strong man who could take it in hand and give it some hope: Gregory the Great (pope from 590 to 604) was the man.

Gregory addressed some of the internal needs of Rome and wrote the first manual of pastoral theology. He also had a missional spirit. In 597 AD he launched an attempt to reestablish the Church in southern Britain, sending a party of monks north under the leadership of their prior, Augustine.[3] Augustine managed to plant a church at Canterbury in south-east England and then used that as a base to reach west and north. This gives us some idea of how powerful that fifth century revival of paganism actually was.[4] These churchmen thought that the job of evangelization had to be done all over again.

## Central Church

This is what we westerners call the "Eastern Church," forgetting that there was a Christianity beyond it even farther to the east. When we use that name, we are referring to the Greek church and to other churches which grew out from it. It has a very different story from the one in the west.

Its center was Constantinople, established in might and grandeur by Constantine the Great. By the fifth century reality was setting in, and it was becoming harder and harder, given the collapse of the west, to keep on calling it the capital of the Roman Empire. It was then well on its way to becoming the "Byzantine Empire." It had been spared the impact of the fifth and sixth century migrations. The Huns, for example, had swept right past. Over in the east beyond Turkey, it had had to maintain constant vigilance with regard to first the Persians and then the Sassanids.

From the second century and on for hundreds of years, what is now Turkey was the most densely Christianized part of the world. Churches were everywhere, and that certainly included Constantinople itself. The capital was the hotbed of theological discussion. The patriarchs were early-day heros who attracted attention wherever they went. Most of

---

3. This is St. Augustine of Canterbury, who lived two hundred years later than the famous theologian by the same name, bishop of Hippo in North Africa.

4. See p. 66-67 above.

the townfolk were interested in theology, and could they ever scrap. Patriarchs, like John Chrysostom for example, were chased away from their pulpits and altars if they did not deliver their sermons with more than a dash of political and deferential savvy. And yet, there were those who looked beyond their own political and theological hobby horses.

One of these was Ulfilas. Having grown up among the Goths north of the Danube, he moved to Constantinople as a young man. He was consecrated bishop in the 340s and shortly thereafter he returned to the Goths as a missionary. This was one act of translation such as those I referred to earlier,[5] but he went on to perform another one, translating the scriptures into Gothic. His ministry led to the establishment of the Church among those people. The historian Sozomen presents Ulfilas as agreeing to become an Arian in order to guarantee imperial favour for the people to whom he ministered.[6]

### Eastern Church

A very different picture of the Church emerges to the south and east of the Mediterranean. We begin in Egypt. The founding of the Church there is rich in tradition. First, we hear of the Holy Family's escape from the wrath of King Herod by fleeing there and then of Mark's, the author of the second gospel, travelling there to establish Christianity. By the early third century, Christianity, in various forms, was established from Alexandria in the north to Chenoboskion in the south. The range of theological beliefs among those associated with Christianity in Egypt in the early centuries was truly extraordinary. The discovery of the Gnostic Library of Nag Hammadi in Chenoboskion in 1947 made this very clear.

The library was made up of just under fifty documents all written in the indigenous language of Egypt, Coptic, and most of them are gnostic. They breathe the atmosphere of that rather non-cohesive flood of religious groups that burst to the surface in the mid-second century. In one way or another, they all emphasized the idea of salvation through a secret knowledge, and they constituted a major challenge to that part of Christianity that came to be known as mainstream. Some of these writings have an almost surreal feeling to them as they pull in ideas from many religious sources, blending them in quite extraordinary ways. Inspite of this competition, the mainstream version of Christianity did

---

5. See pp. 14 and 15 above.

6. Sozomen, *Ecclesiastical History*, 373.

prevail. Remember, this is the stage people as different as Origen and Antony the Great played on. Early Egyptian Christianity was diverse.

Farther to the south was the ancient warrior kingdom of Nubia. Christianity did not take hold there until the sixth century. When it was introduced, it came in two forms with different ideas about the incarnation of Christ. Ironically, one version was sponsored by Emperor Justinian and the other by his wife, Theodora. They must have had interesting pillow talks.

Still farther south was Ethiopia. We know of the servant of Candace spoken of in Acts 8. It is impossible to trace him beyond verse twenty-nine of that chapter where he is portrayed as heading home with great joy in his new faith. Christianity grew into significance there, gradually, in the second half of the fourth century. The process is quite traceable through early historians and archaeological work. The church which ultimately became predominant there has a continuous history running from that day to this.

Farther still to the south is India. Tradition has the Apostle Thomas travelling to India in the mid-first century and planting Christianity. There is no question but that there was a trade route that ran from Rome through Egypt, down the Red Sea, and across the Indian Ocean to the south-west part of India.[7] A Thomas could have made that trip. However, concrete historical information does not begin to appear until late in the second century.[8] Then more is available from around 300,[9] and Alexandrian mariner Cosmas Indicopleustes reported on voyages he made through the area in the early sixth century, claiming that he had met large numbers of Christians. This is supported by archaeological artifacts.

Finally, there is Syriac Christianity. Damascus was important in the very early days of the new faith, but thereafter Antioch became dominant. The spread east is actually difficult to trace from the beginning, but the best suggestion seems to be that in the first instance the faith was carried by Christian merchants who were trading along the

---

7. *The Periplus of the Erythraean Sea: Travel and Trade in the Indian Ocean by a Merchant of the First Century.* Translated and Edited by Wilfred Schoff. New York: Longmans, Green and Co., 1912. Online: http://www.archive.org/stream/cu31924030139236#page/n5/mode/2up.

8. Eusebius, *Ecclesiastical History*, 1, 462.

9. Moffatt, *Christianity in Asia*, 1, 266.

well-travelled Silk Roads. By this time those routes had been around for

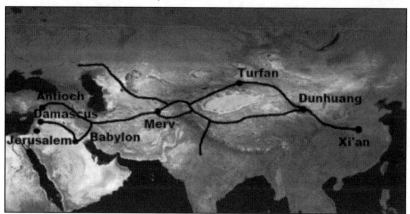

Silk Roads

centuries in one form or another.[10] One branch ran through Edessa in east Turkey, then on Nisibis and farther to beyond the Tigris to the area of Adiabene. Bardaisan tells us that there were Christians as far east as the Hindu Kush, a difficult tangle of mountain ranges roughly north of Afganistan, by the end of the second century.[11]

Under the Persians, Christians at first were able to move freely without the threat of the kind of persecution fellow believers were experiencing farther to the west. However, that came to an end about 225 AD. Once the Sassanid dynasty had established itself in the area, political, social, and religious concerns unleashed persecution, some of it wildly vicious. During the Great Persecution which ran for forty years in the late fourth century something approaching 200,000 Christians died for their faith.[12] A shocking number. Somewhat later the persecution came from a short-lived Jewish dynasty which ruled the southern part of the Arabian peninsula, where Yemen is now. In spite of the blood-letting the Church grew.

Between 200 and 600 AD there were 2,000 churches built in Syria alone. Literary sources and archaeology are filling out the picture for us. This branch of Christianity spread down the Persian Gulf and out into the Indian Ocean; north around the Caspian sea; east through Iraq and Iran, and by the early seventh century to Afghanistan and Uzbekistan

---

10. See Parzinger, "The 'Silk Roads' Concept Reconsidered," 7–15.

11. Bardaisan, *Book of the Laws of the Countries*, 61.

12. Baumer, "Survey of Nestorianism," 449.

and beyond. In a word, while it had not penetrated far into Africa yet—at least that is the current scholarly view—or to South and North America, Christianity was growing everywhere, and especially in the east.

### Step Two

In sketching the setting for the event we will focus on, we have moved through a rapid review of developments in Christianity in various places. The second step will involve casting not much more than a side-long glance at the theology of the period.

One cannot do justice to Christianity before 600 AD without some reference to St. Augustine of Hippo (354–430 AD). Granted he did not cut a very imposing figure in the Church of the East, but everywhere else his influence was monumental. At least in the west, he shaped theology for 1,300 years, and he still preoccupies scholars.

Augustine was born in Thagaste, Numidia (now Algeria); went to school in the area and at Carthage; at age 19 began to live with a woman with whom he fathered a son; became a Manichaean; later moved to Rome and then Milan following a successful career path; converted to Christianity under the influence of Bishop Ambrose in 386; returned to Africa and became the Bishop of Hippo Rhegius (Annaba, Algeria). Although his life can be easily sumarized, it really was as complicated and challenging as anyone else's, marked by joy, sorrow, frustration, sin, and service. We have extensive knowledge of the first thirty-three years of it because he wrote an autobiography, sparing few details, in his famous *Confessions*.[13] For the rest, we can pick up what we can out of the *Retractations*, a work he wrote late in life, listing and commenting on everything he had written, and, by the way, there were no "retractions" as we would understand them.

Focusing briefly on Augustine's prodigious theological work, I touch on only two points. First, his view of God. Augustine rested in the absolute majesty and might of God, emphasizing the unity of the Godhead while finding the diversity among the members of the Trinity expressed in the mutual relationships they share. He introduced what have been called "psychological analogies" to help explain the Trinity. As an example, he asked us to think of love, which involves the lover,

---

13. The biography of Augustine which I find the most helpful is Brown, *Augustine of Hippo*, 2nd. ed, 2000. The bouncy, self-assured study by O'Donnell is also useful.

the beloved, and love itself—three dimensions of one emotion. But, of course, the discussions of the Trinity swirl on.

Second, original sin. The issue, for him as for preachers throughout the centuries as well as many philosophers, was how to explain the persistence of evil. Augustine's working solution was to see it as passed on to everyone from Adam, assuming that in some sense all human persons were in Adam at the time of his great disobedience. Augustine saw it as linked to "concupiscence" as expressed in sexual desire through which all of us were conceived. There were those who disagreed with him passionately, the monk Pelagius would be a prime example, and the Church of the East came to a very different understanding.[14]

Augustine was most certainly not the only Christian who was thinking hard about what he and others of his religion believed. He can be seen as a representative of the Latin-speaking west, but the Greeks and the Syrians were very, very active, too. I have referred to ecumenical councils, that is, important meetings to settle doctrine, The middle of the fifth century saw another one. The issue again was how full divinity and full humanity co-existed in the man Jesus of Nazareth. The person at the center of the storm this time was Eutyches. He had been teaching that once the Son of God had come into this world he had only one nature, the divine, and that there was nothing in him that was really human. A meeting was called at Chalcedon near Constantinople, and he was condemned as a heretic.

As strange as some of this sounds to our ears, these discussions certainly had the attention of the general populace in those days. In fact, on one occasion a mob caught up with a bishop who came down on the "wrong" side of one of these questions and they lynched him.[15] And on top of that, the council's conclusions did not bring the arguments to an end for a long, long time. In fact, some of the discussions are still being revisited.

## EVENT

For many centuries the event we are going to focus on was virtually unknown. It happened in 635 AD, during the time the Tang Dynasty (618–907) ruled the Chinese Empire. That era is widely recognized as one of

14. Baumer, *Church of the East*, 116–17.
15. Pelikan, *Emergence of the Catholic Tradition*, 267.

the most brilliant periods in Chinese history. The borders of the empire were extended, and throughout most of the dynasty's rule there was economic and social stability. Under the Tang, foreigners were welcomed who not only provided a prolonged stimulus to trade but also opened the empire to religions that were not indigenous to China. One of these, Buddhism, had already been in China for a long time, but Zorastrianism and Manichaeism appeared, and along with them, Christianity in its Syriac version. Its appearance is recorded in a remarkable document.

This document is a stele, a slab of rock approximately three feet wide and nine feet high with an inscription on it. It is now found, along with more than 2000 others like it, in the Stone Steles Museum, part of the Shaanxi Provincial Museum in Xi'an, China. It was created in 781 AD by a prominent calligrapher, and some time after that date it was lost. It only became known again in the early 1620's when labourers digging a trench in the area of Xi'an came upon it. Eventually it was moved to its present location.

As impressive as the stele itself is as a work of art, it is the iconography and inscription which it bears that has captured the attention of many. The inscription is bilingual, Chinese and Syriac. The text was written by a Christian monk, Jingjing, or Adam. It offers a list of Christian clergy, all in Syriac, and, in beautiful Chinese characters, an account of the official founding of Christianity in China with its subsequent history until 781 and a summary of its doctrine. The stele drew notice immediately after its discovery in seventeenth century, but has only reached to an ever-broadening circle of academics in the last two decades.

The details of the appearance of Christianity are striking. The message was carried by Aluoben, who was completing a very difficult journey from the west. The Tang emperor, Taizong, had sent one of his ministers out to meet Aluoben as he entered Xi'an and to escort him back to the court. He was welcomed there by the emperor himself. Shortly thereafter, the emperor issued a remarkable decree:

> The great virtuous Aluoben of the kingdom of Da Qin, bringing his Scriptures and images from afar, has come and presented them at our capital. Having careful investigation, we find his doctrines to be most mysterious. Having examined the principle of his religion, we find it complete and the fundamental points being included in it. Its language contains no complicated verbosity. The success in understanding its principle can be com-

pared to forgetting the trap once the fish is caught. The teaching is helpful to all creatures, and profitable for men;—let it have free course throughout the empire.[16]

Taken at first reading, this is an astonishing statement. What's going on? Who is this Aluoben and why was he welcomed so warmly?

First, it needs to be acknowledged that there will be no detailed biography of Aluoben written on the basis of the sources we now have. They are sparse. However, there is something like consensus that he was a Syriac monk, and possibly even a bishop. Christoph Baumer thought that his Syriac name may have been Yaballaha or Abraham and that he was acting on the orders of the head of the Church of the East, who at the time was Ishoyahb II.[17] Baumer added that the warmth of Aluoben's reception could be explained by his having accompanied an official delegation from King Yazdgerd III whose dynasty, the Sassanids, ruled Persia at the time.

Glen Thompson essentially agreed and created an interesting scenario. Significant numbers of Christians may have followed the Silk Roads into China before 635. These then may have sent a messenger to Ishoyhb II asking him to send a bishop so that the Christian community could be properly organized. Ishoyhb agreed and went to the Sassinian court to ask the king to write to the Chinese emperor requesting that he permit a bishop to come to China to meet that need. King Yazdgerd consented, prepared the documents, and off went Aluoben with the dignity and authority of both the Church of the East and the Persian monarch behind him.[18] The diplomatic network did its work so that when he arrived the Chinese court was ready, and he was welcomed with the respect appropriate to a person of consequence.

This was a very good start for Aluoben's ministry in China, and it seems to have blossomed into a strategy. The way the story on the stele reads, he appears to have built and retained that contact with the upper classes of the empire conscientiously.[19]

16. Tang, *A Study of the History of Nestorian Christianity,* 106.

17. Baumer, *Church of the East,* 181. Ishoyahb II was in office from 628 to 646 and lived in Seleucia-Ctesiphon on the Tigris River.

18. Thompson. "Was Alopen a 'Missionary'"? 275.

19. Wang, "Remnants of Christianity," 150.

## DEVELOPMENTS

It truly was a very good start for the Church of the East in China, not just for Aluoben. Within three years a monastery had been founded in Xi'an which eventually was home to twenty-one monks. By 642 the literature Aluoben had brought with him had been translated. Under Emperor Gaozong (650–83) churches were built in all of China's provincial capitals. In spite of a period of persecution under Empress Wu (690–705), the church continued to grow and in the next century continued to find powerful friends. In 745 Emperor Xuanzong once again extended official recognition to Christianity and underlined this action by issuing tablets to Christian monasteries affirming them. Somewhat later Christianity found another champion in Guo Ziyi, a general in the army and a minister in the government. He donated large sums for the restoration and building of churches, and for underwriting conferences for the leaders of the church. One of Ziyi's friends served under him as vice-commander of the army. This was Issu, to whom the stele of Xi'an is dedicated. He was also a priest in the Church of the East.[20]

We can actually get a little closer to the experience of these Christians in China by looking at the literature they left behind, and this turns out to be far more than a purely academic exercise. It sheds light on a group of Christians trying to introduce the Gospel of Christ to a new socio-cultural context. The process can be called "inculturation" and it has been a challenge from Christians from the beginning until now. With Andrew Walls it can also be called "translation," an idea I referred to earlier. In fact, there is only a very small number of documents which have been discovered so far that can be called Christian, maybe seven, eight, or nine. The uncertainly comes from doubt whether one or two of these documents actually belongs to Christianity or some other religion.[21] Needless to say, these documents are being exposed to meticulous examination.

Two observations can be identified. First, there was carried on a "fairly in-depth dialogue."[22] Christians had developed contacts with Daoists and Buddhists and were working with them to find language in

20. Baum and Winkler, *Church of the East*, 47–49.

21. See Vermander's discussion in "Impact of Nestorianism," 180–94, of a seventh-century Chinese document written in Xi'an.

22. Eskildsen, "Parallel Themes," 64. See also Nicoline-Zani, "Past and Current Research on Tang *Jingjiao* Documents," 44.

which the Christian message could be shared. One of the most intriguing collaborative projects involved the Christian Jingjing, who wrote the text that was eventually carved on the stele of 781, and Indian master, Tripitala Prajna, who recruited Jingjing to join a translation team which was going to work on Buddhist texts. The project was aborted by the emperor.[23]

The other observation is that there are traces of a theological drift over time. In other words, concepts essential to Christianity which are very much parts of earlier documents appear to be played down in later years. For example, the idea of crucifixion is clear in seventh century material, but absent in eighth century documents, arousing the suspicion that it was being suppressed in order to be as inoffensive as possible to a Chinese audience.[24] This is a challenge Christians have faced constantly: when do accommodation and communication become sell-out?

In Persia, Central Asia, and China, the Church of the East continued to grow throughout the seventh and eighth centuries. It has been estimated that by the middle of the eighth century its reach stretched three times farther than that of the Greek and Latin churches together and that it had twice as many churches and members.[25] Details are available. For example, Rayy, a city just south-east of present day Teheran, had a large Christian community overseen by a bishop in 410 AD[26]; and Merv in Turkmenistan, a major trading center on the ancient Silk Roads, had a Christian metropolitan, a bishop overseeing other bishops in a very large area, living there by 544.[27] Hunter draws attention to Metropolitan Elias of Merv. In 644 he baptized many people from a Turkic tribe following a mass conversion led by their chieftain. Pagan priests had conjured up a storm which Elias brought to an end by using the sign of the cross.[28] However, all was not smooth sailing.

In 651 AD, the Arabs overthrew the Persians, and with that, the world changed. Islam came roaring out of the Arabian Peninsula. The

23. Wang, "Remnants of Christianity," 160 and Chen, "Connection Between *Jingjiao* and Buddhist Texts," 96.

24. Eskildsen, "Parallel Themes," 70. It is also signficant that the cross as it appeared, and appears, in the Church of the East emphasized the resurrection rather than the crucifixion—it did not carry the crucified Christ.

25. See Baum and Winkler, *Church of the East*, 73 and Hunter, "Church of the East in Central Asia," 130.

26. Reynolds, "Medieval Islamic Polemic," 220.

27. Hunter, "Church of the East in Central Asia," 131.

28. Hunter, "Church of the East in Central Asia," 133.

founder was Muhammad (570–632). Around 610 Muhammad began to receive a series of revelations. At the center of them was a thoroughgoing monotheism resting on Allah with Muhammad as his prophet. By 632 Arabia was Muslim and within ten years most of Persia and the Byzantine provinces had fallen to Islamic armies. In 661 Imam Ali, the last of what are known as the four "righteous caliphs," was killed, and the Umayyad dynasty seized power, ruling until 750. By 695 Carthage had been conquered and by 711 much of Spain was in Muslim hands. The Muslim onslought was finally stopped at the Battle of Tours-Poitiers in 732 by a Frankish army led by Charles Martel.

Islam went through a dynastic change c. 750 when the Abassids succeeded the Ummayads. The new dynasty established its capital at Baghdad, the "Round City," so named because of its circular design, in July 752. It rapidly became a center of commerce and learning. In fact, its "House of Wisdom" became home to scholars of many races and religions engaged in research in many fields and in the translation of Greek, Persian, and Syriac literature. And the Church of the East continued to grow, a fact that is quite significant given the circumstances and the subsequent history.

Baum and Winkler suggest that, "Even long after the Arab conquest, Christians outnumbered Muslims in Egypt, Palestine, Syria, and Mesopotamia. Gundeshapur, Nisibis, and Merv remained intellectual centers of the Church of the East, where writers, translators, and clerks were educated."[29] They also draw attention to monasteries that continued to be established during this time. Altogether, the location of some 150 monasteries have been determined.[30] Hilary Kilpatrick offered some surprising insights regarding the Christian monasteries just mentioned that are too interesting to rush by. Her reading of Muslim sources extending into the tenth century showed a remarkably open view toward Christian customs and institutions, and the monasteries figure prominently. They served as ideal destinations for day trips for ordinary Muslims with their atmospheres of peace and harmony, their beautifully chosen and maintained locations, and their good wine. They also provided hospitality for travelers, and, most notably, health care. Various monasteries specialized in treating particular problems, but more generally they were valued for

---

29. Baum and Winkler, *Church of the East*, 43.
30. Baum and Winkler, *Church of the East*, 44.

offering safe places for the mentally ill.[31] This is an extraordinary case of inter-religious understanding.

Unfortunately and in contrast to the above, Christian monasteries suffered different fates under Islam.[32] One well-known one survived into the eleventh century. It is located on Kharg Island in the Persian gulf, which is now an important depot for shipping Iranian oil. The ruins, somewhat larger than a football field, hold the remains of a church, library, dining hall, and monks' cells. It may have been founded in the seventh century.[33]

## CONCLUSION

In all of this the Church of the East was experiencing something very different from what Christian groups in the West were facing. The latter had been born in Judaic and Greco-Roman cultures, and they had absorbed a great deal from both. As they expanded, they quickly began to encounter largely illerate peoples. In the east Christians encountered the Persians, south Asians, and the Chinese, all highly sophisticated cultures. Even a quick walk through the Asian galleries in the British Museum makes that very clear. Nonetheless, missionary evangelism continued. We will return to early Muslim-Christian relations later.

Was anybody doing this sort of mission work in the west at this time? Yes, and it was the Celts. Saintly brothers Cedd and Chad were carrying out their ministries in central Britain which had largely reverted to paganism. One is reminded of their work by a visit to the "Chapel of St. Chad's Head" in Litchfield Cathedral. Another, St. Boniface, had launched a ministry on the continent. In 719 he was formally commissioned by Pope Gregory II "to preach to the heathen," and he successfully established monasteries in Germany. Pope Gregory III reaffirmed this work in 732, and then Boniface became Archbishop of Mainz in 746. His life ended in martyrdom in 754. Yet in places as far removed from each other as China and Britain, Christians were establishing a path of evangelism, and that would continue.

31. Kilpatrick, "Monasteries through Muslim Eyes," 22–24.

32. See Baumer, *Church of the East*, 138.

33. D. T. Potts, "Kharg Island." See also Boucharlat, "Steve, Marie-Joseph, *L'île de Khârg*."

# 5

## Debate in Baghdad

### 781 AD

## INTRODUCTION

THE LAST CHAPTER CENTERED on an event that occurred only a little over a hundred years earlier than the one we are about to approach. That event took us to one imperial center—Xi'an, China in 635. The event we will look at here takes us to another imperial center—Baghdad in 781. It will give us a picture of Christians who had a sharp vision of the expanding Kingdom of God brought by Jesus Christ. They were living powerfully in the midst of very difficult circumstances, but in most western treatments of the Christian story, they have been overlooked. This is an attempt to raise awareness about them.

## SETTING

We pause again to survey at least some of what had transpired leading up to the event in question. First, in the early eighth century tensions had begun to simmer between the Byzantine emperor, Leo III (r.717–40), and the Bishop of Rome, and from that cascaded a remarkable series of developments.

The initial issue was "iconoclasm," which centered on pictures of Christ, the Apostles, and the saints that enjoyed wide popularity especially within the monastic communities. In fact, these icons had become objects of veneration. For reasons difficult to determine now, Emperor Leo III banned icons in 725 AD. This action was met with strong opposition from the people as a whole and especially from the monks. As Leo and then his son, Constantine V (r.741–75), carried out this policy, violence erupted. In response, first Pope Gregory II (in office 715–31) and then Pope Gregory III (in office 731–41) spoke out against imperial policy in support of the icons and their supporters. Leo saw this as unacceptable interference, and answered by wrenching Sicily and other areas which were under the pope's spiritual jurisdiction away from him. Leo had the military strength to support this decision, while Gregory II and his successor, Gregory III, were left scrambling to find someone to help defend their interests.

This created a very difficult dilemma for the various Bishops of Rome. Feeling pressure from the Avars farther east, the Lombards under King Alboin had moved into Italy in 568 AD[1]—and stayed until the late eighth century! By around 750 the Lombards had taken Ravenna, a major city in northern Italy, and the pope, by then Zacharias (in office 741–52), feared for the security of Rome. In happier times he might have turned to the emperor in Constantinople, but now he could not. And he did not have to.

Pippin the Short, the most powerful man among the Franks (ancient France) had a problem that morphed into a two-sided solution. His people were ruled by a Merovingian, a descendent of Clovis, but who in fact was powerless. He, himself, Pippin, occupied a position of unequalled influence, but he had no moral authority to assume the legal leadership of the Franks. He petitioned Pope Zacharias for the right to ascend the throne. For his part, Zacharias saw the resolution of his difficulty in Pippin, and on his instructions Pippin was anointed and crowned King of the Franks. The unfortunate Merovingian was sent to a monastery. Zacharias died shortly thereafter, but his successor Stephen II (in office 752–7) crossed the Alps, travelled to Paris, and repeated the ceremonies not only for Pippin, but also for his sons, Charles and Carloman. The soon-to-be-famous Carolingian dynasty was created. Stephen also received the much desired relief as Pippin led his troops across the Alps to wage war on behalf of the Throne of St. Peter.

As it turned out, Popes Zacharias and Stephen had achieved far more than they realized, much to the chagrin of some of their successors. They had paved the way for Charles the Great, Charlemagne. On Pippin's death in 768 the twenty-six year old Charles assumed the mantle

1. Brown, "Transformation," 1–58.

of leadership of the Franks along with his younger brother. Three years later Carloman died, and the realm fell into the hands of the man who would live in history as Charlemagne.

Charlemagne cut an extraordinary figure. He was tall, fair-haired, well-built, and athletic. He swam regularly, ate well, and drank moderately. He succeeded in expanding the realm he had inherited in several directions, and he had hopes for the intellectual welfare of his people. He created a center of learning at Tours under the leadership of Alcuin of York. Work done there and beyond led to the creation of a characteristic script used in the production of manuscripts known as "Carolingian." For a time he even attended school himself, sitting among the youngsters present and calling himself "David." It appears that he did not want to intimidate his classmates. I wonder if they guessed who he was?

Charlemagne was also a pious man and felt a heavy responsibility to bring non-Christian tribes around him to the faith. But he could be cold-blooded and ruthless. Summer after summer he led his troops on campaigns against pagan neighbors, the Saxons earlier and the Avars later. One event, horrific beyond words, occurred in the spring of 782. Year after year conquered Saxons had accepted baptism and made vows to fulfill the tithes which were imposed upon them, and then later had risen in anger and revolt. Charlemagne determined to put an end to this cycle of submission and rebellion. He ordered 4,500 captured soldiers to be executed.

Alcuin, a British monk-scholar whom Charlemagne had brought to France, and who had had the king's ear for years was profoundly shocked. Steven Stofferahn argues that Alcuin used his relationship of trust with the emperor to insist that a different approach had to be followed when dealing with conquered pagans. The evidence suggests that his plea had a moderating influence on Charlemagne's later treatment of the Avars.[2]

It could be argued that in Charlemagne Christianity found another Constantine. In fact, statues featuring these two notables on horseback guard either end of the portico of St. Peter's Basilica in Rome—the Church and larger-than-life politicos hand-in-hand. This stands in marked contrast to the experience of Christians in the East. True, during the eighth century, Christians found powerful friends in China and across Central Asia and Persia. There was the occasional war lord or

2. Stofferahn, "Staying the Royal Sword," 461–80.

Arab who embraced the faith for a longer or shorter period, but there never was a ruler who aligned himself and his family with Christianity for the long term.

David Thomas states that for hundreds of years the center of the Islamic world, nowadays Iraq, was religiously pluralist. "At first, the Jews, Christians, Persian dualists and others who had lived there for centuries, and in some cases for millennia, hardly seemed aware of any need or requirement to conform to the faith of their Muslim rulers."[3] That sounds a bit overstated, but some Christians certainly did play prominent roles in the Islamic world of their day. Their skills meant that some were sought out as physicians, financiers, personal secretaries,[4] and translators.

Yes, translators. Many Christian monks and clergy were highly literate, often in three languages—Syriac, Greek, and Arabic. Under the first few leaders of the Abbasid dynasty, mid-eighth century, the attempt was made to gather the wisdom of different peoples and religions. Christoph Baumer calls this era the "Period of Translation."[5] These Syrian Christians had contact with the west, and as they moved east they carried products of Greek culture with them. When they found themselves at the table with representatives of their political masters they had some rather interesting material to inject into the discussion. They translated philosophy, poetry, and science from Greek into Syriac and on to Arabic. In other words, they provided a key bridge between cultures stimulating the younger with the fruit of the older.

So here they were, Muslim and Christian along with representatives of other religions, reading and studying each others' work, but it seems that nobody was being convinced by anybody else's arguments. In fact, reading each other's writings through the filter of their own beliefs led fairly consistently to mutual distortion.[6] This all sounds quite civil, even rather encouraging—Christians and Muslims sitting around arguing theology with each other. But there is a very important caveat. The Christians were absolutely vulnerable.

The Muslims were the masters, and no one dared forget it. While being paid appropriately for work done, the Christians were feared and de-

---

3. David Thomas, "Introduction," vii.

4. Thomas, "Introduction," x.

5. Baumer, "Survey of Nestorianism and of Ancient Nestorian Architectural Relics," 455.

6. Thomas, "Introduction," viii.

spised and treated with suspicion and disrespect. As David Thomas said, Christians "always had to remember that circumstances could quickly become vicious."[7] At no point under Islam was the outlook for Christians good. Baumer emphasizes that Christians lived under very real financial and social restrictions which tempted many to convert, and many, many did. He describes Islam as a simple, down-to-earth religion with no difficult ideas, making it comparatively easy to change religions.

An actual account of one of these conversions which occurred in 769–70 has been given to us by the author of *The Chronicle of Zuqnin*. A Christian church leader, a deacon, went to a Muslim whom he knew and asked him to help him become a follower of Islam. Surprisingly, the Muslim tried to keep him from taking the step. When the Christian insisted, he led him through a series of questions:

> "Do you renounce Christ?" He said: "Yes." Then he said to him: "Do you renounce Baptism?" He said: "I renounce it." He then said to him: "Do you renounce the Cross, the Eucharist and everything which Christians profess?" He replied: "I renounce them." At this point the son of the Devil added to these words insults not requested by the Arabs. After he made him apostasise in this manner, he asked him: "Do you believe in Muhammad as the messenger of God, and in the Book that descended upon him from Heaven?"[8]

Churches and Christians were always at the absolute mercy of the ruler of the moment.[9] Among many other demands, Christians had to sew large yellow patches on the front and the back of their clothes[10]—a means of both identification and humiliation. This idea was used most famously in the twentieth century by Nazis to identify Jews, but also in thirteenth century Europe by order of Lateran Council IV under Pope Innocent III with reference to Jews and Muslims.[11]

What is surprising was that Christians ever spoke out, and sometimes rather boldly. For example, in 691 the head of the Church of the

---

7. Thomas, "Introduction," x.

8. *The Chronicle of Zuqnin*, 328.

9. Baumer, *Church of the East*, 152.

10. Moffatt, *A History of Christian in Asia, Volume*, I, 346.

11. "Constitutions, Fourth Lateran Council—1215," sec. 68, 266. In this place justification for the practice is wrongly attributed to Lev 19:19 and Deut 22:5 and 22:11—266 n. 2.

East, Henanisho I, was summoned before the Caliph of the day and asked what he thought of Islam. He replied, "It is a power that was established by the sword and not a faith confirmed by divine miracles, like Christianity and like the old law of Moses." The enraged caliph wanted to cut out the patriarch's tongue, but later pardoned him in condition that he never appear before him again.[12]

## EVENT

This is the context in which one of the truly arresting figures in the Christian story lived. He is Timothy I who served as the "Catholicos," the head of the Church of the East, from 781 until his death in 823. Born in 727 or 728, he came from a well-placed family and first appeared as a bishop when he was about 40.[13] His ascent to the position of Catholicos was rocky and disputed, but when he took office he turned out to be remarkably effective.

One of the keys to the success he enjoyed was the relationships he was able to develop with Caliphs Muhammad ibn Mansur al-Madhi (775–85) and Marun-ar-Rasid, al-Madhi's son (786–809). The former gave him jurisdiction over all Christians in the Muslim world,[14] and both permitted him to approach them personally.[15] Timothy referred to this right of access on a number of occasions. Early in his career, in the midst of an event I will discuss later, he said, "The next day I had an audience of his Majesty. Such audiences had constantly taken place previously, sometimes for the affairs of state, and some other times for the love of wisdom and learning which was burning in the soul of his majesty."[16] Timothy must have been able to gain the ruler's trust quickly because the event to which he refers took place in the first year or two of his position as Catholicos. Twenty years later Marun-ar-Rasid sent the seventy-year-

---

12. Baumer, *Church of the East,* 144.

13. Bidawid, *Les Lettres,* 1–5.

14. Comneno, *"Nestorianism in Central Asia,"* 25.

15. Bidawid, *Les Lettres,* 76.

16. "The Apology of Timothy the Patriarch before the Caliph Mahdi," 196. At about the same time, 781, he explained to Metropolitan Ephrem that he had not been able to visit him because he had been to the caliph six times recently trying to get some churches which had been destroyed rebuilt (Timothy, *Lettres,* 38) and about fifteen years later he told his old school friend, Metropolitan Serge, that he had been to see the Caliph Harun-ar-Rasid three times toward the end of October, 795 (or 796). (Timothy, *Lettres,* 21). On this occasion he came away with a large sum of money, 84,000 zuze.

old Timothy off on horseback to an official meeting in Roman territory.[17] Clearly, he had been able to hold the confidence of key Muslim figures. One quite remarkable comment he made about al-Madhi must be noted—"He is a lovable man, and loves also learning when he finds it in other people."[18] That despite the fact that just before Timothy became Catholicos al-Madhi had destroyed a number of churches and pillaged areas in which there were significant Christian populations.[19] However good his relationships with the caliphs were, he later breathed words of thanks for the lobbying of a court insider, Gabriel, a royal physician, who helped him accomplish an important mission.[20]

The surviving letters, which come from only the first half of Timothy's time in office, give a picture of what was preoccupying him then. He was a builder and was ready to get his hands dirty. Around 790 he allocated 20,000 zuze for the construction of a hospital, and he bought some property for 10,000 zuze on which to build a residence for himself and his successors as Catholicos.[21] Then there was that 84,000 zuze which Marun-ar-Rasid had given him to be spent on a monastery.[22] He also had a deep interest in language and literature. He kept an eye out for rare books, [23] and he worked diligently to make the treasures of Greek antiquity available in his Arabic context.[24] He had a keen sense of the ecclesiastical world of his day, fully aware, for example, of Rome and Constantinople. Timothy was convinced that his own church, located in Seleucia-Ctesiphon, should be acknowledged as superior even to Rome. After all, Christ was born in the East and the East was the first region to embrace Christianity. [25] That would have upset some people in the West if they had ever heard of it. And on top of it all, he was a theologian.

17. Timothy, *Lettres*, 37. Timothy was to leave Baghdad on June 7, 799. At the time he was also collaborating with the Patriarch of the Melkites, another Christian group, and some other Greeks on a translation of Aristotle's *Topics*, and they were all having trouble. He was quite a vigorous septuagenarian.

18. *Apology*, 196.

19. Bidawid, *Les Lettres*, 76. This might have been in response to a defeat Byzantine Emperor Leo IV had inflicted on a Muslim army just previously.

20. Timothy, *Lettres*, 42 and 25.

21. Timothy, *Lettres*, 36.

22. Timothy, *Lettres*, 21.

23. Timothy, *Lettres*, 24.

24. Timothy, *Lettres*, 35.

25. Timothy, *Lettres*, 27.

He addressed many themes, but it was Christology which received his sharpest attention. When he wrote to the monks of the Mār Māronis Monastery, he insisted that Christ must be understood as totally identical (con-substantial) with both the Father and with us,[26] i.e., as the incarnate God-man.

Along with all these interests, he actively promoted the expansion of his church, and I am sure he would have understood that as expanding the Kingdom of God brought by Christ. Leaders in the church, bishops, should be virtuous, spiritual, well versed in the Scriptures, and know three languages, probably Syriac, Arabic, and Persian.[27] He was appointing bishops in what is now Iraq and Iran, but also north among the Turks and even in Tibet.[28] Many have noted the dramatic growth of the Church of the East which reached into Turkestan[29] and beyond. Timothy's period in office may have been one of the most active eras of missionary outreach that ever occurred in the whole of the Christian story. Under him his church claimed tens of millions of members in 230 dioceses and had a reach that was wider than that of the Bishop of Rome.[30] Those are staggering statistics.

One of the most extraordinary events of Timothy's career was a two-day discussion he had with Caliph al-Madhi in 781. It has been suggested that the text we have is actually a literary creation of an event which did not happen, but there seems to be a scholarly consensus that it is authentic.[31] This was not a chat among equals by any means. Timothy can refer to his Sovereign's "humorous smile,"[32] and can say that al-Madhi gave him permission to "Ask anything you want,"[33] but the caliph was in charge and on the offensive throughout. Understanding fully the precariousness of his position, Timothy addressed him constantly with deferential terms like "O God-loving King," "My illustrious Sovereign," and "Commander of the Faithful."

26. Timothy, "Ad Monachos Monasteri Mār Māronis," 101.

27. Timothy, Lettres, 40.

28. Timothy, Lettres, 28, 25, and 37.

29. Hunter, "Church of the East in Central Asia," 138.

30. Baum and Winkler, Church of the East, 60–62.

31. Note for example, Moffett, History of Christianity in Asia, 349–51 and Jenkins, Lost History, 17 and 18.

32. Timothy, "Apology," 195.

33. Timothy, "Apology," 209.

The two leading issues in the dialogue were the divinity of Jesus Christ and the Trinity. Al-Madhi questioned these ideas over and over again, and Timothy kept calling on analogy after analogy trying to explain them. Al-Madhi was not buying. He rejected Timothy's arguments flatly. But that did not stop Timothy. Several times he backed al-Madhi into a corner, and when the caliph realized he had no way out, he simply and decisively changed the subject. In spite of that Timothy did not give up. Before he was done he had rejected the Koran as scripture equal to the Old Testament and the New Testament,[34] refused to acknowledge Muhammad as a prophet,[35] and came within a hair's breadth of charging al-Madhi with unbelief.[36] Then as the end of the discussion was obviously approaching, Timothy used a parable of a pearl to make a point. The point he parted with was that the miracles of the Old Testament, of Jesus, and then the disciples demonstrated that Christianity was superior to Islam.

## DEVELOPMENTS

We leave a very forward-looking, mission-minded Catholicos and move on to review what happened in his world and beyond in the centuries which followed. As suggested above, in Timothy's part of the world, the Christian orientation was outward. Citing a ninth-century document Erica Hunter gave us a typical example in the person of the missionary bishop Mar Subhal-Iso. Timothy made sure Subhal-Iso had received preparatory instruction in Syriac, Arabic, and Persian. He bound him in loyalty to himself by anointing him with oil and giving him a pastoral staff in ordination. Then off Subhal-Iso went into barbarian nations to which no other preacher had gone before. As a missionary evangelist, he baptized people, built churches, ordained clergy to give leadership, and then moved on.[37]

A contemporary of Timothy and Subhal-Iso, Abd al-Masib b. Ishaq al-Kindi, showed just how confident some of these Christians could be. In correspondence with a Muslim, al-Kindi boldly revealed the dark side of Islam. He attacked Muhammad's murderous plans, vindictiveness,

---

34. Timothy, "*Apology*," 172.
35. Timothy, "*Apology*," 197.
36. Timothy, "*Apology*," 216.
37. Hunter, "Church of the East in Central Asia," 141.

and polygamy involving fifteen wives. He characterized Islamic wars as no better than Bedouin raids and contrasted the Muslim demand for jihad with Christ's law of love. Then when his correspondent tried to tantalize him with the delights of Muslim marriage and paradise, he dismissed them as mere sensual pleasures no more worthwhile than the material benefits being a Muslim would bring.[38] Some exhibited this kind of courage and stayed safe, but others encountered very serious trouble trying to maintain their balance on the high wire of religious, social, and political impotence.[39]

Around 850 under Caliph al-Mutawakkil the more or less relaxed climate of toleration changed sharply. Churches were turned into mosques or destroyed, Christian graveyards were razed, and the Christians were forced to wear the yellow patch.[40] Particularly hard days had arrived, but many stood firm. As one example among many others, in the Chu Valley in Central Asia (modern Kyrgyzstan), the church which had been planted in the 700s survived for centuries.[41] In the face of challenges, the Church of the East continued to prosper, and our journey through it has placed many previously unknown pieces of the puzzle into our hands. But what was happening elsewhere?

Iconoclasm was still bubbling in the west, meaning now that part of the world to the west of Syria.[42] In the complex and fluid political and religious world of Constantinople, the Second Council of Nicaea in 787 spoke to that very question. It proclaimed that representational images, painted, in mosaic, or some other suitable material, of Jesus Christ, the Virgin Mary, angels or saints were certainly acceptable. In fact anyone who denied this should be "anathema," placed under a curse. However, these images should be venerated only and not approached with full adoration. That should be reserved for God alone. It also proclaimed that body parts of saints or possessions closely associated with them, known as "relics," had to be built into all churches to add their special holiness to places of worship. Not surprisingly, a response to these decisions came from even farther west.

---

38. Baum and Winkler, *Church of the East,* 67 and 68.

39. Baumer, "Survey of Nestorian and Ancient Nestorian Architectural Relics," 445.

40. Thomas, "Introduction," x and Baumer, "Survey," 455.

41. Dickens, "Syriac Gravestones," 14.

42. See p. 81 above.

Charlemagne continued to wield tremendous influence which grew exponentially following his being crowned as Roman Emperor in St. Peter's Basilica in Rome on December 25, 800. In fact that influence would survive even beyond his death in 814. In 791 the *Libri Carolini* (*Charles' Books*) appeared expressing theological opinions bearing the authority of Charlemagne. These books waded into the issue of icons. They went along with Nicaea II when the council said that only God should be adored (worshipped), but they departed from the council's decisions elsewhere. *Charles' Books* insisted that only saints and their relics should be venerated, not pictures. The pictures were to be welcomed for their aesthetic and educational qualities. They beautified churches and reminded people of the heroic lives of Christians of the past. They brought pleasure and inspiration, but they were not to be treated as objects of religious devotion.

Iconoclasm was only one of many theological questions that was attracting attention in the west in the ninth century in the west. Another was the "*filioque*" clause. The word is Latin, and it can be translated "and from the Son." The question was how did the Holy Spirit come to play a prominent role in the world? The creed that was perhaps most common across Christianity was the one which came out of the Council of Nicaea and was revised at the Council of Constantinople. These gatherings were viewed as ecumenical councils which supposedly spoke for all Christians. It said the Holy Spirit "proceeded from the Father." At some point, Latin-speaking Christians added "and from the Son." One of the first to have done this may have been Ambrose, famous bishop of Milan in the fourth century.[43] The addition was affirmed at the Council of Toledo in 589 and again at the Synod of Aachen in 809, during Charlemagne's reign. However, Pope Leo III refused to approve it. We shall see shortly that the addition of "from the Son" upset the Greek Church in no small measure.

The last theological wrangle that I will mention had to do with the Lord's Supper, also called the Eucharist. The ninth century saw the first major discussion of the Eucharist. Radbertus (d. 853) who was head of the Corbie monastery produced a work entitled *On the Body and Blood of the Lord*. In it he argued that once the priest leading the eucharist had prayed the prayer of consecration the bread and wine became the actual, historical body and blood of Christ. However, only those who spiritu-

---

43. Beck, "Greek Church," 83.

ally understood that this transformation had occurred, actually received Christ's flesh and blood. Others just got bread and wine.

Another monk at Corbie, Ratramnus, a contemporary of Radbertus, was asked his opinion, and he too wrote a book with the same title, but disagreed with his abbot. He argued that the bread and wine do not change at any time, that Christ is certainly present but spiritually, and that the bread and wine are only symbols.

This was also a time of significant differences between the Greek and Latin churches. Leading the church of Rome at a particularly critical point was the very strong Pope Nicholas I (in office 858–67). His assumptions about how the Christian church in general should run seem to have been influenced by what came to called the *False Decretals,* one of which was *Donation of Constantine.* This document showed Constantine ordering all leaders of the Church to be subject to the Bishop of Rome and granted the pope authority over the whole of the Latin Church. It later turned out to be a forgery created in the ninth century, not the fourth, but it had a role to play. When a layman, the brilliant Photius, was made patriarch in Constantinople by Emperor Michael III, Nicholas refused to recognize him. The emperor had thrown Photius predecessor out of office in part at least because he had disciplined the emperor's uncle. An examination of events led to Nicholas' deposing Photius in 863. Not to be outdone, on grounds of heresy, including the insertion of the *filioque* clause in the creed, Photius deposed Nicholas. The mutual depositions were lifted in c. 879, but they definitely added more poison to the waters between Constantinople and Rome.

As the ninth century wore on, conditions became increasingly bleak in Rome. The weakening and then the collapse of the Carolingian dynasty that had started with Pippin left the bishop of Rome in a difficult position. Both the territory the papacy controlled and the papacy itself became vulnerable to an ambitious Roman nobility who wanted to take charge of the highest office of the Latin church. The sad story tells of depositions, imprisonments, murders, and occasionally two or even three men claiming to be pope at the same time. The state of affairs at the time prompted one scholar to pass on a name that has been applied to the decades in question: ". . . the pornocracy of the holy see."[44]

A particularly gruesome instance involved Formosus who had served as pope from 891 to 896. While there were ambiguities in his rise

---

44. Kelly, *Dictionary of Popes,* 120. See also Scholz, "Christopher," 20 and 86.

to office, the chief concern of his successor, Stephen VI, seems to have been that Formosus represented the wrong family or party. In 897 several months after Formosus' death, Stephen had Formosus' body exhumed, dressed in the full vestments of the papal office, and placed on a throne before a synod that has colorfully been called the "cadaveric synod." A deacon placed behind the throne answered for Formosus confessing guilt in response to all charges laid against him. The corpse was then mutilated by cutting off the fingers on the right hand which Formosus had raised in blessing as pope.The body was stripped and thrown into the Tiber. It was fished out and reburied by one of Formosus' loyal followers,[45] but that is not the end of the story. Later the same year those loyal to Formosus managed to get Stephen deposed and strangled.

And this troubling period went on for a long, long time. Half a century after the Formosus affair, and arising out of events very similar in nature, Pope John XII managed to fight his way into office. Once there he found his position difficult to retain. Casting around for allies, he settled on a powerful German king, Otto I. Happy to seize control of as much of Italy as he could, Otto made his way to Rome and while there, John crowned him Holy Roman Emperor in 962. In doing this, John created a new political structure which lasted for more than eight hundred years. The basic idea was that the pope and the emperor would work hand-in-hand, but it became much more complicated than that.

Behind and around all of this, more promising steps in mission were being taken in western European Christianity, too. There were those who had found something in their faith that inspired them with the passion to share it. One of these was St. Boniface who launched his mission to Germany from Britain. He planted the Church in north-central Germany, was appointed Archbishop of Mainz, and sealed his work among the Germans with a martyr's death in 754. As I mentioned above, later that century Charlemagne took a very different approach on his campaigns in Germany. He brought the Church converts he had made by another method: the edge of the sword. In the first half of the ninth century a missionary, Ansgar, pushed into Denmark, Sweden, and Norway, only to be driven out by marauding Northmen. It was not until around 1000 that Christianity took root in Scandinavia.

The story of the conversion of Iceland is a wild account preserved but generally unknown to most people in one of that country's most

---

45. Herbers, "Formosus," 37 and Ewig, "Western Church," 154–57.

famous Sagas. King Olaf Tryggvason of Norway, who had embraced Christianity, sent Thangbrand, a German, to Iceland just before 1000. He fought and killed some who opposed his preaching, on one occasion using a crucifix instead of a shield for protection. Some came to faith, but eventually his mission failed, and he returned to Norway. Olaf sent out two others whose approach to missionary work was less antagonistic. The number of Christians grew, but animosity flared between believers in the old and the new religions. The critical moment came at the annual meeting of the Icelandic parliament, known as the *Althing*. It met beside a river adjacent to a geological rift related to tectonic plates. The key player was Thorgeir Tjorvison, the "Law Speaker," the one who announced decisions of the parliament.

When the Icelanders assembled around the Law Rock from which decisions were proclaimed, tensions ran high between Christians and non-Christians, and it looked as if violence could break out at any moment. The Law Speaker whom the Christians had chosen went to Thorgeir and asked him to decide what the law regarding religion should be. It was a risky move for him because Thorgeir was an adherent to the old religions.

Thorgeir spent the whole day in silence with a cloak over his head. The next day when he spoke to the whole assembly he insisted that all of Iceland must accept one or the other of the religions, and he asked non-Christians and Christians alike to pledge to accept his ruling. They agreed. The crowd waited: "The first principle of our laws," declared Thorgeir, "is that all men in this land shall be Christian and believe in the one God—Father, Son, and Holy Ghost—and renounce all worship of idols."[46] He then added some restrictions on behavior and called for observance of Sundays and all other days important in the Christian year. The non-Christians felt betrayed, but the ruling held and Iceland has never departed from it.

Missionary outreach was close to the hearts of eastern Europeans also. In the late ninth century two brothers, Cyril and Methodius, from Thessalonica were selected by the emperor in Constantinople, Michael III, to answer a request from Moravia to help establish Christianity. They invented a written script for Slavic and moved north ministering effectively and beginning a translation of the gospels. The greatest growth took place a hundred years later under Vladimir (r.980–1015),

---

46. *Njal's Saga*, 225–26.

who ruled at Kiev. He was baptized in 988, established churches and monasteries, and carried Christianity north, laying the foundations for the Russian Orthodox Church.

It was a time of upheaval and success in the west, but in the far east Christians were facing tremendous challenges. Early in the ninth century they appear to have been doing well in China. Their literature had been translated into Chinese, some occupied positions of considerable power,[47] and the recent discovery of a Christian pillar on the second city of the Tang dynasty, Luoyang, shows that there was a strong community of Christian expatriate merchants there.[48] That was about to change.

In 845 Tang Emperor Wuzong issued an edict against foreign religions, aimed primarily at Buddhism, but impacting Manichaeism, Zoroastrianism, and Christianity, too. Reflecting on that, Xie Bizhen said, "This brought Nestorian Christianity in China to an end," and later, ". . . no sign remained of the two hundred years' history of Nestorianism in China."[49] That seems too strong.

The state of the available evidence means that opinions must be tentative. By Wuzong's time Christianity had been in China more than two hundred years. Since it had been there that long, there is no doubt that Christianity had gone through some kind of inculturalization. Surviving texts show that a "buddhisization" had taken place. However, it is becoming increasingly clear that a form of Christianity recognizable as that which was brought to China by Aluoben in 635 continued to exist for centuries. The very fact that someone cared enough about Christian manuscripts to preserve them points in that direction,[50] and so does a growing body of artistic artifacts. With regard to the latter, Ken Parry noted,

> It does appear from the iconographic evidence that the East Syrian community at Quanzhou was aware to some extent of the artistic adaptations under the Tang. This would seem to be evidence for the continuity of "Nestorian" Christianity in China

---

47. Baum and Winkler, *Church of the* East, 49.

48. Tang, "Preliminary Study of the *Jingjiao* Inscription of Luoyang," 110, 125, 130.

49. Xie Bizhen, "History of Quanzhou Nestorianism," 272.

50. Huaiyu, "Connection Between *Jingjiao* and Buddhist Texts," 113 and Nicolini-Zani, "Past and Current Research," 38.

between the edict of 845 proscribing foreign religions and the start of the Mongol period.[51]

Samuel Lieu agreed.[52]

Part of the explanation for the ongoing survival of Christianity in China related to the edict of 845 itself and to events surrounding it. Christoph Baumer pointed out that the emperor succeeding Wuzong was Xuanzong II, who came to office in 846/7. He, in fact, revoked the 845 edict and allowed some reconstruction.[53] In a paper read at the Third International Conference on the Church of the East in China and Central Asia held in Salzburg, Austria in June 2009, Wang Yuanyuan carried the discussion further. He pointed out that Wuzong's offensive against foreign religions was actually spread over several years (842–45) with Buddhism and Manichaeism being dealt with early and rather viciously, and Zorastrianism and Christianity coming into focus later.[54] Yuanyuan argued that if Wuzong had really wanted to wipe out all foreign religions it is unlikely that he would have overlooked the latter two when he was dealing with the first two. He also drew attention to the fact that the action against the Christians was launched only few months before the emperor's death. Consequently, it would not have had time to be carried out as thoroughly as earlier measures were. Last, Yuanyuan underlined that the ban, as it applied to Christians, focused on the laicization of the clergy, not on ordinary believers. Not only may some clergy have escaped the ban, but the laity could have carried on without them.

Before returning to western Europe we will pause on the African continent to visit the warrior nation of Nubia that once extended along the west coast of the Red Sea. It became a Christian nation in the mid-sixth century. One hundred years later the Muslims struck south from Egypt. They were handed an unprecedented defeat by the Nubians at Dongola, the capital of the northern Nubian kingdom of Makuria. The Muslims then entered into a diplomatic relationship with the Nubians which guaranteed Nubian autonomy for more than 600 years.[55] Most of

---

51. Parry, "Art of the Church of the East," 326. The Mongol period started in the second half of the twelfth century.

52. Lieu, "Nestorian Remains from Zaitun," 287.

53. Baumer, *Church of the East,* 186.

54. Yaunyaun, "Doubt on the Viewpoint of Extinction of Nestorianism," 5.

55. Spaulding, "Medieval Christian Nubia," 582.

what we know about the strong and rich Christian culture which flour-ished comes to us through its archaeological remains.[56]

Turning now to Europe north of the Alps, we encounter a new social structure evolving: feudalism. The roots were in France, but it spread in all directions and dominated that part of the world for around 400 years starting in the ninth century. It was built on power and land with both being seen as private possessions of often charismatic figures who had the military strength to support their claims. The arrangement which rounded out the picture was the approval of the Roman Catholic Church which provided sacred legitimization. Charlemagne, who lived into the early ninth century was a model for political figures for centuries.

Charlemagne's experience illustrated a first level of feudalism in which a king gathered around him armed supporters (knights) who were bound to him by oaths, ceremonies, and gifts, often of land. As the ninth century unfolded some of these supporters were able to gather their own knights and acquire control of more and more land leading to hierarchies of allegiance involving knights, great and not so great, princes, counts, dukes, and kings. It must be remembered that the larg-est section of the population—the serfs or peasants—were completely outside the structure. There were customs and laws which defined the places of the serfs, but they had comparatively few rights and were more or less bound to the land of the lord whom they served.

This social structure had two common features. The first was a struggle for dominance between representatives of the Church and the political figures. The clergy insisted they were outside, or above, subor-dination to laymen, while the kings claimed that they ruled by divine right, that is, God had placed them in their offices. The other feature was war. The hierarchy of nobles was a war machine. At all levels the men were trained fighters, and fight they did, knights vs. knights, princes vs. princes right up to kings vs. kings, with subordinates fighting in the wars of their lords. Our view of the era is sweetened by romantic chivalry, but it was a time of tension, conflict, and bloodshed.

## CONCLUSION

The period from around 700 to 1000 was hardly a tranquil period as one tries to hold global Christianity in perspective. There is much that is

---

56. See http://rumkatkilise.org/nubia.htm.

deeply troubling: terrible persecution that Christians met at the hands of Muslims over and over again; the revolting corruption rampant among those who clawed their way to leadership in the Christian Church; the culture of violence that emerged in Europe.

There is also encouragement. There are the determined attempts to insert the gospel into the cultures of China, the passion to find the best thought-forms and the language to get the message across. There is the missionary drive of Timothy I and his bishops, going boldly where no Christian had gone before. There is the thirst for education— east, central, and west—to understand the Bible clearly and to shape doctrine correctly.

And there is encouragement also in less visible, spiritual activities. People were praying in monasteries and convents, and wherever else there were Christians. Peasants were surrounding and punctuating their ordinary days of work with prayer. Many who sat on thrones of great power prayed too. It is easy to overlook that. People associated with Christianity everywhere understood the complexity and the challenges of life, and they sought God's guidance. We often do not like their decisions, and I expect that they would be troubled with many of ours.

People served, and they did it in the name of Christ. It is hard to catch them at it. That kind of thing does not make the headlines either then or now, but they were being faithful in service. Christian monasteries were renowned, even among Muslims, for welcoming the desperately ill or the unmanageably insane. The priests did the rounds of their parishes; the village "prayer warrior" installed beside the sick bed helped the dying to a good death. It is humanity, that is what it is, but it is in the name of Christ.

# 6

# Take the Cross! "God Wills It!"

## *1095 AD*

IF ONE IS TO acknowledge the designation, "Middle Ages," then 1095 is the middle of the Middle, fenced by the markers 450 at the beginning and 1450 at the end, blending into the Rennaisance. Other terms, the "dark ages," or what some prefer, the "medieval period," may highlight some aspect—the loss of art, learning or commerce, for instance—or its "inbetweeness" with reference to other times. There are some problems with all the names. In the first place, they are European names and that means they do not work so well in breaking down the human story into manageable pieces in other parts of the world. The Chinese, for example, may be more comfortable with structuring time by imperial dynasties.

Secondly, the names—"middle" or "dark"—could imply that the time between c.450 and c.1450 was not as valued as some other periods, such as antiquity or modernity. What does "dark" mean? There are certainly aspects of the years in question that were unquestionably regressive, but there were features of the times before and after the middle ages that were troubling, too. Think of the slave trade in antiquity and the global terrorism of—what shall we call it?—post-modernity.

This 1,000 year period in Europe is a source of great fascination. Wandering through the monasteries and cathedrals built at that time gives us a sense of the size of people's souls. The architecture, the engineering, the carving are spell-binding. The music, both secular and religious, haunts us, and people continue to pour over the poetry and theology of the era. Certainly there are other dimensions of the time that are a little more challenging to come to grips with, and we turn to one now—the European crusading era. In the popular imagination, the Crusades represent a low point, one of Christian violence and mayhem. One hears this in the cool raging of the rock group "System of a Down" in their song "War?"[1] On the other hand, the assessment of a current historian sounds quite different. Peter Lock said,

> It might once have been fashionable to dismiss the Crusades as violent, barbarous and cruel, based on morally dubious grounds. We must never forget, though, that the crusaders were men of their time operating within the values of that time, and that they should not be judged by modern ethical and moral standpoints any more than their Muslim opponents should.[2]

Judging them "out of their time" would be like wondering why they did not keep in touch with their wives using their cell phones. But there are no grounds here to collapse into sheer relativism. While allowance may be made for the era in which they lived, it must be remembered that theirs was a culture that embraced absolute standards of behavior much more strongly than ours does. Be that as it may, their actions continue to define the relationship between Christians and Muslims for many of us. Keep in mind that the Muslims were just as effective in commiting appalling acts of violence as the Crusaders were even if that is overlooked in current thinking in the west.

## SETTING

Many events set the stage for the crusading era. Some grew out of tension within the Christianity of the day. Earlier on we have encountered the misunderstanding and anger between the Greek Church centered on Constantinople and its Latin counterpart in Rome. In the eleventh century, 1054 to be exact, the bad feeling erupted again, ending with solemn curses being flung in both directions that severed formal relations between them until 1965. The players were Emperor Constantine IX, Monomachos (r. 1042–55) and Patriarch Keroularios (in office 1043–58) in the East and Pope Leo IX (pope 1048–54) supported by Cardinal Bishop Humbert of Silva Candida (in office 1050–61) in the West.

---

1. View a performance on YouTube.

2. Lock, *Routledge Companion to the Crusades*, 442. Please note that that implies that all current values are superior to all values held back then, which of course is debatable.

The convoluted political and religious realities seemed to call for some sort of coordinated action between Rome and Constantinople to control the threatening aspirations of Normans who continued to make claims to territory in southern Italy. Unfortunately, correspondence between the two Christian leaders was fraught with bias and suspicion. Building on the *Donation of Constantine* among other things, Leo insisted on his superiority while Keroularios spoke out of a growing sense that it was only in Constantinople that true Christianity had been preserved unharmed.[3]

Rome sent a delegation to negotiate with Constantinople, but it was doomed from the beginning. It was led by a hothead, Humbert, who had to deal primarily with Keroularios, another hothead. The air soon thickened with charges and countercharges. Keroularios faulted Rome for fasting on Saturday, using unleavened bread in the eucharist (watch this one), and inserting the *filioque*[4] clause into the creed. Enraged, Humbert went after similar issues, the procession of the Holy Spirit and Greek priests being permitted to marry, but he focused on the Greek use of leavened bread in communion. Humbert verbally attacked an elderly monk who had written against using unleavened bread and had his essay thrown into the fire.[5] The outcome of this ill will was Humbert and his colleagues' laying a document excommunicating Keroularios and those who supported him on the high altar of the main church in Constantinople, Hagia Sophia, on July 16, 1054. This was matched eight days later by Constantinople's excommunicating Humbert and his supporters.

Here is where a nasty twist occurs. In the super-heated passion and rhetoric of the day, both of these documents were viewed as excommunicating a whole branch of the Christian Church not just a few individuals. Technically, they were not doing that. As Beck said, ". . . no act had been performed which would permit one to speak of a schism in the strict sense,"[6] and there is nothing to indicate that those living at the time thought this tiff would last very long. Unfortunately, the falling out did come to be seen as a schism, and the ruptured relationship remained unhealed until 1965 when Pope Paul VI and Patriarch Athenagoras I

---

3. Beck, "Byzantine Church," 412.

4. See p. 91 below.

5. Beck, "Byzantine Church," 415.

6. Beck, "Byzantine Church," 417.

mutually cancelled the excommunications in both Rome and Istanbul. Incidentally, Leo IX under whose authority Humbert acted, had been dead for three months when the excommunication was laid on the altar.

The place of the kind of bread used in communion played a curious role. Both sides had a cogent rationale for their practice, but the argument came at a time when Rome was preoccupied with getting people to accept papal primacy and with tightening up doctrine and practice.[7] Using leavened bread became the key charge Humbert laid against Keroularios. There is irony here. First, in a document written about the time the delegation went to Constantinople, Leo never said that using leavened bread was illegal, but that unleavened bread was better. Second, Whalen points out that two leading eleventh-century Latin theologians, Lanfranc of Bec and Anselm of Canterbury, both argued that the nature of the bread was not an issue because after the prayer of consecration by the priest "there was no bread on the altar."[8] Whatever was there had become the flesh of Christ!

As the ecclesiastical clouds darkened over Constantinople so did the political ones. Danger had arrived from the east. A Turkic people, the Seljuks, had flowed west south-west from Central Asia. They were integrated into the Sunni branch of Islam, and they carved out a place for themselves on the eastern side of the Abbasid Empire in 1040. They entered Baghdad in 1055 where their leader, Tughril Bey, was recognized as protector of the caliph, or sultan. Between 1070 and 1075 they proceeded to wrest Aleppo, Damascus, and Jerusalem away from the Fatimids, Shiite Muslims who ruled Egypt. The Fatimids managed to regain control of most of the towns along the Mediterranean coast in 1089 and they drove the Seljuks out of Jerusalem in 1098. For the Byzantine Empire centered in Constantinople, the critical date was August 26, 1071.

This was the date of the Battle of Manzikert. Young emperor Romanus IV Diogenes with a motley army of mostly mercenaries faced Sultan Alp Arslan and his army of Seljuks on the borders of Armenia. By the time the day ended, the imperial army had been defeated and what is now Turkey ultimately became open to the Turks. Now nothing is that simple and especially nothing in the Byzantine Empire. Paul Markham argued that the battle was waged in a context of truly byzantine intrigue

---

7. Whalen, "Rethinking the Schism of 1054," 4–5 and 8–9.

8. Whalen, "Rethinking the Schism of 1054," 22.

and treachery.[9] It was followed by civil war and chicanery of a sort that would have made Machiavelli himself proud. It was a military defeat, but it was not a devastating defeat. Scheming before and after inside the empire was what made it turn out to be devastating. Events surrounding the battle also illustrated the profound cracks in Islam of the time, featuring the Seljuks, the Abbasids, and Fatimids, and any number of local operatives trying to elevate themselves.

At approximately the same time as these clashes at the eastern end of the Mediterranean, there were significant stirrings taking place in Rome. You may remember what I called the "cadaveric synod"[10]– Formosus, Rome, late ninth century. Circumstances were pretty much in disarray. The crowning of a Holy Roman Emperor in 962 (although the name came later), bringing together the power of the German king Otto I and the mysterious glamor of the imperial crown,[11] improved conditions marginally, but major difficulties persisted throughout the tenth century and into the eleventh. 1050 saw the beginning of 75 years of papal reigns during which real reform was attempted. Those living at that time, particularly the leadership in the Roman Catholic Church, saw the same problems we see when we look back and, no doubt, they felt them more acutely.

There were certain pressing issues that they were convinced had to be dealt with. First was "lay investiture," the practice of laymen like the Holy Roman Emperor, choosing people like archbishops, bishops, and priests, installing them in office with appropriate symbols (shepherd's crooks and so on), and then controlling them for their own interests. Second was "simony," using money or promises of favors in order to "buy" a position in the Church, archbishoprics, for example. Third was clerical "fornication" or "adultery," priests, bishops, etc. living with women whether married or not. The desired antidote to this problem was "celibacy," clergy living unmarried and without sexual contact of any kind with women.[12] Added to these is a fourth, obedience: Christians, both ordained and non-ordained recognizing and submitting to the au-

9. Markham, "Battle of Manzikert."

10. See p. 92–93.

11. Kempf, "Church and the Western Kingdoms," 204–207.

12. Charles A. Frazee has offered a thorough study of the issue. Among other things, he argued that in Rome's Easter Synod of 1051 Pope Leo IX called for the enslavement of clerical wives. See Frazee's, "Origins of Clerical Celibacy," 121.

thority of those above them in the hierarchy. Friedrich Kempf insisted that "The reformers wanted to find the way back to the ancient pure church, to the free play of the forces proper to her,"[13] and they probably were that high-minded. Nevertheless, these are the big four which stand out in the surviving letters of Pope Gregory VII (1073–85), which is the only significant collection of its kind from the popes who worked in this era.[14] Furthermore, it is this pope who is universally recognized as dominant in the seventy-five year period of top level reforming. Kempf's comment is "Gregory's pontificate was a turning point in the history of the Roman primacy."[15]

The issue which overrode all others for Gregory VII was lay investiture. He wanted the Church to get control over itself by being able to put in office suitable people according to appropriate criteria and procedures. There were other sides to the question, too, and the person who pressed some of them was Henry IV, king of Germany in 1056 (at age six), Holy Roman Emperor in 1084, a position which he held until 1105, one year before his death. The dust-up between these two careened through the whole of Gregory's time as pope. It is one of the great melodramas in the whole Christian story.

It reeled its way through civil wars in Germany, two excommunications of Henry by Gregory, and a standoff at the gates of "Duke" Matilda's castle in Canossa, north Italy where Gregory had taken shelter. For the occasion Henry appeared in the clothes of a penitent and barefoot in the snow outside the castle, and Gregory did not let him in until he had repeated the performance twice. This shows how desperate Henry was to keep Gregory from getting to a meeting that had been called for February in south Germany. He had actually crossed the Alps with an entourage including his wife and her ladies who glided down the Mont Cenis Pass on ox-skins—in January! The effort paid off. Henry was able to return to Germany with his excommunication cancelled and set about revenging himself against the politicians and churchmen who had opposed him at home.

In the early 1080s Henry led an army into Italy which besieged Rome for years. Finally, with Gregory holed up in the then impregnable Castel Sant Angelo, Henry installed his own antipope who crowned

13. Kempf, "Changes," 426.

14. Cowdrey, "Introduction," xi.

15. Kempf, "Changes," 372–73.

Henry as Holy Roman Emperor in 1084. Henri Daniel-Rops said Gregory did offer to install Henry as Holy Roman Emperor by lowering the imperial crown onto Henry's head on a rope.[16] Apparently Henry declined preferring his own plans. Eventually some of Gregory's friends managed to get Henry out of Rome, but they then created such havoc in the city that Gregory had to leave when they did, and he finally died in Salerno. Henry lived on to make trouble for Gregory's successors.

Without question, Gregory was one very determined pope, and Kempf can say that his greatness is to be seen "in his religious, perhaps mystically gifted, personality, in the abundance of the divine experience given to him, taken up by his genius, and converted into action,"[17] and that may be so. But his letters give us a clear window into his soul, and it was a soul beset by agony.

Occasionally, he poured out his heart to intimate friends. He had great regard for Beatrice and her daughter, Matilda. The former was Countess of Tuscany (d. 1076). (Occasionally Gregory called her "duke."[18]) Matilda, who succeeded her mother, ruled much of north Italy and acted like a duke.[19] In his torment Gregory said to them "Having still been preserved for our accustomed labors and infinite cares, we hour by hour suffer as it were the pains and afflictions of a woman in labor, when by no steersman's skill are we able to rescue a church that is almost being shipwrecked before our eyes."[20] To his mentor, Hugh, the powerful and influential head of the famous Abbey of Cluny he wrote, "I am buffeted by a thousand storms and as it were, dying I live, and I await for him who has bound me with his chains[21] and who has brought me, though unwilling, back to Rome and there girded me about with a thousand afflictions."[22]

It is surprising to see him display this level of candidness even with William I, King of England. In 1074 he used the nautical image again

16. Daniel-Rops, *Cathedral and Crusade*, 180.

17. Kempf, "Gregorian Reform," 369.

18. *Register*, 4.

19. Reynolds, "Reading Matilda," 1.

20. *Register*, 103. I can see these two women look at each other and raise their eyebrows as this man, much less one who has never even been married, talks about childbirth.

21. Probably Christ.

22. *Register*, 140.

describing the Church as a ship battered by tornadoes and huge waves, managing to avoid hidden rocks, "yet also near exhaustion,"[23] and then went on to cite the problems he faced, saying, "by day and night we are particularly consumed by our concern with them." There was political manipulation behind this candor I suspect—he was also looking for a prompt payment of the *quasi* tax called Peter's Pence. However bad it was at the moment, there was worse to come. And once he was in the midst of it, in May 1077, he wrote an open letter to the German faithful describing his Church as the "holy church which is now almost collapsing."[24] More politics? Blatant or subtle politics or just flat out transparency, it is clear that when he was about to die the scars of battle were livid on his soul. Gregory's final words—"I have loved righteousness and I have hated iniquity, therefore I die in exile."[25] And so he did, in Salerno.

Circumstances were difficult in the Christian world, both east and west, but we are looking at that part of it north and west of Jerusalem. Islam was firmly rooted in Spain, along the north coast of Africa, and through the Middle East up toward Constantinople. At the same time, the head of the Roman Catholic Church was groaning under the burden of his office and wringing his hands in public about the church. What kind of a reaction might one expect in these circumstances? Probably not large numbers of Christians heading for Jerusalem. Yet, that is exactly what was happening.

Peter Lock described the eleventh century as a period of mass pilgrimages of Christians to Jerusalem,[26] and Ronald Finucane made the point that Islam acknowledged their right to come there as "people of the book."[27] Furthermore, as guides and shopkeepers the Muslims profited from the Christians' pilgrimages. Finucane also drew attention to the spiritual motivation for these pilgrimages. He suggested it may have been behind an *en masse* trip of some 7000 Germans to Jerusalem in 1064–65.[28]

---

23. *Register*, 74.
24. *Register*, 238.
25. *Register*, 446.
26. Lock, *Routledge Companion to the Crusades*, 306.
27 Finucane, *Soldiers of Faith*, 15.
28 Finucane, *Soldiesr of Faith*, 15.

The experience of these German Christians illustrates the difficulty involved in pilgrimages at that time. First, most of the "Holy Land" was the site of considerable internecine war among various Muslim groups. A trip through a battlefield is not the safest route to take at any time, and at this time travelers had to cope with with tremendous difficulties in communications and accommodations. This would be multiplied many times over for groups the size of the 7,000 that followed the Bishop of Bamberg to Jerusalem. Certainly the fighting was not directed specifically at Christians, but pilgrims and soldiers would be competing for the same roads, the same sources of water, and the same food supplies.

Beyond these difficulties mentioned, there was actual violence and the threat of violence directed toward these visiting Christians. For example, the German group above had to defend itself against bandits while on route. There was no political infrastructure which kept the peace. Added to this, there were tolls demanded of Christians as they passed through towns and regions. There was no regulation of this either. People with weapons could ask for whatever they liked, and it seems as though toward the end of the eleventh century these conditions worsened.[29]

As we move through the eleventh century, we are increasingly in the presence of an idea waiting to be born. Muslims were threatening the existence of the Greek empire in Constantinople. Pilgrimages were becoming a more hazardous undertaking. In the West peace movements had arisen to try to control the carnage wrought by Christian knights in Europe. People talked about the "Peace of God" and the "Truce of God." In this context the idea of "holy wars" resurfaced and came to be directed against those who threatened the peace of God, specifically, the Muslims in Spain and south Italy. Military action against them was seen as defensive. In addition to this, at least twice in surveying Gregory's correspondence for 1074 we find him encouraging military action against the Muslims in the East as a means of providing relief for eastern Christians.[30] The seeds of the moment were swollen with future conflict.

## EVENT

The idea found its champion in north-east France in the tiny village of Lagery surrounded by rich farm land. Odon de Lagery, also known as

---

29. Lock, *Routledge Companion to the Crusades*, 412.
30. *Register*, 51 and 128.

Eudes de Châtillon, was born into the nobility of Champagne in 1042. He is a favorite son in Lagery with a square named after him. The Church of St. Martin with its beautifully carved capitals was built a hundred years after he lived there. He grew up in the Church and for the Church becoming first prior of Cluny, then Cardinal-bishop of Ostia in Italy, and finally in 1088 Bishop of Rome as Urban II. The final eleven years of his life had fascinating consequences. "Fully assenting to Gregory's principles, but elastically adapting their implementation to the present situation, Urban II led the reform papacy out of the narrow pass and toward victory."[31] Of course Kempf, who described Oden/Eudes' ascent to the throne of Peter and success, would not want us to assume that it was as easy as the statement implies. And it was not.

Urban could not get into his palace for a couple of years after his election as pope. The Holy Roman Emperor, Henry IV, Gregory VII's major thorn in the side, was still around and so was the antipope, Clement III, whom Henry had installed on Peter's Throne. It seems as though Urban only managed to take up residence when he employed bribery. As his ability to neutralize Henry and Clement began to grow so did his exercise of authority. In 1089 at the Synod of Melfi, still far south of Rome, he renewed Pope Gregory's prohibitions of simony, clerical marriage, and lay investiture, firmly embracing Gregory VII's agenda. Writing to someone he knew well, he said,

> Trust and have confidence about me thus in all things, just as about my most blessed lord Pope Gregory. Desiring completely to follow in his footsteps, I spit out everything which he spat out, what he reproached I reproach. But what he deemed valid and catholic I embrace and approve, and I believe and confirm altogether, in all respects, what he in the end believed about each side.[32]

It was perhaps around the same time that he was meeting in Melfi that Urban first heard the request for military assistance from the Byzantine Emperor Alexios I (r.1081–1118). After establishing himself in Rome, he set out north summoning a council to meet at Piacenza. It was there in March 1095 that a plea for help from Alexios reached him and it sparked a response.[33]

---

31. Kempf, "Gregorian Reform," 386.

32. Pope Urban II, Collectio Britannica, 45.

33. Lock, *Routledge Companion to the Crusades*, 338.

Urban did not preach the sermon that propelled Europe into action until six months later, November 28, 1095. In the meantime the concepts of a holy war and a pilgrimage seem to have come together in his mind. He felt compelled to help Christians in Spain, but the need in the East seemed even more urgent. The venue he chose at which to unveil his vision was Clermont in France. A council had been summoned. Hundreds of churchmen and a large number of political figures were present. For the special moment a podium was hastily constructed in a field outside the city. Urban mounted the platform and launched into his appeal. Ironically, "What Urban actually said at Clermont does not survive."[34] The record of his historic address only comes down to us in several partially contradictory accounts written a full three and a half years later. Between the speaking and the recording was the tremendous difficulty in carrying out the venture and its surprising success.[35]

Urban emphasized the dire straits in which Christians in the Greek East found themselves. He elaborated on the viciousness of the Turks. He raised the idea of the Peace of God, urging Europeans to divert their aggressiveness from the ongoing large and small battles among themselves to a defensive and holy war against those who were profaning Christian holy sites and torturing and killing Christians. His preaching struck a responsive chord. The throng began to chant "God wills it!" and knights surged forward to take cloth crosses to show that they had committed themselves to the vision which came to be seen as a crusade.

There was also the promise of spiritual benefit from participation. This would, after all, be a pilgrimage to Jerusalem and that had long been seen as the ultimate act in gaining God's favor and forgiveness. However, the hope that Urban held out appears to have been somewhat vague. R. W. Southern thought that it involved the assurance that if soldiers died in a state of repentance and confess while on crusade they would gain immediate entry to heaven.[36] Lock's opinion was that "Urban . . . seems to have offered commutation[37] of penance rather than remissions of sins."[38] Somewhat cynically perhaps, Riley-Smith said that Urban offered Crusaders indulgences which at that time were "probably no more

---

34. Lock, *Routledge Companion to the Crusades*, 298.
35. Lock, *Routledge Companion to the Crusades*, 298.
36. Southern, *Western Society*, 136.
37. Commutation—the changing of one punishment to a lighter one.
38. Lock, *Routledge Companion to the Crusades*, 295.

than guarantees that the crusade would be so severe a penance that it would make satisfaction for all sin previously committed."[39] The spiritual benefit of going on crusade actually was only spelled out fully as late as 1145. Simply put, death on crusade equaled martyrdom and guaranteed immediate entry to heaven.[40]

A wave of enthusiasm rose from Clermont. Urban focused on recruiting bishops and other prelates to spread the word, and many took up the cause. Unauthorized preachers like Peter the Hermit also seized the vision out of deep religious intensity which had been widely felt for some time in Europe. He and others were also motivated by popular expectations of the immanent end of the world. Urban, himself, stayed in his home country for six months preaching at services throughout south and central France. Riley-Smith gave a compelling account of Urban's travels as the pope swung the full weight of the authority of Peter, the Prince of the Apostles, behind the dream of the liberation of Jerusalem.[41]

The response was overwhelming, far beyond anyone's expectations, including Urban's. The number of people involved in the first crusade is impossible to gauge accurately. Estimates range from 136,000 to 60,000. The departure date that Urban had set was mid-August, 1096, but the first group led by Peter the Hermit set out several months earlier. There may have been 15,000 men in that group. Some think it was much larger, perhaps as many as 70,000, but that guess may include non-combatants. Furthermore, no one knows the ratio between mounted knights and foot soldiers.[42] For sure, direction and control quickly slipped out of Urban's hands. He had envisioned an army of professional fighters. However, he had presented the undertaking as a pilgrimage with comprehensive spiritual benefits, so when just anyone chose to take the cross there was little he could do to stop it. He would only have heard about that happening after the fact anyway.

But the question needs to be asked, why did so many eagerly take up this cause? Because of the multitudes of pilgrims travelling to and from Jerusalem many people in western Europe knew all too well the dangers inherent in such a journey. Pirates, bandits, inn keepers, crowded and stifling boats, disease, bad food, water shortages—not to mention battles

---

39. Riley-Smith, "Crusades, 1095–1198," 543.

40. Lock, *Routledge Companion to the Crusades,* 295.

41. Riley-Smith, "Crusades, 1095–1198," 538.

42. Finucane, *Soldiers of Faith,* 72.

with people who were thoroughly intimidating enemies—all added up to what should have been effective deterrents. Unimpressed, they went in their tens of thousands.

It has been popular to assume a variety of motives driving these pilgrims. Stories have abounded of young sons lacking a landed inheritance who set out to create futures for themselves. There has been talk about the greedy who sought easy plunder, and about the bored and who wanted adventure. Comment has been made about technological advances—the horse collar for instance—improving agriculture which in turn led to population growth, thereby taxing food supplies. All of these suggestions may have been in play to varying degrees amongst different groups. However, other proposals have called the validity of these prevailing explanations into question.

First, it has been observed that younger sons were not disproportionately represented among the knights who made up the armies. In fact, many whole families, lords, their heirs, and their younger sons were among the troops. Some might have been looking for land, a prime indicator of power under feudalism, but many were expecting to fight, and, if they lived, return home.[43] Second, the opportunity to acquire booty seems not to have been as important as it has sometimes been assumed. Rodney Stark emphasized that the crusaders understood that the enterprise would be a costly business, and they made arrangements to pay their own way. Stark also pointed out that when Pope Alexander gave French knights the opportunity to make themselves rich by fighting in a religious war in Spain in 1063 the response was underwhelming. Why? Stark answered, "Spain was not the Holy Land! Christ had not walked the streets of Toledo, nor was he crucified in Seville."[44]

The basic factors motivating Crusades were spiritual. Peter Lock said, "Piety was at the root of all crusading vows and penance was fundamental to those who voluntarily took the cross."[45] Around this time the thought about Christ was reveling in the incarnation—the idea that Christ had become a human person and walked among people on earth in order to provide salvation.[46] At some point the idea caught with Europeans that if they went on crusade, they would be going to

43. Lock, *Routledge Companion to the Crusades*, 301.

44. Stark, "Religious Effects," 294.

45. Lock, *Routledge Companion to the Crusades*, 317.

46. Pelikan, *Growth of Medieval Theology*, 117–20.

the Holy Land, that part of the world in Jesus actually lived, and they were going to reclaim it. They were going to help brothers and sisters in Christ who were being abused and oppressed. They were going to do something which would help their own salvation and possibly even in some way aid loved ones who had died before them. These people took the cross for a variety of motives, but deeply embedded spiritual concerns—whether sound or otherwise—were never far from the surface. And they achieved their most immediate goal. On July 15, 1099 they entered Jerusalem. In the process of reaching their ultimate objective, they also carved out Christian states in the Holy Land that survived for two hundred years. Pope Urban died two weeks after this great victory.

Urban never lived to hear that the project he had launched was a "success." Perhaps he was fortunate. The few letters of his that have survived permit us to get a sense of who the man was. In the light of the character qualities these letters reveal, he may well have been deeply troubled by some of the things that transpired both as the crusading era began, and as it rolled out over the next two hundred years. Perhaps this is an instance of projecting our current sensibilities back onto him. Evaluating peoples' behavior first by the standards of their own time, an approach any historian needs to acknowledge, is not the only way to look at what they did. In this case, there are many facets of the story that are revolting by almost any standards.

Starting with the worst, there were the vicious attacks on the Jewish population along the Rhine valley and beyond at the beginning of the first crusade. Peter Lock's account in particular informs my viewpoint, although most historians address this. Groups of crusaders that assembled along the Rhine, involving people from England, Lorraine, and France as well as Germany[47] set out early in 1096 sometime just after the departure of those led by Peter the Hermit. As they moved south they gave vent to their anti-semitic feelings. Jewish communities in Cologne, Mainz, and Worms were destroyed with between 700 and 1300 victims being murdered in Mainz.[48] Further hatred was poured on Jews in Rouen, Trier, Metz, Speyer, and Regensburg. Where they can be determined, the number of fatalities was lower than in the towns farther

47. Riley-Smith, "Crusades, 1095–1198," 539.
48. Lock, *Routledge Companion to the Crusades*, 398.

north, 22 in Metz, 11 in Speyer, and none in Regensburg,[49] but a sense of the horror and the terror remain and the shame is indelible.

Moving to the next blot on the record, we find cannibalism. The number of crusaders who actually made it to the Holy Land dropped considerably the farther south they plodded. Statistics are difficult to establish. Disease, desertion, and dissention kept shifting the size of the group that showed up for specific sieges and battles. Shortage of food was a constant problem. Lack of money and markets necessitated much foraging and prayer. That was the background to the decision on the part of some to cook and eat parts of dead human bodies.

Lock and Finucane acknowledged that cannibalism occurred at Marra (or Marrat an-Numan—same place),[50] while Jay Rubenstein agreed with them, but also found evidence of the practice at the sieges of Nicaea and Antioch.[51] Both he and Finucane argued that there was more to it than just the inability to find provisions. Finucane associates the cannibalism with the Tafurs, who were a part of the group led by Peter the Hermit.

The Tafurs were among the poorest of the poor who had survived the slaughter around Nicaea. In the battle there, the Muslims had virtually obliterated that stream of enthusiasts who had set out from Europe early in 1096. The Tafurs fought like men possessed. Using only pointed sticks or just bare hands, protected by no armor, they surged to the front of engagements and threw themselves on the enemy. Their very wildness was terrifying. Finucane said Peter the Hermit encouraged Tafurs to see Turkish corpses as "new manna." This led to "sacred cannibalism carried out by a closed community of the poor dedicated to throwing themselves, without inhibition, against the enemy in hopes of reaching either

49. Lock, *Routledge Companion to the Crusades*, 398. W. B. Bartlett's account of these events is particularly powerful—Bartlett, *God Wills It!*, 36–8. Lock summarizes, "It is impossible to quantify the consequences of crusader violence against the Jews. It is not known how many Jews were actually resident in Europe. Estimates vary between 30,000 and 50,000 *in toto*. In terms of loss of life it is reckoned between 3,000 and 5,000, or 1 per cent, were casualties of the First Crusade, most of these perishing as a result of the assault on Jerusalem. For all the other crusades put together a total of 1,000 has been estimated. Any estimates of the material and cultural damage are not available." Lock, *Routledge Companion to the Crusades*, 402.

50. Lock, *Routledge Companion to the Crusades*, 327 and Finucane, 64–65.

51. Rubenstein, *Cannibals and Crusaders*, 550.

the earthly or heavenly homeland of God."[52] The explanation serves to make the practice even more repulsive.

The first crusade ended with Christians in possession of Jerusalem. The day they took the city, July 15, 1099 included more mind-numbing events. Crusaders swarmed the city, killing everyone who moved: Mulsim soldiers, non-combatants, Jews, and even Christians. Promises of safe passage out of the city following surrender were broken, Jews were burned alive in a synagogue, and here and there blood ran ankle deep. Then the day ended with a service of worship in the Church of the Holy Sepulcher. These were dark times.

There is no justification for the butchery, but perhaps some light can be shed on these events by recognizing the prevailing social standards. The crusaders came from a culture that valued war and military prowess. From the time they were teenagers, men perfected the skills of combat. Competence and success meant defeating and probably killing enemies. There was some moderating influence. This was the time when the ideals of "Chivalry" were beginning to be developed, and definite rules of combat were evolving. None the less, as in all wars everywhere throughout time, the crusaders assumed that their enemies were sub-human agents of evil. Soldiers do terrible things in war. I have never been a soldier. I have never been face-to-face with people who are hacking my friends to pieces and trying to do the same to me. I do not really know what a person feels in those circumstances. What is clear is that in these battles "The rulers and warriors of Islam were no less vicious or ruthless than their crusading counterparts,"[53] a fact that could only lead to horrific struggles.

Whatever else happened as a result of this crusade, it had remarkable implications for Pope Urban II. About him, Kempt wrote :

> When, disregarding the kings and relying only on his apostolic authority, he summoned the knights to the holy war and found so powerful a response that for the first time in Western history a supranational army set forth for the defense of Christendom, he became the spontaneously recognized leader of the Christian West.[54]

---

52. Finucane, *Soldiers of God*, 128.

53. Lock, *Routledge Campanion to the Cursades*, 406.

54. Kempf, "Changes," 449.

## DEVELOPMENTS

Following 1099, the crusading spirit survived for a very long time. The attempts to take and hold the Holy Land, itself, finally ended in failure toward the end of the thirteenth century—that is after two hundred years of struggle to maintain a Christian presence there. Some of the events that transpired during that time stretch credulity. Eagerly or reluctantly, over and over again, armies were pulled together and headed off by land and/or sea. They were assembled by saints and rogues. They established and lost five states in and around the epicenter, Jerusalem. They cooperated carefully, and they fought with each other. There was at least one time when two Muslim leaders—who hated each other and who were at war—both hired Crusaders mercenaries. Consider the spectacle of two Muslim armies both made up Muslims and Christians locked in battle against each other. Strange inter-religious dialogue.

In 1204 the crusading army en route to the Holy Land never reached its destination, but decided instead on a side trip to Constantinople where soldiers pillaged mercilessly and then went home satisfied. Remember one of the prime motives behind the whole crusading venture was to help oppressed Greek Christians. 1212 saw thousands of French and German children marching off toward Jerusalem believing that when their feet touched the waters of the Mediterranean the waves would part and they would walk to the Holy Land on dry ground. The waters did not part. Many died en route. It was reported that some were sold into slavery—by Christian merchants, to Muslims.[55] The rest were sent home.

Despite all the savagery, the Crusades were not uniformly appalling, however challenging I find that to say. In the midst of the war, confusion, and chaos there were also positive exchanges between Muslims and Christians and the sharing of ideas on many levels. Further, for two hundred years pilgrimage to Jerusalem was a little easier.[56] Finally, Peter Lock's assessment was, "For me they [the Crusades] are a very positive series of events involving adaptation, invention and innovation on the part of a significant group in western society."[57] This sounds like a bold comment, but he said they have to rank with the efforts of

55. Lock, *Routledge Companion to the Crusades*, 166.

56. As an example, there is a note to that effect in the letters of Hildegard of Bingen mentioning a priest on his way back from Jerusalem in 1176—*Letters of Hildegard of Bingen*, 35.

57. Lock, *Routledge Companion to the Crusades*, 442.

the Byzantine Empire and Charles Martel in delaying the impact Islam has had on the west.[58]

There were also many other currents flowing in Europe during this time which are of great interest. One was a robust spirituality which carpeted the area from the Atlantic to Moscow and beyond. It was in the parish life of local communities, and in the many monastic communities of either women or men which were integral parts of their settings. It also had its superstars. Hildegard of Bingen (1098–1179) was one. Known by popes and emperors, her fame rested on her reputation as a prophet. She wrote up her visions and published them along with other works of music and even medicine. Her correspondence illustrates her being consulted by many seeking guidance for their lives. One monk pours out his thanks to God for her, saying, "Venerable mother, we reflect on the singular gifts bestowed upon you by the Holy Spirit, gifts scarcely heard of through all the ages up to the present day."[59] An example of her counsel is a comment made to the head of a monastery who sought her advice: "Do not regard your Lord as your servant, but look to Him faithfully like an honorable knight who, armed with helmet and breastplate, fights bravely in the battle. These times are the times that cast God into oblivion, times weary of waging Christ's battle. Through the vain love of novelty and change, lies fly abroad, as if the people see God—and yet they know Him not."[60]

In addition to Hildegard, we should keep in mind the mendicant orders, the Franciscans and the Dominicans, whose foundations were approved in the early thirteenth century. They both ran into political entanglements, but they grew out of profound spiritual longing and produced many whose passion for God was extraordinary. Two Dominicans who stand out particularly are St. Thomas Aquinas (1225–74), "The Angelic Doctor," one of the greatest minds the Church has ever witnessed, also a man of overriding spiritual concern; and Meister Eckhart (1260–1328), a controversial German theologian who emphasized a "disinterestedness," a breaking through the outside world to union with God.

---

58. On that question, a study by Philip Jenkins is useful—*God's Continent: Christianity, Islam, and Europe's Religious Crisis.* Oxford: University Press, 2007.

59. *Letters of Hildegard of Bingen*, 16.

60. *Letters of Hildegard of Bingen*, 6.

Finally, I draw attention to the Fourth Lateran Council (1215), the zenith of power for the Roman Catholic Church. It was called by Pope Innocent III (1160/1–1216, elected in 1198). James Powell wrote, "Innocent was a youthful pope who dreamed great dreams and attempted to realize them. The *Gesta* [actions] plays out those dreams against the realities of an unreceptive world."[61] In most general terms, the goals of Innocent's life appear to have been to reform the Church and to promote a crusade. Powell's assessment of the council he chaired is important:

> It was the first Western council to shape the life of both laity and clergy in the Latin Church in significant ways and even to reach beyond toward the Eastern Churches. In the process it set the West in a path of centralized government that was more clearly defined than it had been. Virtually all the sacraments came out of the council under a body of definition and regulation much different than existed before. Most notably, the Eucharistic presence of Christ found doctrinal expression in transubstantiation, while the Eucharist and penance were linked much more closely than had ever been the case before.[62]

## CONCLUSION

The life of western Christianity during this key 250 year period was not always attractive, nor was it always black. The Church moved toward sharper definitions of some paramount dogmas, tried vigorously to deal with some of its problems, and launched actions which have had profound implications for the human story from that day to this.

It is clear to me that old ways of thinking about the period and old labels that have been attached to it need to be laid aside. In the 1960s Time-Life published a series of books called *Great Ages of Man*. The volume dealing with the crusading era was given an interesting title—*Age of Faith*. Perhaps we should consider that as an alternative rendering for this period. I can immediately think of problems.[63] There were all those intertwining layers of mixed and confusing belief, thought, and behavior—the humanity that defies the tidiness of categories. And scattered among them were the pieces so easily overlooked—the vision of a boy from a tiny French village who became pope, and the spiritual passion of a Hildegard.

61. *Deeds of Pope Innocent III*, xliii.
62. *Deeds of Pope Innocent III*, xlv.
63. See Bornstein's comment—"Living Christianity," 17.

# 7

## *Christian Monarch of the Kongo*

### *1506 AD*

### INTRODUCTION

WITH THE OVERARCHING PERSPECTIVE of a brooding historian, we have gazed on as a millennium has passed in review. Along the way we have fitted some little-known pieces into the puzzle that is the Christian story. In a sense we have been watching the world grow. Our planet itself has not changed size or complexity. Rather, during this timeframe earth's inhabitants have gradually enlarged their awareness of it.

Think of some developments occurring before our era: great empires, people movements, social and commercial interests that carried people from one part of our globe to another. Without attempting to be comprehensive, there was the Macedonian from northern Greece, Alexander the Great, whose presence eventually stretched in the fourth century BC from Greece into Central Asia. A century later Ashoka the Great expanded his rule throughout most of the Indian subcontinent. Then after two more centuries the Romans began to strike out from the Eternal City in all directions. Trade spanning centuries and centuries stitched continents together—Asia to Africa to Europe, and within the first two of the continents I just mentioned, west, central, and east Asia, north and east Africa all found each other. The fourth, fifth, and sixth centuries saw masses of people from east and north flood south and west. From the Arabian Peninsula Islam exploited every route it could find beginning in the seventh century, and in the same century the Chinese under the Tang dynasty surged west. Later the Crusades took Europeans to the Middle East in droves.

All this ebbing and flowing thrust together people who were afraid of each other, who questioned the humanity of each other, who used whatever means they had at hand to oppress and dominate each other. To this point, the account of cross-cultural exchange has not been a uniformly pleasant one. *Au contraire*. And in this chapter, it will all continue. We will recognize some familiar paths as we also light upon a whole new continent. There we will find an important new piece to slip into place.

The new land mass before us is Africa. Parts of it were encountered earlier: first, in Christianity's movement in the north-east corner and the north, and secondly, in Islam's slash across the same area. Now it will be sub-Saharan Africa that is important. In the Tropics, south of the equator, we will face new cultural and racial groupings including a powerful west African king, Mbemba Nzingo, or Afonso. He was not only a fascinating, multi-dimensional person, but he and his kingdom provide a remarkable study of what those who study Christian missions might call "inculturalization." But, first, what was the world like in which he found himself? We start thousands of miles east of him and centuries before.

## SETTING

Mongols. The name alone jolts images to mind—murder, mayhem, pyramids of human skulls. Certainly there is justification for those images, but by themselves they are a distortion. The most famous Mongol of all is Temujin who became Genghis Khan when he pulled Mongolia together in 1206. In fact, in July 2006 there were celebrations of the eight-hundredth anniversary of his feat complete with elaborate reenactments of some of his most outstanding battles.

It is with considerable wonder that I say there was a Christian dimension to the Genghis Khan epic right from the beginning. Early in the eleventh century there was an *en masse* conversion of a west Mongol tribe known as the Keraits,[1] and later Christians were in the Mongol army which defeated the Muslims in a maritime battle on the Aral Sea in 1141.[2] In 1199 Toghril Khan, with Temujin's help, became the most

---

1. Comneno, "Nestorianism in Central Asia," 27.

2. Baum and Winkler, *Church of the East*, 79. It might have been here that the rumor regarding "Prester John," a Christian king/priest who would lead an army out of Asia against the Muslims arose. A hundred years later William of Rubruck said that

powerful figure among the Mongols and could reasonably have hoped to be recognized as their supreme ruler.[3] Since many of the Mongols had accepted Christ and Toghril himself belonged to the Keraits, a Christian tribe, this could have been construed in some respects as a Christian empire. But that was not to be. Toghril Kahn was unseated by Temujin, who forcibly united the Mongols and was proclaimed "emperor of all emperors," Genghis Khan.

Under Ginghis Khan a Mongol tsunami rolled east and west. The merciless, rapacious horde of highly adept fighters swept everyone before them, razing cities and liquidating inhabitants who resisted, leaving behind them mountains of smoldering ruins and fields of rotting corpses. One estimate says that in two years between 1220 and 1222, 150,000 Mongols killed 6,000,000 people.[4] And all this with no modern weapons.

The terror and revulsion they caused flashed far and wide and echo to the present. The Muslims were so horror-struck at what they saw coming that in 1238 they actually sent embassies to the West to beg for help. They were rejected. Peter de Roches, Bishop of Winchester, who heard the appeal advised, "Let us leave these dogs to devour each other, that they may all be consumed." Christians could then move in, kill the survivors, and cleanse the earth, "so that the world will be subject to the one Catholic church, and there will be one shepherd and one flock." [5]

Between 1237 and 1241 under Great Khan Ogdai, the Mongols destroyed most of the cities of Russia, the Ukraine, Bohemia, Hungary, Poland, Moravia, and Dalmatia.[6] They were knocking at the door of western Europe. What stopped them was the death of Ogdai. All the leading Mongols were required to be present for the election of the great khan, so they pulled back. Another election like that lost the control of Palestine for them in 1260. After successful military ventures which saw them take Aleppo and Damascus, officers left for Mongolia with most of their troops after the death of Mongke. The Egyptians Mamluks, another

---

"Prester John" was a figment in the imaginations of those whom he scornfully called "Nestorians." He said nobody else in China knew anything about this fantasy king/priest (*Journey*, 122).

3. Baumer, *Church of the East,* 198.

4. Baumer, *Church of the East,* 211.

5. Matthew Paris, *English History,* 131.

6. Baumer, *Church of the East,* 212.

Muslim dynasty, overwhelmed the 1000 or so soldiers who had been left as a garrison and reestablished control of the area.

Christopher Dawson credits the Mongols with opening a road across Asia,[7] and the phrase *pax mongolica* (Mongol peace) is sometimes used to describe the 125 years or so when most of Asia was under their control. The phrase is more than a bit ironic because it rested on a vicious brutality. Along with the internal freedom from war which his conquests provided Genghis Khan fashioned a strict system of law for his empire, a written language, and a postal service. These factors all contributed to a dramatic increase of activity on the old silk roads. 1219 saw a Taoist monk travel through Central Asia to meet Genghis Khan.[8] That marked the onset of a period of foreign travel. From then until 1328 there were seven official embassies and missions sent by popes and western kings to the Mongol court. While those were struggling back and forward along what has been called the coldest and hottest route in the world, two Venetians, Nicolo and Maffeo Polo, made an extended excursion through to China (1260–69) exploring trade possibilities. They set out again in 1271 this time accompanied by Nicolo's now famous son, Marco Polo. They did not return until 1295. Marco dictated what he remembered of his experiences some time later while sitting in a Genoese prison.

What about the Christians? They were not absent from the scene. It is estimated that between the ninth and thirteenth centuries there were fifty to sixty million Christians in the area of whom seven to eight million belonged to the Church of the East.[9] Reporting on his trip in the 1250s, William Rubruck said he came across "Nestorians" (Church of the East) in fifteen cities in China,[10] and Baum and Winkler observed that "The Church of the East could operate freely throughout China."[11] Later they referred to the head of the Church of the East, Yahballaha III who died in 1317, saying, "His church extended from the Near East, across Central Asia to China and India."[12] Marco Polo mentioned "Nestorian" Christians frequently. Two examples of places where he came across them

7. Dawson, "Introduction," xxxv.

8. Dickens, "Syriac Gravestones," 25.

9. Baumer, *Church of the East*, 4.

10. William of Rubruck, *Journey*, 144.

11. Baum and Winkler, *Church of the East*, 87.

12. Baum and Winkler, *Church of the East*, 100.

were Mosul, in present day Iraq, where they were among other Christian groups,[13] and the province of Tenduk in south Mongolia thousands of miles from Mosul. Of Tenduk he said, "[The king] is both a Christian and a priest; the greater part of the inhabitants being also Christians."[14] The impression one gets is that during the period of Mongol rule Christians who belonged to the Church of the East were practically everywhere, and that impression is supported by the archaeological and iconographical research that is being done across the region.

The fascinating question is how the Church of the East came to enjoy this kind of freedom. First, the smile, or at least the nod, of Genghis Khan himself was critical. Along with Muslims and Buddhists, Christians were viewed favorably by his court.[15] Another factor was the presence of Christian wives at the top of the Mongol world. When Genghis Khan overthrew the khan of the Kerait, he took one his nieces as a wife and gave another, Sorkaktani Beki, to his son Tolui. Of Sorkaktani Beki's sons, two grew up to be Great Khans (Mongke, 1250–60, and the mighty Kublai, 1260–94) and a third (Hulagu, 1256–58) became an Il-Khan, the branch of the family that ruled Persia.[16] The practice of taking Christian wives passed to the next generation, too. Doquz Khatun, a Christian woman, married Sorkaktani's son, Hulagu; Despina Khatun, a Christian and the illegitimate daughter of a Byzantine emperor, married Il-Khan Abaqa; and another Christian, Orüg Khatun, became the wife of Il Khan Argun.[17]

These women were influential. Sorkaktani Beki exercised great wisdom in difficult situations which won her the ear of the Great Khan Ogdai and the immense respect of the Mongol court. She also had Mongke (future Great Khan) brought up by a monk of the Church of the East who made sure Mongke knew something of the scriptures.[18] Doquz earned her husband, Hulagu's, complete confidence. He would do nothing without consulting her. In turn, "Her confidant was the Armenian monk Vartan, whom she told that she hoped Christianity would increase

---

13. *Travels of Marco Polo,* 19.

14. *Travels of Marco Polo,* 78.

15. Tang, "Sorkaktani Beki," 353.

16. Tang, "Sorkaktani Beki," 349.

17. Aigle, "Letters," 157.

18. Tang, "Sorkaktani Beki, 353.

with each passing day."[19] She was also a patron of the Church of the East and had her children baptized. Finally, Argun and Orüg had their son Oljaitu baptized giving him the name Nicholas in honor of the pope.[20] These sound like honest attempts at Christian education if not without political dimensions entwined.

There can be no doubt but that the Mongols fought brutally and ruled with an iron rod. Nonetheless, Christians made their ways into key positions in Mongol life. One was Mongke Khan's chief secretary whose "advice is followed in almost all matters,"[21] reported William of Rubruck, a Franciscan monk and an eye witness. Again under Mongke another Christian became chancellor of the empire and yet another, the commander of the army.[22] To his chagrin John Monte Corvino discovered that clergy of the Church of the East wielded enough influence to make it difficult for any other Christian group to establish places of worship or teach doctrine which did not agree with theirs.[23] Then, here and there, there are little hints that the Christian teaching may have had an impact. Marco Polo was struck by Kublai Khan's generosity toward the poor.[24] Polo thought it had to do with the intervention of idolaters' wise men, but I think it just as likely to be attributed to his mother's Christian influence. In another example Hulagu offered some welcome grants to Christians. Peace was extended to all Christians, they were exempt from tribute and taxes, their property was respected, and all churches had freedom of worship.[25] In the midst of barbarity, can there be something that is Christian?

Taking this a step further, the overtures the Mongols made to the West need to be considered. Baumer counted thirteen official approaches that were made beginning in 1264 and ending in 1305.[26] It is probably significant that all of these contacts, some for alliances, some for friendly relations, came after 1260, the year the rump Mongol army was defeated by Muslims in Syria. It is also significant that they all came from the

19. Baum and Winkler, *Church of the East*, 85.

20. Aigle, "Letters," 157.

21. William of Rubruck, *Journey*, 150.

22. Baum and Winkler, *Church of the East*, 85.

23. "Letters of John of Monte Corvino," 224.

24. *Travels of Marco Polo*, 132–33.

25. Aigle, "Letters," 154.

26. Baumer, *Church of the East*, 227.

Il-Khans who were trying to hold Persia. They were the ones who would feel the effects of Muslim resurgence most strongly.

There were subtleties, enticements, and promises in the Khans' messages. Hulagu's began with reworked quotations from the Old and New Testaments.[27] Argun promised that when the joint army of Christians and Mongols defeated the Muslims, "We will give you Jerusalem,"[28] and Ghazan pledged to accept baptism and become a Christian once the Mamelukes were defeated.[29] All these promising gestures remained unfulfilled. Remember the words of the Bishop of Winchester back in 1238—"Let the dogs eat each other, then we'll go in and mop up." Aigle put it this way: "Perhaps the ultimate reason was that conversion of the Ilkhans to Christianity was a precondition of any political alliance."[30] At any rate, it all came to a violent and bloody end. First, starting around 1368 the Ming dynasty in China began to sever contact with the West. The effect on Christians there was to plunge them into isolation. Then Tamerlane, a Mongol and a fanatical Muslim who particularly hated Christians and Jews, exploded out of Samarkand about 1370. He and his hordes swept west destroying everything in his path, slaughtering thousands upon thousands of people—Muslims, Christians, and Jews. The cataclysm he touched off marked the end of the Church of the East everywhere except in the mountains of Kurdistan and in India.[31]

A footnote to these events concerns Nubia. For centuries it had been able to maintain its independence[32] while the Mameluks and the Ottomans fought each other, while shiploads of crusaders came and went from the shores of the south-east corner of the Mediterranean, while the Mongols surged west and were driven back. The end to this began in 1276 with the conquest of Old Dongola, but southern Nubia was able to survive until the early 1500s.[33] Not only was Nubian Christianity reduced to a resource which would spark western archaeological interest four hundred and fifty years later, but the nation itself was obliterated.

27. Aigle, "Letters," 152.

28. Les Lettres de 1289 et 1305, 152.

29. Baumer, "Survey of Nestorianism," 457.

30. Aigle, "Letters," 157.

31. Baum and Winkler, Church of the East.

32. See Spaulding, "Medieval Christian Nubia," 577–94 and Burstein, "When Greek Was an African Language," 55.

33. Grzymski, "Landscape Archaeology of Nubia and Central Sudan," 8.

Tamerlane had threatened Europe, but it avoided his wrath. In the meantime there were other currents stirring within its own borders which turned out to be significant challenges in themselves. First, nationalism was on the rise. The French were French, the Spanish, Spaniards, and so on. "Christendom" as an all-encompassing idea was breaking loose from its foundations. And within the various cultural and ethnic groupings, feudalism which had given Europe a sense of a common social structure, was beginning to feel pressure. A middle class was appearing as merchants flexed their entrepreneurial muscles, and some of them came to have much deeper pockets than were to be found among some supposedly above them in the nobility.

Another issue that overwhelmed all Europe in the mid fourteenth century was the plague. It arrived in Europe from the East in 1346, causing terror across the continent from 1347 to 1351. That was not the end of it. It kept coming back in Europe until toward the end of the seventeenth century. Spread by rats and fleas, its most common sign was a swollen lymph gland, a "bubo," in the groin or armpit. A painful death usually followed quickly.

The impact was astounding. For example, three quarters of the population of Florence died. It is estimated that a third to one half of the European population was carried off during its first wave. That is mind-numbing as one compares those numbers with "global pandemics" we have braced ourselves for recently. Appalling actions took place. As people continued to fight each other, infected bodies occasionally became weapons. They were catapulted into besieged cities. The plague also became a pretext for latent anti-Semitism. As people looked around for explanations for the waves of death during that five-year period around 1350 they often settled on the Jew. Word spread as quickly as the plague that the Jews were trying to destroy Christianity by poisoning food, pools, and streams. In many cities and towns across Europe, confessions were extracted by torture, whole communities of Jews were herded into town squares or synagogues, and then they were burned alive.[34] It was a sobering experience in 2008 to stand beside the Old Synagogue in Erfurt, parts dating from the eleventh century, with a group I had taken to Germany on a study tour. What scenes that building must have seen in 1349 when 3,000 Jews were murdered in that city.

34. Cohn, "Black Death," 3–36.

As if these conditions were not challenging enough, other factors deepened the suffering and gnawing burden of life for most Europeans alive at the time. The Hundred Years' War (1337–1453) pitted the French House of Valois against the House of Plantagenet with its roots in France but then ruling England. The prize was the French throne. The series of battles interspersed with periods of longer or shorter truce or un-settled peace involved many thousands of combatants. It also wrecked havoc on the lives of the civilian population of France among whom most of the battles were fought. And behind all of this was a period of climactic chaos in Europe. It began with an abrupt drop in temperature immediately after 1300, accompanied by extraordinarily wet summers from 1313–14 to 1321, crop failures and widespread famine. H. H. Lamb said: "Thereafter the fourteenth century seems to have brought wild, and rather long-lasting, variations of weather in western and central Europe, the later 1320s and 1330s and also the 1380s with mostly warm, dry (often seriously droughty) summers and a few other decades, notably the 1360s, predominantly wet."[35]

The social upheaval, the international threat from Mongol and Muslim, the shocking devastation of the plague, war, and climatic up-heaval added uncertainty to life which was already extremely tenuous. Not surprisingly, religion was important. Research is showing that for the most part Europeans were involved in the lives of their local parish-es.[36] This period also offers great champions of prayer like the unknown author of the thirteenth-century *The Cloud of Unknowing*, a human be-ing immersed in the relationship of a person and God:

> But now you put me a question and say, "How might I think of him [God] in himself, and what is he?" And to this I can only answer thus: "I have no idea." For with your question you have brought me into that same darkness, into that same cloud of un-knowing where I would you were yourself. For a man may, by grace, have the fullness of knowledge of all other creatures and their works, yes, and of the works of God's own self, and he is well able to reflect on them. But no man can think of God himself.[37]

One should also remember his contemporary Margaret Kempe (c. 1373–1438) of King's Lynn, Norfolk, England with her consuming

35. Lamb, *Climate, History and the Modern World*, 178.

36. Duffy, *Stripping of the Altars* and *Voices of Morebath*.

37. *Cloud of Unknowing*, 130.

passion for God and her disturbing gift of tears brought to overflowing repeatedly by the sight of Christ's cross.[38]

There were tremendous problems in the Roman Catholic Church, the hope of salvation for most western Europeans. There was something called the "Babylonian Captivity of the Church" in the fourteenth century during which time, about seventy years (1309–77), the Bishop of Rome was not resident in Rome, but in the south of France. Then there was the "Great Schism" a little later (1378–1415) in which a wondering world was treated to first two and then three men all claiming heatedly to be the one and only legitimate Pope, Bishop of Rome, representative of Christ on earth.

Back in the eleventh century a series of popes had tried to reform the Church. In the fourteenth and fifteenth centuries the need to deal with problems was just as pressing. The voices crying for profound reform became more and more strident, more and more difficult to ignore. The Englishman, John Wycliffe (1328–84), tapping into his country's nationalism, attacked the wealth of the Church and the large sums of money being sent out of England to Rome. He also insisted that the Bible was the only law of the Church, and among other things, he denied the doctrine of transubstantiation.

He was followed by the reformer John Huss (1371–1415), a Czech, a nationalist, and a very popular preacher. He put forward an agenda comparable to Wycliffe's, and went to the Council of Constance (1414–18) where he expected to be able to discuss it. Instead he was betrayed by the Holy Roman Emperor, Sigismund, who had promised him that he would be able to travel safely to and from the council. Huss found himself thrown into prison as soon as he arrived, tried, and convicted of heresy, and burned at the stake on July 6, 1415.

Another group of reformers, quite different from these two, was also making its presence felt. They believed that the supreme governing body on earth of the Church was a General Council made up of bishops and their advisors. They were known as Conciliarists, and they were led by philosopher/theologians from the University of Paris.

The Council of Constance referred to above did meet, and it was prodigious in both size and impact. It had a three-fold agenda. First, it wanted to deal with heresy, and it did. In addition to killing Huss, it proclaimed Wycliffe a heretic, too, and ordered that his bones be dug up

---

38. See *The Book of Margery Kempe.*

and burned. They were exhumed and reduced to ashes. Second, it was determined to end the Great Schism. In various ways it drove the three claimants to the papal chair off the stage and elected Martin V. As it turned out, he ruled a little more independently than they had expected. Third, it planned to carry through various moral reforms, but that point of the agenda remained untouched.

Constance was not the last council the conciliarists had a finger in. The Council of Basel/Ferrara/Florence/Rome convened on December 14, 1431 in Basel and ended in Rome on August 7, 1445. The move from city to city grew out of the power struggle between the conciliarists and Pope Eugenius IV. Eugenius was eager to minimize the conciliarists' influence and build his own. Clearly, struggles in Mother Church were continuing.

It appeared that this migratory council would bring about the reunification of the Latin and Greek churches. The Greeks had arrived in 1437 seeking help against the Muslims. After lengthy and hair-splitting negotiations, reunification was proclaimed in July 6, 1439.[39] The statement regarding the procession of the Holy Spirit was parsed as carefully as possible so that both sides could agree. There was also agreement that the body of Christ was present in the Eucharist whether the bread used was leavened or unleavened. The Greeks were permitted to maintain their liturgy and to practice the marriage of priests. Unfortunately, when the Greeks got home to Constantinople, the agreement was rejected, and the much hoped for help from the west never arrived. Constantinople fell to the Muslims in 1453.

### EVENT

Momentum now shifts back to Europe and specifically to little Portugal. It was a maritime country and many of its people were comfortable with the sea and the travel routes it offered. After successes in North Africa, the Portuguese launched an attempt to explore further into the land mass to the south. Stimulated by the interests of Prince Henry (1360–1415), also known as the Navigator, the Portuguese sailed south. Early in the fifteenth century they came across Madeira and other Atlantic islands. Moving further along the coast, Diogo Cao led them into the mouth of the Kongo River, leaving behind a stone marker bearing the inscription

---

39. *Decrees of the Ecumenical Councils*, vol 1, 525.

"August 28, 1482."[40] They met the Kongo, people who lived in a country known as Kongo, which had been brought together between 1350–75 through conquests and tribal alliances with its capital south of the river at Mbanza Kongo.[41] Cao left four Portuguese with the Manicongo, the dominant king in the area, and took four Kongo back to Portugal with him as hostages. When he returned two or three years later with the four Kongo in 1485, the Manicongo was so pleased that he sent some of his other subjects back with Cao asking that they be baptized and taught the Catholic faith.[42] He also requested priests, farmers, and tradesmen be sent from Portugal.[43]

Another fleet, under Goncalo de Sousa this time, sailed into the Kongo River on Mar. 29, 1491 bringing with it the Kongo who had gone to Portugal earlier and the personnel the Manicongo had requested. Both a regional chief on the coast and the Manicongo, Nzinga Nkuwu, were pleased. Nzinga Nkuwu, King of Kongo, received baptism on May 6, 1491 with his queen and their eldest son, Mbemba Nzingo, (Afonso) undergoing the rite on June 4 the same year.

We need to pause here and account for the seeming speed of events. John Thornton, one of the outstanding voices on Kongo history, helps us understand how the progression could have flowed apparently so smoothly. First, he said, "I believe that Portuguese and Kongolese society were much more similar to each other than many students of Kongolese history believe, at least similar enough to allow us to abandon the idea of economic domination (translated into political domination) of Kongo by Portugal in the sixteenth century."[44] He then listed some similarities: both had monarchies with kings and noble classes; rural life in both had not changed in centuries; and famine and pestilence were common in both. While the Portuguese's navigational technology was superior to Kongo's "it was not a fundamental structural advantage such as the Industrial Revolution was to afford European countries in the nineteenth century."[45] There were some other technological abilities

40. McVeigh, "Early Congo Mission," 501.
41. Thornton, "Origins and Early History," 119.
42. Boehrer, "Franciscans and Portuguese Colonization," 395.
43. McVeigh, "Early Congo Mission," 502.
44. Thornton, "Early Kongo-Portuguese Relations," 186.
45. Thornton, "Early Kongo-Portuguese Relations," 186.

that the Portuguese had that Afonso seemed particularly interested in, carpentry and working with stone, for instance.

Further, Thornton stated that the Portuguese "came to a country as the invited guests of a powerful and unconquered king."[46] They were not invaders overtly threatening a way of life. The importance of this cannot be overestimated. The religious approach the Portuguese took was "soft," too. Thornton calls it "inclusive," meaning "all aspects of the culture of the target country that are not directly contrary to the fundamental doctrine of the Church are considered acceptable."[47] One became a Christian through a simple statement of faith such as was embedded in the Creeds. At least, as we shall see later, that is where it started. So here was a meeting of cultures which seemed to understand each other at a very deep level, which respected each other, and which were seen to be able to strengthen each other. The contrast with what was happening in South and Central America at the same time is stunning.

Enter Afonso, King of Kongo in 1506. He rose to the throne through turmoil. As he described in a letter in 1512, his father, Nzingu Nkuwu, fell away from the faith. Afonso remained true and was exiled to a far corner of the kingdom. Then word came that his father was dying and a younger brother had seized the throne. He returned to Mbanza Kongo quickly to find his father dead and his brother surrounded with a large army. He had been able to marshal only thirty-six men, but he assembled them in the town square facing his brother's army. He and his 36 called on the Lord Jesus Christ and engaged the enemy. To their amazement, instead of pushing forward relying on their numbers, the enemy fled the field in horror. Afonso's men pursued them, many were killed, and his brother was captured and executed.

Later Afonso discovered why the other army turned tail and ran. Above Afonso's men they saw ". . . a white Cross and the blessed Apostle James dressed in white and many armed horsemen appearing in the air."[48] There are lots of echoes here—Elisha's chariots and horsemen of fire, Constantine's cross, Sts. Peter and Paul swords in hand hovering about Pope Leo I as he confronts Attila the Hun. Whatever happened, Afonso saw it as a critical moment in his life. What stood behind it all

46. Thornton, "Development," 153.

47. Thornton, "Development," 152. This had parallels in the sixteenth-century reformations which occurred in both Germany and England.

48. Afonsa to the Lords of the Kingdom, 1512 "Selected Letters," 1, 260–62.

was a very personal moment to which he referred in the same letter, his conversion. He saw it as an enlightening by the grace of the Holy Spirit in which Christian doctrine was implanted and confirmed in his heart.

After about ten years on the throne, Afonso got a rating from an outside observer. Fr. Rui d'Aguiar was sent to Kongo in 1515 by King Manuel of Portugal to help out. A few months later d'Aguiar wrote to the king to share some impressions of Afonso. The report was glowing. Afonso, he said, knows the Bible, the lives of the saints, and actually everything about the Church "better than we do." He taught everyone, even the Portuguese clergy. How did he do it? He was preoccupied by detailed and protracted study, forgetting to eat and drink and falling asleep over his books, even getting distracted by his theological passion while he was supposed to be giving political audiences. Priests would interrupt masses asking Afonso for *his* blessing and asking him to speak. When he began to preach, he spoke out of deep love and urged people to convert and turn to God. D'Aguiar ends his panegyric by saying that Kongo and Portuguese alike were shocked by his virtue and faith.[49] Actually, what we see is a man in a highly complicated juggling act of which he may have been only partially aware.

A major component of the challenges Afonso faced was his relationship with Portugal,[50] a situation Afonso began exploiting immediately. Missinne pointed out that in 1506, the first year of his reign, he began sending young men, including his own son, Henrique, to Lisbon for education.[51] This flow of people appears over and over again in Afonso's letters.[52] By 1506 Afonso had at least known of the Portuguese for more than twenty years, and no doubt, he had had many opportunities to observe them up close. Obviously he had concluded there was much to be gained by exposing his people to the European world.

49. Aguiar, to King Manuel I, May 25, 1516 "Selected Letters," 1, 361.

50. We must remember a caution that Thornton raised. Unique among sub-Saharan countries, a remarkable collection of papers generated by an African is available to provide most of the material for a reconstruction of the history of Kongo/Angola, but they are found in Portugal. That could lead one to think that the Portuguese were all that Afonso ever thought of. That is almost certainly not true. However, we have to guess at what else might have been happening if it does not appear in the letters.

51. Missinne, "Notes on Education," 145.

52. Afonso to the Lords of the Kingdom, 1512, "Selected Letters," 1, 260; Afonso to Manuel I, May 31, 1515, "Selected Letters," 1, 333; Afonso to Joao III, December 28, 1535, "Selected Letters," 2, 53; and Afonso to Joao III, March 25, 1539, "Selected Letters," 2. 73.

In addition to whatever general benefits Afonso anticipated through interaction with the Europeans, there were specific skills that he was looking for. He hoped builders, stone masons, and carpenters would come to Kongo.[53] He was looking for grammar masters who could take literate Kongo to higher levels so that they themselves could teach the Catholic faith more thoroughly and deal with the difficult questions of interpretation and theology.[54] And he earnestly asked for fifty priests.[55]

Afonso also acknowledged that he had been asking for a lot of things. He assured King Joao III that the Kongo were doing everything they themselves could, given skill levels and resources available, before asking. We also hear of presents of jewelry and marble to the Portuguese to provide some redress to the imbalance in gifts.[56] Afonso did have a commodity in which the Portuguese were very interested—human beings.

The question of slavery is a riveting theme that runs through Afonso's correspondence. Thornton's comment stops one short: "It is quite clear that Afonso, and probably Kongo law in general, had little problem with either the holding of slaves, their alienation [that is, an owner's giving up control of slaves] by sale or gift, or their export from the country,"[57] and he thought that this was most likely the case before the Europeans arrived.[58] He mentioned that Afonso sent slaves to Lisbon so that they could be sold to cover the expenses of Kongo students studying there and even to pay for clothes for himself.[59] He summed up Afonso's position on the question by saying, "Afonso never opposed either the idea of the slave trade or slavery."[60]

All of this is reflected in a report Afonso gave in a letter of April 3, 1516. He told Manuel I that he had given one of the Portuguese king's officials enough money to buy twenty-five slaves.[61] He clearly understood

53. Afonso to Manuel I, May 31, 1515, "Selected Letters," 1, 335 and Afonso to Joao III, August 25, 1526, "Selected Letters," 1, 477.

54. Afonso to Joao III, August 25, 1526, "Selected Letters," 1, 477.

55. Afonso to Joao III, March 18, 1526, "Selected Letters," 1, 459.

56. Afonso to Joao III, August 25, 1526, "Selected Letters," 1, 483 and Afonso to Joao III, January 28, 1530, "Selected Letters," 1, 540.

57. Thornton, "African Political Ethics," para. 8.

58. Thornton, "African Political Ethics," para. 13.

59. Thornton, "African Political Ethics," para. 11.

60. Thornton, "African Political Ethics," para. 19.

61. Afonso to Manuel I, March 4, 1516, "Selected Letters," 1, 356.

that the purchase would be made in Kongo and that the slaves would be exported. He also used some language which is troubling to those who place unique value on each person *qua* human being made in the image of God. In this passage, and consistently, he referred to slaves as *peças*. The Portuguese word *peça* means "piece," and used in this context it seems dehumanizing. In another place he refers to "Cacheu, mulatoes, and Benins," describing them as morally inferior and as almost a kind of glut in his kingdom.[62] In this situation he appears to be pointing to them as the ones who should be marketed.

This is Afonso. This is the king who described his conversion. This is the Christian leader who received the glowing report from the missionary. This is a man in a very complicated juggling act. He knew that drawing his country into allegiance with Christ would mean change. Even so, it would be surprising if at the beginning he had any clear idea of how deeply into the life of his people that transformation would insist on going. Opening one's life to Christ is a process that takes time. One keeps being made aware of issues that require change.[63] Perhaps Afonso never really came to understand the problems with slavery as clearly as we might wish he had.

However Afonso was fully aware of another set of complications that the issue of slavery forced him to consider. The relationship with Portugal was threatening the control of his country. There is an intriguing series of letters coming from the second half of 1526. In one written on July 6 he said that there were Portuguese merchants everywhere in his kingdom who were buying freeborn Kongo, children of nobles, and even some of his own relatives to the point of depopulating the nation. The only solution: stop slavery completely.[64] Then on August 25 he wrote referring to the disrespect with which he has been treated by some Portuguese ship captains who had left for home without having their cargos of slaves properly vetted by his officials. This had meant the loss of nobles and some of his own relatives. He urged Joao III not to buy unvetted slaves.[65] Finally he wrote on October 18 and said no slave who had not been examined by his officials should be sold.[66] Two decisions

---

62. Afonso to Joao III, August 25, 1526, "Selected Letters," 1, 477.

63. Walls, *Missionary Movement*, 50 and 51.

64. Thornton, "African Political Ethics," para. 14.

65. Afonso to Joao III, August, 1526 "Selected Letters," 1, 476–77.

66. Thornton, "African Political Ethics," para. 15.

have been reached. First, freeborn Kongo, nobles, and his relatives may not be enslaved, while others may. Second, he Afonso will determine which is which.

Here we see the shrewdness, the savvy, of the man. Here is an awareness of the mechanisms of international politics and intercultural dynamics that stands out in the annals of colonialism. This is no benighted savage of darkest Africa being jerked around by smirking white men. Afonso had been to school, the school of international—we would say intertribal—politics in Africa. He did not need Europeans to show him the ropes. The stakes were higher now. The hands being played were intercontinental. Afonso saw the challenge, sat down, and went to work. His grasp on diplomacy and bargaining could have put him in a desk at the United Nations. He was so good at negotiating that some of the Portuguese later tried to assassinate him.

All of this played out in the Church he forged, too. It was orthodox. The Scriptures were of critical importance to him. At the center of his faith was a clear and precise expression of Trinitarian theology and the incarnation of Christ.[67] Afonso understood the Christian doctrine of salvation. Commenting on the work of Christ, he said, "By His death we are redeemed and saved."[68] Thornton's assessment was, "We can . . . say with confidence that a form of Christianity, practicing its own local variations but recognized in Rome as orthodox and accepted by European priests operating in the country, had become the national religion of Kongo probably as early as the reign of Afonso I."[69]

His Church was orthodox, but it was African too, and specifically Kongo. Afonso was not going to have it subject to a European bishop, so he set out to have it built around his son Henrique whom he had sent to study in Lisbon. With the active support of King Manuel I, Henrique made a trip to Rome while living in Lisbon, and then in 1518 he was elevated to the status of bishop. Notification came to Manuel I in a formal document dated May 3, 1518 from Pope Leo X,[70] and the decision was recorded in Vatican records dated two days later. He is declared to have

---

67. Afonso to the Lords of the Kingdom, 1512, "Selected Letters," 1, 260, 261 and Afonso to Manuel I, May 31, 1515, "Selected Letters," 1, 335.

68. Afonso to the Lords of the Kingdom, 1512 "Selected Letters," 1, 261.

69. Thornton, "Development," 159.

70. *Historia De Congo*, 46.

the full powers of a bishop in the city of Utica "*in partibus infidelium*."[71]
This is a little complicated. Utica was a city near Carthage in North
Africa. There was no bishop there because the area was completely
under the control of the Muslims. The appointment gave Henrique the
authority of a bishop which he could wield elsewhere, such as in Kongo,
to which he went in 1521.

When Henrique did return to Kongo, he most certainly had the
full backing of his father. What emerged was "a well-organized church,
doctrinally adjusted to Kongo and possessing income, personnel, and
a place in Kongo's political and social system."[72] The importance of
Henrique for Afonso probably personally but also for his overall plan
can be seen in some of his comments. In a letter dated March 18, 1526,
Afonso refers to Henrique saying he does not want him to leave the capital Mbanza Kongo. He is afraid that someone will attempt to assassinate
him.[73] This does not say much about the king's confidence in the security
of his realm, and it might have indicated something about his paranoia.
Perhaps he was just a sober realist.

Later he shared his concern for his son, telling King Joao of
Portugal that Henrique was very sick, reminding Joao that Henrique is
"the sole candle before our eyes. If it goes out, we'll be in darkness."[74]
These troubled words carry a lot of freight. Here was a father speaking
out of love. Here was a king speaking out of hope, hope for a son who
has devoted himself to play a role of leadership, hope for a church which
he longed to be an avenue of salvation, and hope for a nation which he
had been nurturing in freedom. Afonso saw the need for another bishop,
and he suggested that Joao will know why Kongo has only Henrique.
Did he mean that Joao would understand his determination to control
European interference?

The church which was emerging under Afonso's and Henrigue's
hands was remarkable. Christianity was being "inculturated." That is an
old idea now, but it was happening with a significant difference in Kongo.
Usually the missionaries arrive, throw themselves into language study

71. Bull of Leo X to Manuel I, May 3, 1518, "Selected Letters," *Monumenta
Missionaria Africa*, Edited by Antonio Brasio (Lisboa: Agencia Geral do Ultramar,
1952), 1, 416.

72. Thornton, "Developments," 162.

73. Afonso to Joao III, March 18, 1526, "Selected Letters," 1, 460.

74. Afonso to Joao III, August 25, 1526, "Selected Letters," 1, 483.

and, hopefully, absorption of the culture, then try to figure out how to integrate Christianity into the mix. This time it happened the other way around. Some Kongo accepted Christianity, studied the languages of the missionaries, read their books, watched them, and then decided how the new ideas could best be shared in their culture and language. Here was a people, a cultural grouping with a well-defined way of looking at the world, including a religion, with eyes wide open choosing to embrace something profoundly different. This is without parallel in the missional story of the church, and it is a fascinating piece to put in place.

I wish someone could have made a video of their worship services. However, God spoke and was spoken to in Kikongo. The word for "God" was *"Nzambi Mpungu,"*[75] for "religious leader," *"nganga,"* for "soul or spirit," *"moyo."* The general idea of "holy," in the sense of a material object in which were found spiritual forces, was expressed using *"nkisi."* "Holy Bible" becomes *"Mukanda nkisi"* and "Church" becomes *"nzo a nkisi."* And all this came from the Kongo themselves, likely from the king and his son. Foundations had been laid for a thorough-going manifestation of a truly African Christianity.

## DEVELOPMENTS

How those foundations were built upon is a story that would carry us further than we can go. It seems safe to say that while some details might have troubled him, Afonso would likely have been reasonably contented with the general contours of the Church as it continued to unfold. In official quarters, it was recognized as orthodox. In 1596 a panel representing the widely-feared Inquisition came to Kongo to sniff out any baptized Jews who were still practicing their old religion. They did not find any, and they did not catch any whiffs of paganism either. The Kongo Catholic Church which they found was orthodox.[76] Further testimony to the ongoing orthodoxy of the church comes from the middle of the seventeenth century. Gray said, "When eventually in 1645 Propaganda Fide [a bureau of the Vatican] managed to introduce its own emissaries into Kongo, they went not as evangelists to a non-Christian country, but as

---

75. I am relying on John Thornton here—"Developments," 152, 155 and 156.
76. Thornton, "Development," 156.

Antonio Emanuele ne Vunda

dedicated priestly reinforcements, bringing the sacraments of salvation and committed to strengthening the link with Rome."[77]

Relations between mother and daughter churches had been moved forward in 1608 when a Kongo ambassador reached Rome. This was Antonio Manuele ne Vunda, thirty-year old cousin of King Alvaro II. Sadly, he died two days after arriving.[78] He was given a magnificent funeral in the Church of Santa Maria Maggiore, and is commemorated by a remarkable bust in the same church by Francesco Caprale.

The future of the Church in Kongo rested in the hands of lay missionaries. These were young nobles taught in local schools. After 1600 when for political reasons Portuguese bishops stopped ordaining Kongo, these lay missionaries scattered through the kingdom, teaching in local schools themselves, engaging in evangelism and instructing people in the faith. When priests did make it into Kongo, it was these nationals who prepared the way for the priests' ministry of the sacraments. Thornton says, "It was, in fact, the catechists, interpreters and masters who preserved the religion and kept Kongo a Catholic country."[79] This

77. Gray, "Kongo Pirncess," 152.

78. Gray, "Kongo Princess," 147–48.

79. Thornton, "Development," 165.

would have been a stabilizing influence in the political disorder that followed the loss to the Portuguese in the Battle of Mbwila in 1665.[80]

## CONCLUSION

In spite of some troubling aspects of his performance, Afonso of the Kongo certainly cut an impressive figure. He is a stellar addition to the puzzle. The role he played in the penetration of Christianity into sub-Saharan Africa was exceptional. His political, social, and inter-personal sharpness was uncommon. It feels odd to note that he appears to have known little about the unraveling of Christianity that was going on in Europe at the very time when in his world he was embracing the Church.

80. Thornton, "Warfare," 117.

# 8

## Reformation Among "the People"

### 1523 AD


### INTRODUCTION

W E ARE NOW A millennium and a half into the Christian story. How
have Christians fared in the far corners of the earth? Starting in
the East, the picture is bleak. *Jingjiao*, the Church of the East, was dev-
astated under the Ming and Timerlane. The millions of Christians once
flourishing there were decimated. Those early numbers would not be
approached again until the twenty-first century. Up to now there has not
been any direct connection found between the strong Christian presence of the fourteenth century and the resurgence that is taking place in
China at the present. .

In what I have called the central part of our range of interest, the
picture was somewhat better. In north-east Africa Christians had survived in Egypt and Ethiopia, but under great pressure. Regrettably, they
had been wiped out in Nubia. The same story resonates across the top
of Africa to the West. The bright spot was Kongo in west-central Africa.
Christianity had hung on with varying degrees of success in the Holy
Land, Turkey, Constantinople, and eastern Europe, but in all places it
was under Muslim dominance. The Church had remained surprisingly
strong in the Ukraine and Russia in spite of centuries under the heel of
the Mongols and Tartars.

The West witnessed the growth of both nationalism and capitalism as feudalism began to wane. During this time, the Roman Catholic

Church was by far the dominant expression of Christianity. The Christian message had been carried to the west coast of Africa where it had taken root, and prospects were opening up in the New World on the other side of the Atlantic. Despite these favorable appearances, the feeling that things were not right was growing.

Furthermore, the end of the fifteenth century coincided with some very significant developments. In the great Christian metanarrative, a new era was on the horizon. The "Middle Ages" or "Age of Faith" was drawing to a close and the "Reformation Era" was dawning. Had you been alive at the time, you might not have identified the gradually accelerating momentum of change. Profound social and cultural transformations rarely occur at a gallop.[1] But the Reformation was coming, and it was going to turn the life of everybody in Europe and far, far beyond upside down, and not just for the leaders of the Church and the politicos. Listen for the hammer.

## SETTING

As the stage was being set for this far-reaching upheaval, the political world of Europe and the Middle East was pulsating. In the west, the primary question had to do with how to achieve and maintain dominance. The front runner in that contest was the Holy Roman Empire, and at the end of the fifteenth century it was led by Emperor Maximilian I (r. 1493–1519). The lands which made up his empire included the German states, the Low Countries, Austria, Czechoslovakia, Hungary, and parts of Italy. It was a sprawling, disconnected mass composed of many sovereign states which guarded their borders jealously. Working on the basis of the Golden Bull (1356) which functioned as a constitution for the Empire, Maximilian was attempting to centralize the empire and elevate the importance of its parliament.

This parliament, known as the *Reichstag,* was organized into three "colleges," or groups. The first was made up of the seven dignitaries who elected the emperor. There were three archbishops, Trier, Cologne and Mainz, and four secular rulers who were the Palatine of the Rhine, the Margrave of Brandenburg, the Duke of Saxony, and the King of Bohemia. The second brought together other princes and nobles from both the

---

1. See Wallace, *The Long European Reformation,* 6. His study spans four centuries. See also Luebke, "Introduction," 8.

Maximilian I

secular world and the Church, and the third assembled representatives of the "Free Cities" of the empire. The number of these cities varied from time to time, and they gained or lost the status in many ways. The *Reichstag* did not meet at fixed intervals nor in a specific place. When it came together, its meeting was called a *Diet* and it took on the name of the city in which it met, the *Diet of Augsburg*, for example.

Also fully involved in the tussle for dominance were several western monarchies. These were: Spain ruled before and briefly after 1500 by Isabella and Ferdinand, France under Louis XII, and England experiencing the reign of the first Tudor, Henry VII. The main political players during the first half of the sixteenth century appeared on the stage a little later: Henry VIII became King of England and Ireland in 1509, Francis I, King of France in 1515, and Charles V, King of Spain in 1516 and Holy Roman Emperor in 1520. Charles' significance was greatly increased by the riches flowing to Spain from the New World following Christopher Columbus' first trip across the Atlantic in 1492.

A word should also be said about the ruler of one of the Empire's autonomous states, Frederick the Wise (1463–1525) of Electoral Saxony. He was regarded as one of the leading political figures of the Holy Roman Empire, and he wielded his influence effectively. He was also a deeply pious man with a passionate interest in relics. About 1507 he received papal permission to acquire the relics of St. Ursula and her 11,000 virgins, and by 1520, including whatever he had gathered from that source, he had built a collection of more than 19,000 relics. On All Saints' Day these treasures were arrayed on tables in the Castle Church in Wittenberg, and for the appropriate price of admission the faithful could pass through to venerate the articles. To do so would shorten one's stay in purgatory by 5,209 years.[2]

2. This remarkable collection of relics seems to have disappeared without a trace

Another feature of the religious-political world of that time was Albrecht of Brandenburg's election as the Archbishop of Mainz. Brandenburg was in the north-east of what is now Germany, while Mainz was far to the south-west. Albrecht was already Archbishop of Magdeburg and the administrator of another diocese, but among other things, the position at Mainz made him the head of the Church in Germany and an elector of the emperor. It was contrary to the canons of the Church for one person to hold two not to mention three bishoprics. Consequently, in addition to the fee that went with the office, Albrecht had to produce a considerable sum to cover the special permission he required from the Vatican. This meant he had to negotiate a hefty loan from the House of Fugger in Augsburg.

Off to the east another powerful force had arisen—Russia. The Orthodox Church had reached Kiev in the Ukraine in the tenth century and somewhat later become established in Russia under Vladimir I (958–1015). By 1448 the Church had become fully integrated into Russian life and in that year became autonomous from the Greek Church. After 1453 it assumed leadership in the Orthodox world with Moscow coming to be seen as the "Third Rome."

Behind and to the south of all this were the Turks. They had taken Constantinople in 1453 and were pushing relentlessly north-west. In 1521 they occupied Belgrade and through the 1520s expanded their hold on Hungary, creating a major threat in the eyes of the Europeans. The Muslims hovered ominously in the south-east.

In the midst of the world I have been describing with its rivalries, its saber rattling, and its uncertainties, how was the Church faring? Before answering that we must be clear about which Church we mean. It is not *Jingjiao*, the Church of the East. What remained of it was in India and in the mountains around the Caspian Sea. The issue there was basic survival. It is not the Orthodox family of churches. They were either struggling to survive under Islam or were so far to the north-east that the tides which ebbed and flowed in the west scarcely touched them. The Church we are watching is the Roman Catholic Church. Interestingly, there is no indication in the letters I have seen of one of its most recent sons at the time, Afonso of the Kongo, that he had caught wind of the changing tides farther north.

---

after the Protestant Reformation.

Eamon Duffy thought that the Roman Catholic Church was doing rather well. In the introduction to *Stripping of the Altars*, he said, "My object in this book is to map the range and vigour of late medieval and early modern English Catholicism,"[3] and he made a strong case in support of the idea that both were significant. Later he offered us the parish of Morebath in south-west England to illustrate the point.[4] There was also support for this view from Diarmaid MacCulloch who said, "One conclusion to be drawn from the accumulation of recent research on the Latin Church before the upheaval was that it was not as corrupt and ineffective as Protestants have tended to portray it, and that it generally satisfied the spiritual needs of late medieval people."[5]

Affairs in the Church in western Europe at the beginning of the sixteenth century appear to have been acceptably robust. Life was often "nasty, brutish and short" for many at that time, and it was made worse by unpredictable outbreaks of the bubonic plague. Death lurked around the next corner, and in the best case scenario, after that awaited purgatory—hell with time limits.[6] The sacramental and devotional life of the Church was the antidote. Grace flowed through the sacraments, and the ultimate prayer, the Mass, was surrounded by constant intercession by monks and nuns whose lives were devoted to prayer, the "work of God" (*opus dei*). All this prayer could help as a person prepared to die, shortening the time spent in the horrors of purgatory. The places and the people through which these mercies came were highly valued.

A large proportion of the population of western Europe was involved with the Church. Parish support was often high. People belonged to fraternities and societies which cared for various aspects church upkeep. They raised money through "ales" i.e. parish picnics, and they poured money into astonishingly beautiful churches. Holy Trinity in Long Melford in south-east England is a breath-taking example.

Other signs of the Church's hold on people were the multitudes going on pilgrimage. They were visiting shrines of saints in hopes of blessing in this life and the next, and no one illustrated this passion better than the English woman, Margery Kempe. After twenty years of married life and fourteen children, she and her husband negotiated an

---

3. Duffy, *Stripping of the Altars*, 6.

4. Duffy, *Voices of Morebath*.

5. MacCulloch, *Reformation*, xxiii.

6. Le Goff's study is very helpful—*The Birth of Purgatory*.

Holy Trinity, Long Melford

agreement in which they renounced sexual intercourse so that she could give herself more fully to spiritual devotions. [7] With her very troubling gifts of tears, she then headed off on pilgrimages which eventually took her to the Holy Land, Rome, Santiago de Compostello, and numerous European shrines. The teaching, ideals, and spiritualities of the Church were obviously very important to her as they were to many of her contemporaries.

As robust as that portrayal of popular spirituality of the time is, there are those who question it. On the basis of his work, John Bossy argued that in parts of Europe the participation of ordinary folk in the life of the Church was very different from what I have been describing. Discussing the period leading up to the Reformation, he said, "The people of western Europe fulfilled their parochial duties in so spasmodic a manner that it is hard to believe that they had any clear sense of parochial obligation at all."[8] Doran and Durston also raise concerns about the way historians reach general conclusions about the life of the Church on the basis of sources used to access the religious lives of ordinary people. They raise a cautionary flag about the interpretation of wills. They also point out that when working on English religious life it must be acknowledged that only 8% of parishes have any records at all for the

7. See *The Book of Margery Kempe*, 58–60.

8. Bossy, "Counter-Reformation and the People," 88.

period 1400–1600.[9] These comments point to some of the challenges of "doing history from the bottom up."

Added to this is the general recognition that many living at the time were fully aware of inadequacies in the lives of many churchmen and were completely out of sympathy with much Church policy. This was particularly true of the elites in various places in Europe, and it prompted them to whittle away at the powers of the Church. Other motives were probably at work in some of these cases too, such as nationalist interests and the desire for personal gain. Nevertheless, the people at large had pretty clear ideas of what was going on, too, as some of the doggerel and drinking songs make very clear. Most striking were the cries for reform, and they came from many directions.

The sauve scholar Desiderius Erasmus of Rotterdam (1466–1536) requires attention. He was the leader of the northern (Christian)

Desiderius Erasmus

9. Doran and Durston, *Princes, Pastors and People*, 82.

Humanists, the superstar whom many tried to emulate, the model of the refined intellectual over whom princes competed in attempts to woe him to their castles. In 1511 he published *Praise of Folly*. This was a clever but biting satire in which Folly ridicules the abuses and excesses of the Catholic Church, the chattering class of the day, and the elites. It was an immediate hit. Even Pope Leo X chuckled over it. It went into many editions and was translated into several languages.

In sharp contrast Girolama Savonarola (1452–98), a Dominican in Florence went on a rampage against immorality on all levels, including eventually the papacy. He quickly attracted an enthusiastic following, but after book burnings and particularly vehement condemnations, Florence turned on him. He was hanged and burned on May 22, 1498. Recent examination by the Vatican has exonerated him of charges of heresy.

Somewhere in between these two stood Francisco Ximenes de Cisnernos (1436–1517). By 1495 he was the third most powerful person in Spain behind monarchs Ferdinand and Isabella. He actually ruled Spain for two short periods. He aimed at a pure Church in a pure realm. That eventually contributed to the forcible conversion or expulsion of Jews and Muslims. As Grand Inquisitor he sought doctrinal purity. He also spearheaded the founding of the University of Alcala in the hope of producing for the Spanish Church a disciplined, educated clergy. He was largely successful. The Catholic Church played a definitive role in Spain well into the second half of the twentieth century.

And there were others to the north. Ulrich Zwingli (1484–1531) was born into a Swiss peasant family in the mountains south-east of Zurich. With a glowing education which included a warm admiration for Erasmus, he became a priest in 1506. After working through problems with anger over Swiss mercenary service plus difficulties relating to related to an affair he had with a young woman in his parish, he was finally called to the Grössmunster in Zurich in 1519. There he began to work hand in glove with the political leaders of the city who had already been taking over control from the Church and pushing toward reform.

Another leader was Conrad Grebel (1498–1526), a member of one of the elite families of Zurich. He caught the new currents flowing in the council of Zurich and was excited at what he guessed was happening. On July 31, 1518 he wrote eagerly to Zwingli urging him to tear himself away from responsibilities and travel to Zurich for a visit.[10] He must

---

10. Grebel, "To Zwingli, July 31, 1518," *Sources of Swiss Anabaptism*, 63–64.

have been ecstatic when he heard that Zwingli was going to be coming to Zurich as pastor of the largest church in town. This enthusiasm cooled fairly quickly. Grebel and others decided that Zwingli was going to be too conservative in shaping his reform, and they turned away from him. The primary issue was the baptism of infants (Zwingli) vs. the baptism of people who had already become believers (Grebel and others). The movement of which Grebel became a part came to be known as "Anabaptism."

More familier is another figure who was moving in the direction of reform—Martin Luther (1483–1546). He was born in Eisleben and given a good education including a law degree from the University of Erfurt. In 1505 he entered the Augustinian monastery there. He took vows out of a profound spiritual longing and an intense sense of sin. Advancing steadily, in 1511 he was sent to Wittenberg to teach at the new university that Frederick the Wise had established there. Sometime before 1518, probably as early as 1516,[11] Luther discovered the theological/spiritual truth for which he would be forever famous: the just shall live by faith. The hammer was about to strike.

An agent of the Church came near to Saxony promoting the sale of an indulgence. Luther appears not to have known it, but half of the proceeds of the sales were to go to pay off Archbishop Albrecht's loan from the Fuggers Banking House in Augsburg. What seems to have ignited Luther's wrath was that people were being told that through the purchase of the indulgences their own time in purgatory could be avoided and that loved ones of theirs who were already suffering there could be freed. Luther had other concerns bubbling just below the surface, too. They all coalesced in his "95 Theses." In hopes of stimulating a debate, Luther nailed them to the door of the Castle Church on October 31, 1517. A simple enough act in itself, but it launched Luther into a maelstrom that he could not have imagined. The rest of his life was a battle, but the next four years almost defy description.

The theses were translated, printed and distributed by the thousand throughout western Europe. Luther was not just registering disgust regarding indulgences, he was reflecting German nationalism, speak-

---

11. There is a hint in a letter written by George Spalatin, Frederick the Wise's secretary, to Erasmus. Spalatin explained Luther's position on salvation by saying that Luther taught "We become just first and then act justly." We are changed first through faith in Christ, and then we perform good works—Spalitin, To Erasmus, Dec. 11, 1516, 4, 168.

ing for the individual person and the poor, pointing out where hope of life in God lay, and challenging the authority of the Pope, himself. The theses had the effect of a lightning strike in a tinder dry forest. In the hearts of thousands, his theses and the flow of pamphlets which followed opened up vistas of possibility for this life and the next that they had never dreamed of. In the heart of Rome, on the other hand, he was the ogre of the north.

Events seem to unfold like water over the cataract of Niagara. Masses of high and low were rallying around Luther. Rome wanted him silenced. Frederick, Luther's sovereign, sheltered him. Erasmus whispered in Frederick's ear that that was a good idea.[12] Luther was at pains to explain himself to various audiences all the while exposing himself to danger.[13] He was excommunicated on January 3, 1521. The crowds around him swelled. He found himself with a date at the upcoming session of the Imperial parliament called to meet in the west German city of Worms in April 1521.

At the epicenter Luther was struggling. February 1519—"God is impelling me, driving me on rather than leading me. I cannot master myself, I want to be calm, yet I am driven into the midst of uproar."[14] A month earlier he had written his sovereign and admitted that he was willing to be silent and let the issue "bleed to death by itself"[15] and even write to the Pope and "submit myself with great humility."[16] However, he added, "But there is positively no chance of revocation."[17] He even produced a draft letter. As late as October, 1520 he had claimed to a friend that he was prepared to "offer, as humbly as I can, to keep silent, provided that others keep silent to, so that I am not seen to omit anything in my power to make peace."[18] Twelve years later, as Luther thought back on what had happened, he said, "God knows, I never thought of going

---

12. Erasmus, Elector Frederick of Saxony, April 14, 1519, 6, 299.

13. Sensing he was close to the stake, Luther slipped away from one of these "command performances" in Augsburg in October, 1518 in the dead of night on a "borrowed" horse. He later wrote a friend and apologized for helping himself to the horse.

14. Luther to John von Staupitz, February 20, 1519, 108.

15. Luther to Frederick the Wise, January 5 or 6, 1519, 97.

16. Luther to Frederick the Wise, January 5 or 6, 1519, 98.

17. Luther to Frederick the Wise, January 5 or 6, 1519, 100.

18. Luther to Spalatin, October 20, 1520, 180.

so far as I did."[19] Be that as it may, nothing stopped the approach to the precipice. In the spring of 1521 he was on his way to Worms for a face-to-face meeting with the Holy Roman Emperor, Charles V.

## EVENT

April 17, 1521—Luther stood before the assembled *Reichstag*. He was ordered to recant what he had said in his works, and he bought some time. The next day he returned and issued his famous statement—"I cannot and I will not, so help me God!" or words to that effect. About the same time Charles V made his own declaration: "I have decided to mobilize everything against Luther: my kingdoms and dominions, my friends, my body, my blood and my soul."[20] The battle lines were drawn—bull-headed monk vs. passionate, young monarch.

Luther had passed the test: he stood his ground in the face of the assembled might of the Empire. Over the next few days the temperature rose even higher. On April 24th and 25th Luther was taken into the "back room" to meet with small groups. You can imagine the pressure that could be brought to bear on Luther in those situations. The six who gathered with Luther on April 24th. included a major irritant for him, Archbishop Albrecht of Mainz, and his primary defender, Frederick the Wise.[21]

Luther had met the challenges of Worms unscathed. On April 26th he got into his wagon and headed for home. On the way Frederick had him "kidnapped" and tucked away in the Wartburg Castle for safety. Historian MacCulloch described this period as one of wide-spread tension and great anxiety arising from the fact that almost anything could happen. He called 1521–4 "The Years of Carnival."[22] Luther's writings challenged the authority of the Old Church and its servants. In a truly Lutherish paradox he described a Christian as a perfectly free lord of all, subject to none and a perfectly dutiful servant, subject to all.[23] Whether everyone who read that enigmatic statement could appreciate its two-sided truth is another question. In the same work he also wrote, "All of

19. Luther, Between June 12 and July 12, 1532, No. 1654.

20. Oberman, *Luther*, 29.

21. Incidentally, both Oberman (*Luther*, 22) and Krodel (*Luther's Works, 48*, 48) say that Luther and Frederick the Wise never met personally. However, in *Luther's Works, 48*, 205 n. 6 Krodel said they were both at the meeting on April 24th.

22. MacCulloch, *Reformation*, 152–55.

23. See Luther, "Freedom of the Christian," 55.

us who believe in Christ are priests and kings in Christ."[24] Couple these ideas with a long-established entrepreneurialism in Europe and a self-confident middle class and you have more than the seeds of a religious revolution. You have the beginning of the end of a centuries-old social structure, feudalism.

Luther's writing found an exceptionally receptive market. His publications in the year 1523 alone went through 390 editions.[25] One of his devoted readers was a young mother in Lenting, Bavaria. She was Argula von Grumbach, born into the powerful von Stauffen family in southern Germany in 1492.

Argula von Grumbach

Now she becomes our focus of attention, another one of the neglected puzzle pieces. Her husband, Friedrich, held an imperial post as administrator of Dietfurt while she was at home raising children. It is not completely clear how she got Luther's writings—it was likely through Nuremberg[26]—but it is absolutely certain that she was reading him. She said, "A great deal has been published in German, and I've read it all. Spalatin [close associate of Luther's] sent me a list of all the titles."[27] The

24. Luther, "Freedom of the Christian," 63.

25. MacCulloch, *Reformation,* 152.

26. Krodel, *Luther's Works, 49,* 313 n. 11.

27. Lady Argula, "Letters," 86.

general comments about her catch attention. Gerald Strauss identified her as "one of the most fearless members of Luther's advance guard,"[28] and Gottfried Krodel called her "one of the few fascinating and truly great women of the Reformation in Germany who is known to us in some detail."[29]

Her private life was punctuated by sorrow. At age seventeen she lost both her parents within five days to the plague, and seven years later her guardian uncle became entangled in political intrigue, was tortured and executed. Later still Lady Argula's adult daughter predeceased her. This may have been the norm at the time, but it sounds as though death was stalking her family particularly aggressively. In the midst of this, she was able to make sure that all her children received good educations even while the family's property holdings and revenue shrank. She was the glue that kept the family together, handling much of the business end of things even before her first husband died in 1530.[30] What is remarkable is the public life that emerged from that private life—and dramatically complicated it.

Lady Argula was drawn into the public eye by action on the part of the faculty of the University of Ingolstadt. An eighteen year old student, Arsacius Seehofer, was arrested for breaking a Bavarian mandate forbidding Luther's works to be brought into the region. Seehofer had spent some time in Wittenberg and embraced Luther and Melanchthon's teaching. He smuggled some books in, was arrested, and ordered to recant or be burned at the stake. In tears Seehofer recanted on September 7, 1523.

There was some important background to this. Ingolstadt was the university of John von Eck, Luther's opponent in a debate in Leipzig in 1519. One of von Eck's colleagues was Professor of Medicine, Peter Burchard. He had been president of Wittenberg University in 1520 when he stirred up a student riot against the city council. Order was not restored for months and not before Frederick the Wise sent in troops.

28. Strauss, "Religious Policies of Dukes Wilhelm and Ludwig," 359.

29. Krodel, *Luther's Works*, 49, 313 n. 11.

30. Matheson, *Argula*, 8. Peter Matheson is the English language expert on Lady Argula. He has worked in the family and business papers in Munich, edited the material she published, and recently uncovered material related to her which was previously unknown.

Luther called him "that senseless man."[31] Shortly after this Burchard moved to Ingolstadt where he "became a bitter opponent of Luther."[32] On top of all this and at the same time, the University of Ingolstadt was talking about trying to woo Melanchthon, Luther's closest theological lieutenant, into joining their faculty.[33]

When she learned of the action taken against Seehofer Lady Argula sprang into action. Within the year, she had published seven open letters and a poem, and together they were distributed in an estimated 29,000 copies. She had obviously struck a chord in her readers. Here was a woman writing and writing theology no less. This was shocking, mind-numbing and astonishing, part of the "carnival," the upside-downess, MacCulloch described.

There are some interesting features to her work. First, she speaks as an aristocrat who is entirely comfortable in her station. She finds excuses for those of her class who supported the action against Seehofer.[34] She identifies with the landed and moneyed class's suspicion of the academy.[35] She travelled to both the Diet of Nuremberg (1524) and the Diet of Augsburg (1530) to lobby princes and representatives of cities.[36] While at Nuremberg, she found herself invited to dinner with Johann of Simmern and others.[37] Simmern was nothing less than the stand-in for elector Frederick of the Palentine, and in that role he was representing the Emperor himself in the government of the Reich.[38] As the first female lobbyist the Empire had known, Lady Argula had dined with leaders of the highest rank.

This is worth a moment's reflection. Here was a woman, granted an aristocrat, moving into a man's world without direct male support, arranging her own travel and accommodation. These actions are the norm now in much of the world, but in Lady Argula's day, such independent behavior was unimaginable. When she wrote to Frederick the Wise, she reported she had spoken to Duke Johann (Simmern), and she added,

31  Luther To George Spalatin, July 14, 1520, 168.

32. Krodel, *Luther's Works 48*, 168 n. 2.

33. Luther To George Spalatin, July 14, 1520, 166.

34. Lady Argula, "Letters," 81.

35. Lady Argula, "Letters," 82.

36. Matheson, *Argula*, 20 and 24.

37. Lady Argula, "Letters," 126.

38. Matheson, *Argula*, 124.

"I would also gladly have spoken much more with some other rulers, if people had been there to listen."[39] Matheson noted the way Lady Argula was operating and said, "Argula von Grumbach is not lobbying in desperate concern. She appears genuinely buoyant, joyful and grateful, confident in the certain word of God."[40] Lady Argula also felt totally free to exhort Simmern, Frederick the Wise, and Duke Wilhelm to follow the path which she thought appropriate. Further, when she referred to Luther, she occasionally called him just "Martin."[41] She obviously was not agog in the presence of the great man.

A second, and in fact dominant feature, of Lady Argula's work was her view of the Bible. It was the absolute foundation of everything she did. It was "the book which contains all God's commands."[42] Her father gave her a German Bible when she was ten. She did not read it then as diligently as he would have wished,[43] but she certainly made up for it later. As Matheson said, "The supreme, exclusive authority of Scripture for faith and life is a central tenet for her."[44]

Lady Argula stepped into a leading role at a tumultuous time among her all-male peers. Without question in her own mind, she was ready to teach men and anyone else who would listen. She acknowledged 1 Tim. 2:12 and 1 Cor. 14:34ff. where Paul appears to restrict women's range of ministry. "But now," she said, "that I cannot see any man who is up to it, who is either willing or able to speak, I am constrained," and she then cited ten passages of scripture which she was sure authorized her speaking out.[45] She was way out on a limb culturally and socially, and it did not seem to bother her especially. Matheson described the letter she wrote to her troubled cousin, Adam von Thering, as being "as passionate, incisive, and impressive as it is coolly subversive of virtually all the conventions of sixteenth century Bavaria."[46] Yet, if she was a proto-feminist, she was a very specific kind of feminist. She was acting out of the freedom she had found in Christ. As Matheson understood her, she saw herself as a

39. Lady Argula, *Letters*, 134.

40. Matheson, *Argula*, 130.

41. Lady Argula, *Letters*, 85.

42. Lady Argula, *Letters*, 80.

43. Lady Argula, *Letters*, 86.

44. Matheson, *Argula*, 31.

45. Lady Argula, *Letters*, 79–80.

46. Matheson, *Argula*, 140.

captive to the central message of scripture. Her baptismal vows alone, she was persuaded, gave her as valid a commissioning as any theologian, and she was molding her own version of Luther's "priesthood of all believers." For her, church leadership included women.[47]

So what exactly did she do? After a quick trip to Nuremberg to consult with theologian Osiander, whom she had come to know well,[48] she returned home, wrote two letters, and sent them on October 20, 1523. The first was to the faculty of the University of Ingolstadt and the second was to Duke Wilhelm of Bavaria, who had pledged to watch over her when she was left a teenaged orphan. The first one contained the bomb.

Shocked by the treatment of Seehofer, she urged the scholars to lay aside coercion. Borrowing a line from Luther, she said, "A disputation is easily won when one argues with force, not Scripture. As far as I can see that means the hangman is accounted the most learned."[49] And she challenged them to a debate. "I have no Latin," she went on, "but you have German, being born and brought up in this tongue. What I have written to you is no woman's chit-chat, but the word of God; and (I write) as a member of the Christian Church, against which the gates of Hell cannot prevail."[50] She continued, "I do not flinch from appearing before you, from listening to you, from discussing with you."[51] And she embedded her challenge in a flowing defense of Lutheran theology absolutely saturated with Scripture.

The bomb went off. Her challenge was quickly published, and made some gleeful printer a lot of money in a hurry. I imagine the scholars enjoyed a good belly laugh when they first got the letter, but that must have turned into smoldering anger when they discovered that thousands of people were reading Argula's challenge. This was unprecedented. It violated the way the culture was structured. It was ludicrous. It was exciting. It was carnival! One shoe had been dropped. When would the other hit the floor?

On December 8th. In fact. Dr. George Hauer, fuse lit in his cannon, mounted a pulpit in Ingolstadt and fired. In the course of his talk he rolled out a series of uncomplimentary invectives—"You wretched and pathetic

---

47. Matheson, "Luther and Argula von Grumbach," 10.
48. Matheson, *Argula*, 17.
49. Lady Argula, "Letters," 84.
50. Lady Argula, "Letters," 90.
51. Lady Argula, "Letters," 89.

daughter of Eve," "You female desperado," "You arrogant devil," "You heretical bitch," "You shameless whore."[52] This is one angry academic.

Shortly after this attack, Lady Argula wrote to a cousin of her mother's from the powerful von Thering family, and we get a sense of how difficult things were becoming. Apparently the man to whom she wrote had said that if her husband could not control her, someone else should lock her up. Lady Argula assured him that her husband was doing everything he could to make life difficult for her.[53] In this letter, she also reveals that she had heard that her husband was going to lose his position in the Empire because of her. With determination she said, "I cannot help that."[54]

When she began her campaign, she knew she would be in trouble. Her husband did lose his position and seems to have hated her for it. The family lost property and revenue. In 1524 she was hit with outright character assassination in a 130-line piece of doggerel. That someone would go to the bother to do this is an indication of how strongly the impact of her letters was felt. Krodel said she was imprisoned twice and suggested that only her aristocratic peers kept her from worse treatment.[55]

Still she did not slink away and hide. In 1530 she was at the Diet of Augsburg when Melanchthon made the first full presentation of Lutheran theology before the assembled parliament and Emperor Charles V. She was there pleading her cause. Apparently she even tried to mediate an agreement on the Lord's Supper between the south Germans, led by Bucer from Strassbourg , and Melanchthon. Krodel credited her with later organizing a school and a local congregation of believers.[56] We catch her spirit in her last published letter written to the people of Regensburg on June 29, 1524. Quoting Scripture, she called them forward, saying "Let us fight chivalrously against the enemies of God."[57] She was most certainly not finished.

In the letter she had written to the council of Inglostadt trying to draw them onto her side against the university faculty, she made a very powerful comment. She said, "I am persuaded too, that if I am given

52. Matheson, *Argula*, 14.
53. Lady Argula, "Letters," 145.
54. Lady Argula, "Letters," 149.
55. Krodel, *Luther's Works* 49, 313 n. 11.
56. Krodel, *Luther's Works* 49, 313 n. 11.
57. Lady Argula, "Letters," 158.

grace to suffer death for his name, many hearts would be awakened. Yes, and whereas I have written on my own, a hundred women would emerge to write against them."[58] What a witness to the strength she herself felt and to the confidence she had in the women around her.

Lady Argula blazed onto the stage and then pulled back. She had family responsibilities as first one husband and then another died. But she kept active behind the scenes. As she said in her writings, she was not bound to Luther, but to Christ. This attitude opened her to others on the path to reform beyond Luther and his team, particularly in that wing known later as the "radical reformation." Johann Denck taught one of her sons,[59] and Balthasar Hubmaier, ironically one of John von Eck's students, admired her. They saw her work as "a remarkable sign of the times, showing that God was acting in a quite new way."[60] She continued to write Luther and Spalatin. Her letters are lost, but Luther makes reference to her at least twelve times in his correspondence.[61] She even visited Luther in Coburg Castle where he was sitting out the Diet of Augsburg.[62] As determined, courageous, and savvy as Lady Argula was, it appears that Luther had placed her in a very specific pigeon hole. Matheson noted that Luther made no mention of her when he, himself, attacked the theologians at Ingolstadt. Matheson suggested that, "he did not take her seriously as a theologian, any more than the Ingolstadt theologians did. She ranked high as a brave confessor of the faith, but it probably did not occur to him, a professional theologian, to mention her use of the Bible and her theological arguments. For that he was too much a child of his time."[63] Nevertheless, Lady Argula showed just how powerful the people of faith can be, and brightens the puzzle with her presence.

## DEVELOPMENTS

During the 1520s and beyond extraordinarily deep social and political changes were unfolding. Feudalism in western Europe was certainly dying. But "carnival" was passing, too. Uprisings among tenant farmers,

58. Lady Argula, "Letters," 120.

59. Matheson, *Argula*, 103 n. 17.

60. Matheson, *Reformation Christianity*, 277.

61. Matheson, "Luther and Argula von Grumbach," 14. N. 22.

62. Luther to Katie, June 5, 1530, 49, 312. He even passed on to Katie, his wife, advice Lady Argula had given on weaning a baby from the breast. Nice little human note.

63. Matheson, "Luther and Argula von Grumback," 9.

labors, "peasants" as they all have been called, had been common for some time, but 1525 was different. Early in the year *The Twelve Articles* were written by a furrier and a pastor loyal to Lutherans down near Lady Argula's part of Germany.[64] Among other things, they called for freedom and an end of oppression by nobles. Soon actions matched words, with monasteries and castles of aristocrats being attacked and people killed. Luther's theological ideas seem to have played some role, and the contagion spread rapidly. It began to look as though the Empire was sinking into chaos. Horrified, and with a sense of responsibility, Luther called the nobles to action. He published *Against the Robbing and Murdering Hordes of Peasants* and the language is still bone-chilling. The nobility responded, Catholic and Protestant, and somewhere between 70,000 and 100,000 of the lower classes were killed. From that point on, Luther's reformation was tied to the nobility and came to be called the *magisterial reformation* (referring to magistrates, or rulers).

It was also in this context and in 1525 that Anabaptism blossomed as a movement. It grew around Conrad Grebel, Felix Manz, Balthasar Hubmaier, and others in Zurich. The movement spread quickly throughout Switzerland, south Germany/Austria and north Germany/Holland, crystallizing around the "Schleitheim Confession" in 1527. In 1527, and growing out of concerns similar to those behind the suppression of the peasants in 1525, persecution began in Switzerland. Felix Manz was drowned in Zurich. After that Anabaptists were hunted viciously.

Complicating these social and political upheavals in Europe, Islam was also on the move. The Turks continued to press north-westward. In 1526 Louis II, King of Hungary and Bohemia, along with many nobles and clerics plus 16,000 soldiers died in the battle of Mohacs. Three years later the Turks laid siege to Vienna. Unrelated, but involving Islam, Ahmed ibn Ibrahim al-Ghazi (Gragn, 1507–43), an Imam from Somalia, led a *jihad* north into Ethiopia in 1528. His stated goal was to root out Christianity and the centuries-old monarchy. He and his troops laid irreparable waste to the country. The *jihad* was finally broken by a combined army of Ethiopians and Portuguese in 1543.

Throughout western Europe ideas of reform continued to be both embraced and resisted. Nor did England escape the contagion of religious and political shakedown which was infecting the continent. Henry VIII broke from Rome out of a fixation for producing a male heir, but—he did

---

64. Perhaps they were given courage by what they had read of her works.

not break from Catholicism. In 1534 the Act of Supremacy passed into law, permitting Henry to handle his marriage difficulties as he chose. He promptly dismissed his first wife, Catherine of Aragon, aunt of Emperor Charles V, and married another. But he clung to his title of "Defender of the Faith," awarded for an attack he had launched on Luther years before, and insisted that his Church was "Catholic." In addition, needing money for his aggressive plans for action against Scotland and France, Henry dissolved religious houses throughout his realm, taking them over and selling off property and furnishings . By 1540 that meant the closure of 800 monasteries and convents and the displacement of 9000 monks and nuns. It also placed considerable cash in the royal coffers, but there were consequences. The action sparked a rebellion called the "Pilgrimage of Grace," so named because it started near a monastery called "Grace." It involved an army of 30,000 men assembled in York and preparing to march south. Indeed, "Grace" almost toppled Henry's throne, but the wily king averted disaster.

On the continent, Geneva found its Protestant leader in the French lawyer/theologian Jean Calvin. By 1555 Calvin had rewritten the constitution of Geneva, created a constitution for the Church, which we call "Presbyterian," and gained firm control of the Canton of Geneva. His theology and his efficiency became a model for reformations as far from each other as Scotland in the west and Transylvania, east of Hungary.

At long last the Roman Catholic Church formally acted. The Council of Trent, called by Pope Paul III opened in northern Italy on December 13, 1545. With major interruptions it dragged on until 1563. Its fundamental goals turned out to be the centralization and the standardization of the Catholic Church, and to a large measure it achieved those goals shaping the Church into the 1960s with some of its ideas gaining ground again in the third millennium. Even so , it frustrated Catholics like Charles V and Cardinal Reginald Pole who from very different perspectives hoped the Church would find some way to reestablish relationships with departed sisters and brothers.

## CONCLUSION

We heard the hammer. It was Luther's, swung as he nailed up his 95 Theses. Every blow seemed to break open another festering concern. Social, economic, and religious pressures that had been building for hundreds of years erupted. The eruption left a Europe that was fragmented in ways that would take more hundreds of years to sort out. Lady Argula von Grumbach illustrated how deeply the urge to reform had penetrated the fabric of western Europe. She also experienced how firmly the old ways were entrenched. The tear left in the fabric of western European Church and society would be a challenge to millions of people for a long, long time.

# 9

## Protestants to India

### 1706 AD

### INTRODUCTION

THE LOSS OF STABILITY into which western Europe plunged in the sixteenth century can be traced to many factors, but perhaps the most outstanding one was religion. Centuries had to pass, but conditions in Europe did seem to calm somewhat. Settling down may seem like a strange idea for us. Our globe is enmeshed in profound social, cultural, and political redefinition and restructuring which feels like a permanent state of affairs. Indeed, any sense of calm in Europe at any time might be a delusion. Perhaps the most we can say is that the role religion played in the turmoil of western Europe began to shrink gradually in the eighteenth century.

While that shrinkage was taking place, industrial and economic development surged forward, reaching to and creating ever widening markets. Along with the ships of commerce, but sometimes in advance, went the missionaries. As western eyes saw ever-broadening horizons, some were impressed with both supply and demand possibilities, some were gripped with the need to help, and some harbored both reactions intermingled. This was the context in which European Protestants finally launched into self-conscious, officially-supported, cross-cultural ministry, taking the Gospel of Jesus Christ to people groups at the far-flung ends of the earth. The first missionaries set the bar high in their pioneering work for those who would follow them. We will look at their work, but it took awhile for the right conditions to ripen.

## SETTING

Ongoing turbulence continued to characterize north-west Europe. By the mid-1520s what would come to be known as Protestantism was spreading in many directions. In Scotland blood had been shed for the cause. A young follower of Luther, Patrick Hamilton (1504–28) died at the stake in St. Andrews on February 29, 1528. In Zurich Zwingi had become the leading player. As the new religion reached various cantons, tensions grew within the Swiss Confederation. Conflict finally came to a head in a field near Kappel am Albis in 1531. On October 11 that year, parts of Switzerland that had embraced the reformation met in battle with parts that had opposed it. The Protestants were soundly beaten, and Zwingli died on the battlefield. He was succeeded by Heinrich Bullinger as the leader of Protestant Zurich. Decisions in the Holy Roman Empire ultimately led to war again.

Pope Paul III had called the Council of Trent in hopes of defining Catholic dogma and centralizing the Church in response to the Protestant Reformation. On the other hand, Emperor Charles V was looking for some kind of accommodation which might attract Protestants back into Mother Church. The Council opened in December, 1545, and it quickly became obvious that a meeting of Catholic and Protestant minds was very unlikely. Deeply frustrated Charles decided to act. The Empire would force the German Protestants back into the Church.

In 1546 from their walls beside one of the main roads north, Genevans watched imperial troops moving north. On one occasion 15,000 infantrymen marched by, followed some time later by 400 cavalry. Obviously some kind of initiative was immanent. Charles was successful in recruiting Duke Maurice of Saxony. Maurice was a Lutheran, but the carrot Charles held before him was the office of elector of the Holy Roman Emperor, and Maurice seized it. He changed sides and fought among the Imperial forces that met the Protestants in a key battle on Sunday, April 23, 1547. It can be regarded as a surprise attack on the part of the larger imperial army. The pious Elector John Frederick of Saxony had called his troops to worship and not posted enough sentries. In the defeat of the Protestants and the events which followed, both he and the famous Philip of Hesse, Duke Maurice's father-in-law, were taken prisoner.

A truly significant moment occurred on May 20th. The surrender of Wittenberg having been signed the day before, Emperor Charles V entered the city surrounded by his guards. This was Wittenberg, the city of Luther, who had nailed up his theses there and played a major role in tearing apart Charles' empire—the monk whom Charles had pledged to silence. Death had beaten Charles. Luther had died fifteen months earlier. Here was the emperor in the city of Frederick the Wise, the man who had frustrated him by sheltering Luther and hiding him away. Charles rode the long main street up to the castle. He stopped there, then walked into the church where Luther had been buried. It is said that Charles stood silent before Luther's grave for some time. When urged to dig up Luther's bones and burn them, he refused saying, "I make war with the living, not the dead."[1] Scores were not settled.

They were not even close to being settled. In his moment of victory, Charles V decided to impose measures which would bring the believers in the Old and New religions together. They were embodied in his *Interim* brought down in 1548. Completely brushing aside theology and liturgy, he gave Protestants both wine as well as bread in communion (in Catholicism only clergy were permitted to receive the wine), and he let Protestant ministers keep their wives. If he really thought this would remake them into happy Catholics, he was very wrong. The Lutherans flatly refused the plan, and the Catholics were even more angry at the upstart Emperor for meddling in the affairs of those more holy than he.

Events rapidly turned sour for Charles. Elector Maurice changed sides again and brought the Lutherans into a temporary marriage of convenience with the Catholic King of France, Henry II. Aggressive and effective action from both these men led Charles to decide that his time was up. In 1552 he passed the leadership of the Empire over to his brother, Ferdinand, and left for Spain, never to return to Germany again.

Ferdinand then ended hostilities with Maurice, opening the way for the Peace of Augsburg proclaimed at the Diet of Augsburg in 1555. This divided Germany into a Protestant north and a Catholic south, giving each ruler the right to determine which religion would be practiced in his realm. With all of its complications and inadequacies, the settlement brought peace to central Europe for seventy years. The unfulfilled determination proclaimed at Worms in 1521 to destroy Luther and his work followed Charles to his grave four years later.

1. Dyer, *History of Modern Europe*, II, 48.

If peace prevailed in the Empire, chaos reigned in France. Francis I (r.1515–47) was opposed to the reformation from the beginning and with reason. So many in the northern part of his realm began to embrace Luther's ideas, most troublingly among the higher levels of the aristocracy, that people began to call Normandy "Little Germany." A decade or so into the struggle over reform violent anti-Catholic action hardened Francis's opposition. During the "Affair of the Placards" in 1534, Francis arose one morning to find an attack on the Mass tacked to his bedroom door!

His successor, Henry II (r. 1547–59), as we have seen, was prepared to co-operate with Protestants when it fitted his larger agenda. In 1561, during the period when Henry's widowed queen, Catherine de Medici, wielded great influence in France (1560–9), Catholics and representatives of Genevan Protestantism met in abortive talks at Poissy at her instigation. By this time the issue of religion had become knotted with rivalries among the great families of France. It led to a period from around 1560 to the first decade of the seventeenth century during which France was either in armed truce or fighting civil wars.

August 24, 1572, St. Bartholomew's Day, was a dark day in history of France. Circumstances placed the cream of French Protestantism within easy reach of the Catholic Crown and Council. Orders were given that day to attack the Protestants, and before Catholic energies were spent several months later more than 5,000 people from among the Protestant leadership had been murdered. During the next forty plus years, France whirled through political/religious confusion stained red. Along the way two Catholic kings, Henry III and Henry IV, sympathetic to finding ways to make Protestants comfortable in France, were assassinated by Catholic fanatics.

Britain fared better than France—if good and bad is determined by the number of dead. England staggered through Henry VIII's reign as he ripped his realm free of Rome all the while attempting to remain "catholic." He was an "equal opportunity" persecutor who occasionally executed the same number of Catholics and Protestants—at the same time, in the same place.[2] Then England lurched on: first to Edward VI, king in 1547, under whom England became officially Protestant—of the Genevan, not the Germany variety; second to Mary Tudor, Edward's half-sister, queen in 1553, who set about turning the clock back to make

2. MacCulloch, *Cranmer*, 275.

England Catholic again, burning some 300 hundred Protestants in the process; and third to her half-sister, Elizabeth, queen in 1558.

With her razor-sharp mind, her breath-taking wit, her cast iron will, and the family auburn hair to match, Elizabeth created what some have called "a cuckoo in the nest," an English Church which leaned toward Genevan Protestant on the inside while looking Catholic on the outside. Being determined to govern the state, not her people's religious convictions, she restrained the blood flow. Under her, it was active Catholic/political insurgents who were tortured and killed, and few of the "recusants," that is the many Catholics who kept their heads down and their mouths shut. She and her advisors also maintained her realm of England and Ireland free politically—no mean accomplishment with Catholic Spain launching its huge flotilla of ships, the "Armada," against her in 1588 and with Catholic France just across the English Channel from her.

Imagine the confusion rampant in England in the 1540's through 60's. "Who's on the throne today? And what am I, a Catholic or a Protestant? Or does anyone know, or does anyone care?" Among those who held firm in the face of the fires of Queen Mary, many were just ordinary folks. Enough information was obviously getting through for people to make high-risk decisions. To others it must have felt as though the patients were running the asylum.

Out of these circumstances appeared two strains of Anglo-Saxon Christianity which went on to have influence around the world right down to the present. The first were the "Puritans." Genevan or Calvinist Protestantism was strong in England under both Edward VI and Elizabeth I. They were the activists of the time. They wanted to emphasize preaching, they were concerned about the lack of real church discipline, they pressed to get rid of features of worship which were not prescribed in Scripture, and they were very concerned about what kind of clothes the clergy wore during worship. They also called for the Genevan form of church government that came to be known as "Presbyterianism." Their goal? To make the English Church as much like the Swiss Protestant churches as possible.

Elizabeth's successor, James I (r.1603–25) was not particularly pleased with this, but the Prince of Wales, James' eldest son, Henry, most definitely was—just one of the points on which he and his father disagreed. This young man was popular and witty and definitely a Puritan.

Especially the Puritans, but the whole nation mourned when this heir to the throne died at age eighteen. One wonders what the Church of England would have been like if he had lived. Instead, James kept leaning toward the old ways, and when he was followed by Henry's younger brother, Charles I (r.1625–49), the throne and many of the aristocracy appeared to be moving pell mell toward the bosom of Rome. The results were disastrous as we will soon see.

The other group to surface in England at this time was the Baptists. Prominent in their story are Robert Browne (1550–1633) and John Smyth (c.1570–1612). Both became "separatists," distancing themselves at various times from the Church of England, and both led groups which followed them to the Netherlands when they got into trouble. Both believed that the true church was a "gathered" church made up of people who had come to faith in Christ and begun to worship together in groups that were self-governing, or "congregational," in church government.

Smyth became convinced that only those who had made a profession of repentance and then accepted baptism should be admitted to these groups. In c.1611 he died and at about the same time many of those who had followed him to Amsterdam returned to England to form the first Baptist congregation in that country. Differences arose among those calling themselves Baptist, but by 1641 believers being baptized, and that by immersion, had become a distinctive feature of the name.

None of these events occurred in a vacuum. The Roman Catholics were not just struggling to maintain their footing in England. They were moving aggressively in all parts of the world to which Portuguese, Spanish, and French ships were sailing. The Franciscans and Dominicans descended upon Latin America early in the sixteenth century. There were some ten million baptized Christians there by 1550 and the thrust gained even greater strength when the Jesuits arrived in the 1560s and 70s. The Jesuits also went to India. Francis Xavier, S.J. (1506–52) devoted himself to the lower classes before moving on to Japan in 1549, and somewhat later Roberto de Nobili, S.J. (1577–1656) reached to the Brahmins in India. Another Jesuit, Matteo Ricci, S.J. (1552–1610), moved to China where he identified deeply with the Chinese. In fact the form of worship he developed for them was so Chinese that it got him into trouble with some in the Vatican and other Catholic religious orders. Finally, yet another member of the Society of Jesus, Jean de Brébeuf, S.J. (1593–1649) established a mission in what is now Canada, just east and north of the

Great Lakes. He sealed his commitment to Christ and the gospel with a gruesome martyrdom.

Meanwhile, as western Europe moved into the seventeenth century events took a catastrophic turn. On the continent, long-standing territorial conflicts in the east, west, and north; Imperial jealousy for power; concerns about control of trade on the Baltic; and religion—all blended to form a toxic sludge which flowed across Europe. The "Thirty Years War" (1618–48) dealt death to millions. Imagine armies or bands of soldiers, regular troops and mercenaries, weapons in hand, wounds festering, stomachs empty, surging back and forth across central Europe from the Baltic to the Alps on their way to the next battle or skirmish. For thirty years it went on, compromising infrastructure, such as it was, and altering demographics for generations. That meant countless deaths among soldiery and non-combatants and hellishly difficult living conditions for everyone else. The old Middle Ages had seen more or less constant blood-letting, but this was mayhem of gargantuan proportions. Think about how distant any kind of normal life must have felt for many. Some have suggested that the population of central Europe, and primarily Germany, plummeted from sixteen million to six million.

Nobody had wanted this war, but it only ended when the various configurations of combatants bled each other to a stand still. Mutual hatred and suspicion ran so deep that while the Peace of Westphalia was being tortuously pieced together the negotiators could not only not be in the same room, they could not even bear to be in the same town! Charge and counter-charge, claim and counter-claim shuttled back and forth in the pouches of messengers.

James I had held England out of the melé, but the country soon engaged in its own bloodletting. Large parts of the population hated James' successor, Charles I, so much so that it rose against him under the leadership of Oliver Cromwell in 1640. For eleven years up and down the land and across the Irish Sea, Parliamentarians (or Roundheads) and Royalists slaughtered each other. Before it ended the Archbishop of Canterbury, William Laud (1573–1645) and Charles I, himself (r.1625–49) had died under the executioner's axe. This led to the "Interregnum" or "Commonwealth" or "Protectorate," during which England and Ireland was a republic led by Oliver Cromwell, who styled himself Lord Protector, but refused the crown.

Then as if all this suffering flowing out of human perverseness were not enough, the bubonic plague was still stalking the continent. Epidemics carried off thousands, and there were at least five major regional outbreaks across Europe during the seventeenth century.

It is odd that while this maelstrom of wretchedness was exploding at incalculable cost in human suffering, other currents were beginning to coalesce. At first a trickle and then swelling streams converged to usher in the Enlightenment. The science of Copernicus (1473–1543), Bacon (1561–1626), Kepler (1571–1630), Galileo (1564–1642), and Newton (1642–1727) along with the thought of Descartes (1596–1650), Spinoza (1632–77), Locke (1632–1704) and many, many others led to the impression, counter intuitive though it was, that the human person is rational.

At approximately the same time Lutheran theologians were groping toward a blending of Luther's genuine thought and the insights of Aristotle.[3] This was leading to a period known as "Lutheran Orthodoxy," and it was being expressed in tightly-reasoned, exhaustive theology, and sermons which must have been frightfully boring to many. Out of this arose a movement pulled together by a passionate longing for a deepening of the spiritual life. It was known as "Pietism."

Most agree that the founder of the movement was Philipp Spener (1635–1705). In 1666 Spener was called to Frankfurt am Main to pastor a large Lutheran parish. As he went about his work, he was gripped by a growing desire to know God more profoundly. In 1670 he started to hold small group meetings in his home. Participants prayed and shared insights that had come to them as they meditated on the Bible. It became increasingly clear to Spener that everyone would benefit from a deeper experience with God and that the result would be a demonstration of genuine Christianity in people's lives. He also concluded that preaching had a role to play in this. The pulpit should not be a place where obscure theological essays were read. The preacher's sermons should be lifting people up and helping them in their walk with God.

Many were moved by Spener's teaching, but others were offended. His call to a deeper walk with God carried the obvious implication that he thought things were not as good as they could be in the church of his time. Many found troubling the small group meetings he was holding. Tiring of the ongoing struggle in Frankfurt, he accepted a call to move

---

3. Nestingen, "Gnesio-Lutherans," para. 26.

to Dresden in 1686, and five years later continued on to Berlin. There he enjoyed the favor of Elector Frederick of Brandenburg (r.1688–1713 and King in Prussia, r. 1701–13) and many in the nobility. This was the period of his greatest influence.

One who caught Spener's spirit was August Francke (1663–1727). While studying at universities in Erfurt, Kiel and Leipzig and gaining proficiency in ancient and modern languages, he embraced the spirituality of Pietism. In 1690 Francke was called to teach and pastor in Erfurt, but his Pietism put him out of favor with authorities there, and he was forced to leave early the next year. In December, 1691, perhaps influenced by Spener, Elector Frederick called Francke to become professor of Greek and Hebrew at a university he was establishing in Halle and to pastor a church in the area. Francke's career was launched.

He threw himself into the work with remarkable sensitivity to the community around him.[4] In 1695 he opened a school for poor children and shortly thereafter, an orphanage. These were "faith" ventures. He felt God's leading and determined to trust God to meet all needs. Both ventures flourished. In 1696 he added a kind of prep school for sons of aristocratic families; in 1697, a Latin school; and in 1698, a high school for girls. In addition, he oversaw the establishment of a pharmaceutical business, and a publishing company complete with a printing press. The institution to which all these belonged came to be known as "Die Franckische Stiftungen" (The Francke Institution) and the complex of buildings which grew up to accommodate them still stands in Halle (Saale). His work was respected throughout that part of Germany, and he became a prominent leader in Pietism. When he died in 1727 his remarkable programs were serving 2200 children, 250 non-fee paying, and employing 175 teachers and 8 inspectors.

### EVENT

The development that follows was truly significant in the story of the Church. The Thirty Years War had left Europe traumatized. Jens Glebe-Møller argued that a wave of "end time" fervor swept Europe as people began to feel that the collapse of the world as they knew it could happen at any moment. The Millennium (Rev 20) was around the corner. At least that was the message of Dane, Holger Paulli, as he travelled Europe,

---

4. Bautz, "Francke, August Hermann," para. 1.

but before that could happen the heathen and the Jews had to be reached with the Gospel.[5] It was in that context that "The road to Protestant missionary work in the eighteenth century was opened by King Frederick IV of Denmark."[6] In 1705 Frederick decided to establish a mission station. The late Missiologist Hans-Werner Gensichen saw the outcome of Frederick's action as the real beginning of the history of continuous, methodical Protestant world missionary outreach,[7] and Paul Jenkins agreed.[8] While a growing number of people are becoming aware of this episode in missions, it is one of those pieces which has mostly been overlooked in the retelling of the Christian story.

Frederick's decision was truly ground-breaking. By contrast, the Roman Catholics had been active in cross-cultural, trans-continental religious ministry for more than 200 years by this time. Their outreach began in the maritime countries of Portugal and Spain, and they had access to religious orders of men and women free from family responsibilities whose visions included proclaiming the Gospel of Christ far and wide. On the other hand, throughout the sixteenth and seventeenth centuries, the Protestants had spent considerable energy trying to figure out who they actually were, and then had become deeply mired in the Thirty Years War and its consequences. The Catholic religious orders in southern Europe escaped this catastrophe for the most part.

Commenting on the life of missiologist Hans-Werner Gensichen, Daniel Jeyaraj said that for him "The history of the Church is the history of Missions."[9] From the beginning there has been a passion in the hearts of Christians to take the Gospel of Christ to those who have not heard—wherever they are. We have noted this in century after century. By the beginning of the eighteenth century European Protestants were

---

5. Glebe-Møller, "The Realm of Grace Presupposes the Realm of Power. The Danish Debate about the Theological Legitimacy of Mission," 89–90.

6. Brunner, *Halle Pietists*, 102.

7. Gensichen, "Dänish-Hallische Mission," 319. Gensichen also said that what developed out of this decision influenced Zinzendorf, William Carey, Cotton Mather, Johanes Jänickes, the Berliner Missionsseminar, the early Weslyans, and the first American-Lutheran mission. ("Dänish-Hallische Mission," 321).

8. Jenkins, Review of *A German Exploration of Indian Society: Zeigenbalg's "Malabarian Heathenism*, 217. However, Andrew F. Walls played down its importance. (Walls, "Mission, VI von der Reformationzeit bis zur Gegenwart," 40).

9. Jeyaraj, *Inkulturation in Tranquebar*, 34.

comfortable enough with survival and identity issues to think beyond themselves, and when they did, the passion broke out.

The mission was located in Tranquebar (modern Tharangambadi) on the coast of the Bay of Bengel in what is nowTamil Nadu in south-east India. Bartholomäus Ziegenbalg, one of the first missionaries, described it as a Danish colony with an attractive castle and walls set in an area ruled by the King of Tanjour (Tanjuvar), who was a vassal of a powerful Muslim ruler.[10] It was a tiny colony, 5x3 miles, hugging the coastline. The Danes had held it since 1620 for an annual rent to the King of Tanjuvar.[11] Ziegenbalg estimated the population of the colony to be about 18,000 along with a large number of Muslims and others whom he just calls "darkskinned."[12] Danish historian, Anders Nørgaard, said there were only 250 Europeans there at the time.[13] The mission survived until 1845 when the colony was sold to the British.[14] Nørgaard says that by then it had succumbed to rationalism. There was no significant criticism of the mission. Quite simply, no one could be found who would go to India and carry on the work.[15] Lehmann commented graphically: "When the Mother Church no longer took the Bible seriously and the spiritual life in Europe became cold, the Tranquebar mission was paralyzed."[16]

Just why Frederick IV chose to act when he did has been a topic of discussion for some time. The idea of missions was well known and affirmed by those at the royal court,[17] and Frederick's chaplain was a pietist, Franz Julius Lütkens, who was concerned that the Gospel be preached to the "heathen."[18] Then in 1704 Elisabeth von Vierigg whom Frederick had married bigamously, one in a series of mistresses, died in childbirth with the child dying shortly after. Frederick was deeply convicted about his behavior and promised Lütkins he would do something

---

10. Ziegenbalg to Weitzmann, October 7, 1709, 116–17.

11. Lehmann, *It Began at Tranquebar*, 6.

12. Ziegenbalg to Linde, September 5, 1706, 35.

13. Nørgaard, "The Mission's Relationship to the Danes, 47.

14. Nørgaard, "The Mission's Relationship to the Danes, 90.

15. Nørgaard, "The Mission's Relationship to the Danes, 83.

16. Lehmann, *It Began at Tranquebar*, 172.

17. See Jeyara, *Inkulturation in Tranquebar* 42–43 and Pedersen, *De forste sammenstod mellem ordhodoksi og pietisme*, 23–29.

18. Jeyaraj, *Inkulturation in Tranquebar*, 43.

as penance.[19] On top of all this, he may have known what the Society for the Proclamation of the Gospel was doing in the West Indies,[20] and he might have been motivated by the old Peace of Augsburg principle that "the religion of the people is determined by that of the prince."[21]

Whatever combination of factors prompted Frederick to launch this initiative, he maintained an active interest in it. He received correspondence from missionaries, he entertained them when they came home, and following Lütkens's death, he set up a small board to watch over the mission and a Missions Collegium to prepare future missionaries.[22] Without question the political and administrative power source was in Copenhagen. As Nørgaard wrote with considerable national pride, "It was and always would be the Danish king who gave the necessary dogmatic legitimation to the Lutheran mission."[23] As we shall see soon, the spiritual center of the mission was Halle.[24]

Having made the decision to become involved in missions, the next pressing issue was to find candidates. When representatives of the more mainstream part of the Lutheran Church in Denmark failed to find anyone,[25] Frederick placed the task in the hands of his pietist chaplain, Lütkens,[26] and the Copenhagen-Berlin-Halle network came through.

The first person to sign on was Heinrich Plütschau.[27] Plütschau (1677–1752) had studied theology at Halle. In Tranquebar he was an eager and fully committed participant in the life of the mission. He studied both Portuguese, which had become the language of trade along the east coast of India because the Portuguese were the first Europeans to arrive there, and Tamil, the local language. He spent six years in Tranquebar, returning to Germany for health reasons. He taught Tamil to mission candidates at Halle for a brief period and then pastored a Lutheran church in Germany for 36 years.[28]

19. Pedersen, *De forste sammenstod mellem ordhodoksi og pietisme*, 30.

20. Brunner, *Halle Pietists*, 102.

21. Nørgaard, "The Mission's Relationship to the Danes, 46.

22. Jeyaraj, *Inkulturation in Tranquebar*, 2.

23. Nørgaard, "The Mission's Relationship to the Danes," 46.

24. Jeyaraj, *Inkulturation in Tranquebar*, 3.

25. Jeyaraj, *Inkulturation in Tranquebar*, 46.

26. Lehmann, *It Began at Tranquebar*, 3.

27. Tamcke, "Heinrich Plütschau," 548.

28. Gröschl, "Missionaries," 1498–99.

In addition to Plütschau's dogged determination to learn both languages and his profound spiritual life, two other features of his life in the mission stand out. First, he carried on a preaching ministry in both German and Portuguese, and he taught school for children in Tamil. He was effective in both capacities.

Second, he was very concerned about human relations. He came to the aid of those being taken advantage of by someone more powerful. This happened twice on the ship sailing to Tranquebar.[29] Once he was in Tranquebar, he became troubled by the slavery which he saw being practiced. He took the part of Lutheran Tamils who had been enslaved. He argued that they could not be sold, but that they should be treated as "children of the house."[30] He was also a mediator, or a peace-maker.

The biggest test of Plütschau's skills as a manager of conflict came in a heated disagreement between Ziegenbalg and the Govenor of the colony, J. S. Hassius. The issue was the conversion of a Tamil. The man's relatives were protesting against the conversion, and Hassius saw the danger of social and perhaps even political unrest. As Ziegenbalg described the situation, again it was Plütschau who intervened,[31]and the intervention seems to have been successful.

The other person selected for the mission was Bartholomäus Ziegenbalg (1682–1719). He had started a theology program at Halle, but had to discontinue due to ill health. Having spent time in ministry in a number of places, in August 1705 M. Langen asked him if he would go to the West Indies as a missionary under the auspices of the King of Denmark. His answer was evasive, but when he met Langen and others in Berlin three weeks later it turned out that they had thought he had said yes. He excused himself pleading incompetence, youth, and physical weakness, but they did some arm twisting, and he agreed to go. In October, he and Plütschau went to Copenhagen where they were ordained on November 11th after some pretty heavy-handed pressure applied to the bishop by the king himself. Then it turned out that they were not going to the West Indies or to Africa, as had been hinted, but to India. On November 29, 1705, their ship embarked.[32]

---

29. Tamcke, "Heinrich Plütschau," 550.

30. Tamcke, "Heinrich Plütschau," 552.

31. Ziegenbalg to Lang, October 23, 1709, 145.

32. Ziegenbalg to Linde, September 5, 1706, 32–33.

Two young men, Heinrich, 28 and Bartholomäus, 23, were aboard ship cutting through the trackless sea on their way to a life they knew nothing about, to a country they knew next to nothing about. They were growing into a very close relationship, according to Ziegenbalg,[33] and they had their instructions in hand:

> 1. Learn whatever possible of language while on ship.
>
> 2. Labour among the pagans, as existing circumstances shall make it practicable.
>
> 3. Although it is of some help, to improve the little rest of the knowledge of God, which men still have by nature.[34]

What these instructions might have meant to them is another question. It is unlikely that there would have been anyone in a crew of Danish and German sailors who could help them with Tamil, although some use of Portuguese might have been more possible. Nørgaard argued that this document called for an "incarnation." The missionaries were to "take on" what was Indian as Christ "took on" humanity." Nøgaard said, ". . . it is thanks to the Tranquebar Mission that such an 'incarnation' came into being that has been a model for all later missions."[35] That approximates quite well the way these young men understood their instructions, and Ziegenbalg in particular carried them out to a remarkable degree.

They arrived on July 9, 1706. Plütschau returned to Germany after six years, and Ziegenbalg died in Tranquebar in 1719. The venture was clearly emotionally tough.[36] Colleagues came and went.[37] By October, 1709 Ziegenbalg and Gründler decided they wanted to find wives, so they wrote J. Lange to see what he could do for them. Ziegenbalg even enclosed a ring for a particular girl whom he knew—and a ten-point job description![38] The men did not get the women whom they mentioned in the letter, but both ultimately married.[39]

---

33. Ziegenbalg to Francke, October 1, 1706, 46 and in many other letters.

34. "Royal Appointment and Instructions," 1337.

35. Nørgaard, "The Mission's Relationship to the Danes," 54.

36. Ziegenbalg, to Breithaupt, Antonius, and Francke, September 22, 1707, 58.

37. Johann Ernest Gründler (1677–1720), who arrived in 1709, became Ziegenbalg's closest friend—Gröschl, "Missionaries of the Danish-Halle and English-Halle Missions in India," 1499.

38. Ziegenbalg to Lange, October 7, 1709, 124 and 129.

39. Ziegenbalg to Maria Dorothea Saltzmann (1693- ?) in 1715 during his trip to

Commemorative Monument erected in 2006

There was a chronic shortage of money in spite of Ziebenbalg and Plütschau's plowing half their salaries back into the mission expenses.[40] Losing a very large sum in the sea while it was being unloaded did not help.[41] Disagreements with the governor over evangelizing the Tamils reached their peak with Ziegenbalg spending four months in solitary confinement in a very hot cell next to a kitchen.[42] In 1712 the mission set up the first printing press in Tamil Nadu, and in 1715 Ziegenbalg printed his Tamil translation of the New Testament, "the first such translation in any Indian language."[43] The men opened a little church they had built on August 14, 1707 and were thrilled with a great crowd of heathen, Muslims and Christians who attended.[44] They also held worship services

---

Germany and Gründler to the widow Utila Krahe (1675–1720), who was already in India. See Pabst, "The Wives of Missionaries."

40.  Ziegenbalg to Friends, September 8, 1706, 37.

41.  Ziegenbalg to Frederick IV, December 28, 1713, 372.

42.  Ziegenbalg to Breithaupt, Antonius and Francke, October 1, 1708, 88; Ziegenbalg to Francke, October 1, 1708, 108; and Lehmann, *It Began at Tranquebar*, 69.

43.  Jayaraman, "Tranquebar," para. 13.

44.  Ziebenbalg to Breithaupt, Antonius and Francke, September 22, 1707, 62.

in their house,[45] but in 1718 dedicated a much larger building which still stands, the New Jerusalem Church.

New Jerusalem Church

What is truly remarkable is the way Ziegenbalg went about his work. Immediately upon arriving, he and Plütschau plunged into the study of Tamil.[46] Within two years Ziegenbalg was able to preach extemporaneously.[47] When he was challenged with having a superficial understanding of the local religions, he urged the Tamils to find their best books. He would pay for them and study them carefully.[48] He also read deeply into the theology of what is called Hinduism. Acknowledging that Hindu

45. Ziegenbalg to Lütkens, August 22, 1708, 74.

46. Ziegenbalg to Francke, October 1, 1706, 43.

47. Ziegenbalg to Lütkens, August 22, 1708, 72. Jenkins expressed amazement at his ability to learn the language—Jenkins, Review of *A German Exploration of Indian Society*, 217.

48. Ziegenbalg, *Thirty-Four Conferences*, 53–54. This is an intriguing document. It is 352 pages long and most of it contains accounts of thirty-four occasions when missionaries, likely Ziegenbalg, got into candid discussions with Tamils, who were what we call Hindus, and Muslims. The author obviously tries to report on both sides of the discussions fairly. The document stands as one of the first extended accounts of "contact," the moments West met East for the very first time, moments filled with confusion, shock, revulsion, and, surprisingly, the mutual desire to understand. The work is seen as a very important source for the study of the Danish-Halle mission. See H.-W. Gensichen, "Imitating the Wisdom of the Almighty." It can be accessed on the Internet at www.archive.org.

thought about the divine is more complicated than people in the West often see, Paul Jenkins admitted astonishment that Ziegenbalg grasped the complexity.[49] For example, in one of his conversations with a Tamil philosopher, Ziegenbalg discovered that the man did not believe in the plurality of gods or in the worship conducted in temples. Speaking for himself and other thinkers like him, the man said, "We reverently adore the Supreme Being, who created all things."[50] The philosopher than went on to say that he and his colleagues could not share this belief with others for two reasons. First, because very few can worship God without images, and second, because to do so would take away the comfortable lives of Brahmans and priests.[51] This monotheism, as Jenkins calls it, appears over and over again in Ziegenbalg's reports of his conversations with Tamils.

Will Sweetman argued that Ziegenbalg was able to understand the Hindu pantheon because he read a key unpublished manuscript.[52] That may be true, but he was also hearing about it repeatedly from those he was in conversation with. For example, on one occasion a Rischi (prophet) sketched Hindu theology by saying that the Supreme Being's name is Dewaddadwan. He has many lieutenants, commonly called gods. The three main ones are Biruma, Wishtnu, and Ruddirea. All of the lieutenants have "borrowed beings" and are completely dependent on the Supreme God, and they appear to human beings in many different shapes and images. They believed this configuration of divinity would continue until all things are restored to the primitive state and the Supreme Being will be all in all.[53] When Ziegenbalg protested that the idea of all these gods was ridiculous the Tamils apparently agreed, but said that the Supreme Being liked these kinds of games.[54]

Here was a European who poured himself into learning the language of the people to whom he came and who read well over one

---

49. Jenkins, A review of *A German Exploration of Indian Society*, 217.

50. Ziegenbalg, *Thirty-Four Conferences*, 148.

51. Ziegenbalg, *Thirty-Four Conferences*, 150.

52. Sweetman, Review of *Genealogy of the South Indian Dieties*, 112. The name of the manuscript is *Tirikalaccakkaram*.

53. Ziegenbalg, *Thirty-Four Conferences*, 167.

54. Ziegenbalg, *Thirty-Four Conferences*, 172. At another time, a Brahman told Ziegenbalg that Hindus worshipped the Supreme Being (He called him the "Prime Cause.") through all the intervening gods—Ziegenbalg, *Thirty-Four Conferences*, 2.

hundred theology and philosophy books in Tamil in a concentrated effort to understand profoundly the way in which Tamils viewed the world. This was almost unheard of at his time, and is still fairly rare. Through all this, he developed a deeply-rooted respect for the people to whom he had come. Very early on he said the Tamils were clever and sharp and lived better lives than Christians. They were wrestling with the same questions as those who had studied Greek philosophy.[55] He confessed that he wanted to spend his life among the Tamils.[56]

Ziegenbalg could not keep himself from getting out among the Tamils. He sat on the grass and talked to school children, stopped at local pubs to chat with Brahmans, and listened to poor fishermen on the coast struggling to make a living. "He sought and found the people where they really were."[57] Taking advantage of his hospitality, people came from near and far to see this white man who talked their language and seemed to understand their thought better than they did. Ziegenbalg would drop everything, light sweet incense, and feed them with sweet meats.

He preached the Gospel everywhere and at all times, and his hearers lapped it up. One Imam looked him square in the face and said, "I freely confess, I never heard a Christian talk as you do."[58] A merchant admitted that he had been particularly aggressive in opposition to Ziegenbalg just to see if he could get him angry, but Ziegenbalg had passed the test.[59] They all knew that the white man was not going to try to overpower them, so with comfort they could say, "You have the freedom of speaking and we of approving what we please."[60] At the end of one five-hour conference set up in another town by a Dutch magistrate, both sides complimented the other on how things had gone, and then the whole group sat down to drinks and sweet-meats. Ziegenbalg took down the names of several so he could write them.[61]

However, the Tamils were not passive. On one occasion an old man who had been listening to Ziegenbalg got to his feet to insist that they were not heathens. Their religion was as old as the world, and many of

55. Ziegenbalg to Francke, October 1, 1706, 44.
56. Ziegenbalg to Lange, August 19, 1709, 98.
57. Gensichen, "Imitating the Wisdom of the Almighty," 836.
58. Ziegenbalg, *Thirty-Four Conferences*, 66.
59. Ziegenbalg, *Thirty-Four Conferences*, 259.
60. Ziegenbalg, *Thirty-Four Conferences*, 70.
61. Ziegenbalg, *Thirty-Four Conferences*, 177.

their gods had done miracles.[62] Building on the idea of the antiquity of their religion, a Brahman defended it by saying that it had been believed by so many outstanding people for so many ages that someone would have discovered it was false, if it were.[63]

Again and again Ziegenbalg's contacts argued that the wretchedness of Christians' behavior made what he was trying to teach them sound completely ridiculous. Even a school boy could say,

> we are taught from our youth. . . that the Christian religion is the worst of all religions. . . . If what is reported of their wicked lives, and the strictness and narrowness of the Way to heaven . . . be true, we have reason to fear that few Christians will ever come to heaven: for they commit such abominations that our polluted eyes cannot behold them without horror, nor willingly converse with them.

He went on to ask that if Christians look so bad to them, how much more will God reject them?[64] Clearly Christian lives have not always been great advertisements for their beliefs.[65]

Ziegenbalg's respectful openness led to his meeting opposition thick and fast. In addition to the above, he heard Tamils say,

> I believe all you say of God's dealings with you white Europeans, to be true; but his appearances and revelations among us Black Malabarians have been quite otherwise; and the revelations he made of himself in this land are as firmly believed here to be true, as you believe those in your country: for as Christ in Europe was made man; so here Wischnu was born among us Malabarians; and as you hope for salvation through Christ; so we hope for salvation through Wischnu; and to save you one way, and us another, is one of the pastimes and diversions of the Almighty.[66]

---

62. Ziegenbalg, *Thirty-Four Conferences*, 101.

63. Ziegenbalg, *Thirty-Four Conferences*, 5.

64 Ziegenbalg, *Thirty-Four Conferences*, 80. He concludes by urging Ziegenbalg not to be discouraged by what he has just said, but to pick the thread of his talk and keep on telling them about his doctrine. Ziegenbalg must have swallowed a couple of times before he went on.

65. And by the way, they should stop eating beef, spitting and taking care of other bodily necessities in the house, and wash their bodies more often. Ziegenbalg, *Thirty-Four Conferences*, 324.

66 Ziegenbalg, *Thirty-Four Conferences*, 14.

"A thousand roads may lead to the same capital city."[67] Eloquent expressions of a thorough-going pluralism. The bottom line of people's beliefs was "if we lead lives morally inoffensive and strictly virtuous, we have no need of the Christian religion, to make our persons or actions more acceptable to God,"[68] and the clincher was, if we are wrong it is because God wills it—"For who are we, to resist the will of god, who has decreed everything that is to happen to us in all the course of our lives."[69]

Then there were the difficulties converts to Christianity would face with their families and the larger society. Ziegenbalg realized early on that becoming a Christian would result in total ostracization for a Tamil,[70] and he heard that over and over again.[71] Then he had to live through the sad example of a poet, Kanabadi, who had a determined and very public conversion, but then fell away.[72]

The cross-cultural evangelist encounted an endless welter of arguments, as Christians always have and still do, and now in the West as much as in other parts of the world. Ziegenbalg readily admitted the destructive impact of people who carry the name "Christian," but who have no real faith. He turned aside arguments as well as he could (so effectively that one Imam thought he had a demon who helped him come up with answers on the spot!) He flatly rejected the "politically correct" pluralism,[73] saying as kindly and as lovingly as he could, "Outside of Christ there is no salvation."[74] He acknowledged the free will of the people to whom he had come. They could accept or reject his message. Citing Mt. 28:19, he explained to King Frederick that the text said "teach," not "convert" all nations.[75] Later he added, "The conversion of the heathen is a work God must do. We have nothing more to contribute than to explain to them what the Word of God says about repentance

---

67. Ziegenbalg, *Thirty-Four Conferences*, 212.

68. Ziegenbalg, *Thirty-Four Conferences*, 17.

69. Ziegenbalg, *Thirty-Four Conferences*, 7.

70. Ziegenbalg to ? September 25, 1706, 41.

71. Ziegenbalg, *Thirty-Four Conferences*, 261 and 285.

72. Ziegenbalg to Lange, 140–48, and Singh, "'One Soul tho' not one Soyl'?" 77.

73. One Tamil threw at him "You seem so holy, but it doesn't become a holy man to blaspheme our Gods, . . . for true piety dispises no man upon account of religion." Ziegenbalg, *Thirty-Four Conferences*, 107. See also Ziegenbalg, *Thirty-Four Conferences*, 327.

74. Ziegenbalg, *Thirty-Four Conferences*, 66.

75. Ziegenbalg to Frederick IV, September 19, 1707, 53.

and faith."[76] Here was a wise young man. That conviction made it possible for him to open himself to the Tamils and their beliefs, leaving the outcome of his work in the hands of God.

Ziegenbalg died young in early 1719, at 37 years of age. That physical weakness he had talked about before heading to India seems to have caught up to him. His close friend, Johann Gründler, and Johann's wife, Utila, both died the next year. These deaths must have given Dorothea Ziegenbalg much grief, although she remarried shortly after. The deaths clearly forced a change in the mission's leadership. The mission had not exploded into vast numbers, but it had grown. In 1709, a little over three years after it had gotten started, Ziegenbalg reported that there were 145 people associated with them,[77] and Lehmann stated that there were 250 in 1720.[78] It also eventually established an indigenous ministry. The first ordained Indian pastor was known simply as Aaron. He was converted through

Ziegenbalg's Grave

Ziegenbalg's ministry in 1718. He proved himself in ministry and was ordained on December 28, 1733.[79]

A feature of mission life that has been noted by several is that the influence of both caste and gender were minimized. Lehmann commented that initially higher and lower castes were separated by a yard as they sat in church, "But there was no difference at the altar."[80] Certainly, the correspondence and the conferences showed clearly that the mission's doors were open to anyone irrespective of class, but they also demonstrated that Ziegenbalg and the others went looking for people of all strata of society.

76. Ziegenbalg to Weitzmann, October 7, 1709, 119.
77. Ziegenbalg to Weitzmann, October 7, 1709, 119.
78. Lehmann, *It Began In Tranquebar*, 43.
79. "Biography of Pastor Aaron," 1405–1407.
80. Lehmann, *It Began In Tranquebar*, 64.

With regard to women, the mission was almost radical. One modern Indian journalist called Ziegenbalg a "true champion in the cause of women's education,"[81] highlighting both the school for girls and the women in management there. Ziegenbalg's concern for the position of women prompted him to speak against the prostitution expected of the *devadasis*, or temple dancers.[82] Women frequently appeared in the crowds which came to hear him speak. He encouraged them to ask questions and comment on what he was saying, and they did. Reflecting on the impact of the mission, Irshick said: "It is of some interest that the Tamil cultural area where the missionary arrived in the early eighteenth century, by the twentieth century becomes one of the most modern in India and achieves zero population [growth] in the 1990's."[83]

In 1715 the Mission Board in Copenhagen liked what it saw. It encouraged the missionaries to press on with the propagation of the Gospel as far and wide as possible without worrying about colonial boundaries or commercial bluster. Nørgaard put it well when he said, "In other words it was decided in Copenhagen that Lutheran world mission should commence in Tranquebar."[84] This was just the beginning, and the mainspring was Ziegenbalg. Lehmann wrote, "It belongs to the greatness of Ziegenbalg, who entered the work without any practical training in mission work, or any previous knowledge of Hinduism, that with an almost inspired assurance he led the new mission work on lines, the basic correctness of which has remained undisputed by his co-workers and successors up to this day."[85]

## DEVELOPMENTS

Meanwhile the Catholics had continued to pursue their missionary interests with vigor well into the eighteenth century. Beyond Europe itself, they were channeling people and resources to North and South America, West Africa, Asia, and the Pacific Islands, and they were very effective.

For their part, the Protestants were not content with just Tranquebar. In the 1720's Hans and Gertrude Egede left Denmark for Greenland—more

---

81. Syed Syed Muthahar, "Tercentenary of Tranquebar Mission," para. 5.

82. Ziegenbalg to Breithaupt, Antonius and Francke, October 1, 1708, 89.

83. Irshick, "Conversations," 254.

84. Nørgaard, "The Mission's Relationship to the Danes," 66.

85. Lehmann, *It Began In Tranquebar*, 27.

Lutheran missionaries under the eye of King Frederick IV. In the 1730's the Egedes were joined in Greenland by Movarians sent out by Count von Zinzendorf from Herrnhut. About the same time other Movarians went to work in St. Thomas and Dutch Guiana in the West Indies.

To the north of these tropical settings, the Thirteen Colonies of English settlers, in what would become the United States, were growing rapidly. The rigors and disorientation of putting an ocean between yourself and your homeland, of clearing land and figuring out how to live in a new world, of struggling to develop businesses all contributed to weakening the Christian faith with which many settlers had come. Despite these challenges, a revival broke out which swept most of the colonies early in the eighteenth century. Under the leadership of people like Theodore Frelinghuysen (1691–1748), Gilbert Tennant (1703–64), Jonathan Edwards (1703–58) and many others, whole communities found their relationships with God and Church dramatically deepened.

Events in Russia at this time were quite different from what took place in the Americas and the rest of the world. Czar Peter the Great (1672, r. 1682–1725) took a strong hold on power in 1689. He was not only a modernizer and a westernizer, but he wanted to make sure he had control of the Russian Orthodox Church. There had been a history of unusual violence and suppression under the previous czar. In 1700 when the head of the Russian Orthodox Church died Peter simply did not allow him to be replaced. In 1721 the "Spiritual College" was created. It was a branch of government which controlled the life of the Church and Education. Many disagreed with the way Peter had managed things, but he was not a man to be trifled with.

### CONCLUSION.

The early tremors of the Reformation period were subsiding by the opening years of the seventeenth century. Still, the road ahead was not a smooth one. The Thirty Years War and upheavals in both Britain and France destroyed any hope of peace. Nevertheless, the extraordinary commitment of Plütschau and Ziegenbalg exemplified, inspired, and shaped an urge that was building in Protestantism. One encouraging feature of the period was the evident hunger to seek God more deeply. Such a desire is difficult to trace because often the people who feel most earnestly were the least likely to shout it from the house tops.

## 10

# *A Vision of Freedom*

## *1811 AD*

### *INTRODUCTION*

THE VOYAGE TO INDIA in the last chapter offered a close up look at something quite new in the Christian family—Protestants carrying out formal plans to cross seas and linguistic-cultural boundaries to spread the gospel message. 1706 can arguably be viewed as the birth date of the Protestant missionary program.

The next one hundred years or so revealed another idea catching hold in many ways and in many places around the globe. That idea was Liberty. It was in no sense new. It had inspired people to all kinds of acts from time immemorial. Since the early eighteenth century though, it had soared to a position of unimaginable importance among the world's populations. The profound thirst for freedom found expression in a spectacular variety of ways. At the center of this discussion will stand a tall, powerful, ambitious African-American, Paul Cuffe. His vision of freedom was particularly compelling. What kind of world awaited the arrival of this man?

### *SETTING*

The world bordering the North Atlantic was immersed in a relentless search for freedom: individual, social, intellectual, theological, and political freedom. It is noteworthy that the multi-dimensional frenzy to throw off literal and metaphorical chains should break out at that place and during that time, but it did, and the story cries to be told.

Politically, France and Britain continued to impinge on each other's ambitions throughout the period, and their pent up frustrations drew others in as well. The Seven Years War (1756–63) was primarily a struggle for dominance in Europe with tendrils reaching across the Atlantic to North American. It became what some have called the first "world" war. Britain and its allies, Prussia and Hanover, were ranged on one side against France, Austria, Sweden, Saxony, Russia, and Spain. Britain chose to let Prussia defend its interests in Europe while it focused attention on the other side of the ocean.

In North America the war involved alliances with indigenous peoples, sieges, classic pitched battles, along with guerrilla-like skirmishes, and pivoted on thirty-minutes worth of cannon and musket fire on the Plains of Abraham outside Quebec. When the acrid smoke had drifted away, the British found out that they had won, and they confirmed their victory in the following year, 1760. When the war finally ended in 1763 the British learned that the balance of power had tilted their way. France's armies had been expelled from the upper part of North America, and its naval power had been severely reduced.

Britain had little time to dwell on self congratulation because the "Americans" were staking their own claim to liberty, and the international complexity deepened. In 1775 people living in Britain's southern colonies in North America decided that they had had enough of "foreign" interference in their affairs. There was a variety of issues, including taxation, which brought matters to a head in what started as a rebellion and ended as a war of independence. The first shots were fired early in 1775 and the formal end came eight years later. During that time battles were fought up and down the east side of what is now the United States of America, on the Great Lakes, and forays were made across the St. Lawrence River. The French came into the war on the Americans' side, the British military was defeated, and, most importantly, a new player on the international scene, the United States of America, was created. During and after the war some 100,000 people who wished to remain loyal to Britain had relocated or been moved, many to Britain's northern colonies, now Canada. Among them were almost 2000 former slaves who had been promised freedom and a new future if they enlisted in the British army. They were transported to the colony of Nova Scotia.

Peace had been achieved, but more trouble was just around the corner—France was seething.

The pot boiled over in 1789. Again, liberty was the goal—*"liberté, egalité, fraternité*—was the cry. A spirit of reform seized the Legislative Assembly of the Estates-General which had convened in 1789. Along with the nobility, the Church became the focus of grievances. The customary tithe was abolished and Church property was confiscated. In 1790 the "Civil Constitution of the Clergy" was passed outlawing papal administrative control of the Church in France and requiring clergy to swear to obey the Constitution. Many did, and many did not. On September 2, 1792, in the grounds of the Institut Catholique in Paris, 130 priests who refused to obey were summarily shot to death.

From spring, 1792 to fall, 1794 France writhed under the "Reign of Terror," during which "Madame Guillotine" was in frequent use. Both King Louis XVI and Queen Marie Antoinette died under the blade. An attempt to dechristianize France accompanied those events. Various alternatives to the "superstition" and the "fanaticism" of the old religion were offered. The feast of the "Goddess of Reason" was celebrated in Notre Dame Cathedral in November 1793. In June 8, 1794 strongman of the Terror, Maximilian Robespierre, tried to impose "The Cult of the Supreme Being" on France. It died when he died on the guillotine in July of that year.

Perhaps the last great indignity to which the French exposed the Roman Church during this time was the capturing of the aged Pope Pius VI. He was seized in February 1798 and taken to France where he died in August 1799. The thirst of liberty can lead to some curious behavior. The door was open for General Napoleon Bonaparte (1769–1821), and he did not hesitate to step through.

Behind, underneath, and around all this political activity, there had been strong intellectual currents flowing both in Europe and west of the Atlantic in the eighteenth century. Names of scientists and philosophers such as Newton, Spinoza, Leibniz and Locke, not to mention the *Encyclopédistes* of France, must be added to the representative list given earlier. The educated of Europe were being attracted by the assumption that reality could be understood only by the rigorous application of reason. The Age of Rationalism had dawned, and it shaped most of those behind the French Revolution and many of those active in America's

War of Independence. Looked at from today's perspective, Modernity had arrived.

The effects on religion were significant. Deism arose in England with the central idea that there is a universal religion which accords with reason. God exists; God acts rationally; God is served by virtuous lives. Robespierre had been inspired by this thinking, and it surfaced in the *Wolfenbütel Fragments*, published in Germany between 1774 and 1778. Their author, Hermann Reimarus, had embraced Deism in England as a young thinker and during his career as Professor of Oriental Languages in Hamburg he approached the New Testament guided by the assumptions of rationalism—but very privately. He was shaking off the restrictions of the Lutheranism in which he had grown up.

The results of his work were only published posthumously, and they caused more than a mild stir. He concluded that Jesus was a politician who carefully chose venues in which to roll out his program in order to establish a new political entity in Palestine.[1] Jesus, Reimarus claimed, was horrified when he realized he had failed and would be executed.[2] His disciples wanted so badly the power and prestige that their places in Jesus' kingdom would have brought them that they stole Jesus' body, disposed of it,[3] and then fabricated the grand lie of the resurrection and the miracles upon which Christianity is built.[4] The more outlandish aspects of this aside, the methodology cleared a path for many biblical scholars of later generations. Reimarus was not the only one engaged in innovation in the second half of the eighteenth century. In fact, there was a distinct clash between various assumptions about where reality really lay and how one could identify it. Reimarus' approach was one option, but others were demanding attention, too.

In 1739 in England, Anglican priest John Wesley (1703–91), following the promptings of George Whitefield (1714–70), began to preach in the fields and beside pitheads. This was unquestionably revolutionary and it got him into trouble. His brother, Charles (1701–88), soon joined him. Before John Wesley's career ended he had travelled about 40,000

---

1. *Fragments*, 18 and 22.

2. *Fragments*, 27.

3 *Fragments*, 95–97.

4 *Fragments*, 85 and 86. These ideas have been responded to many times over. I refer only to Bauckham, *Jesus and the Eye Witnesses: The Gospels as Eyewitness Testimony* and Wright, *The Resurrection of the Son of God*.

miles, most of it on horseback, and had preached thousands of times and at least once to a crowd estimated to number about 10,000. He was an innovative, deeply devoted, challenging, and courageous person[5] whose ministry focused primarily on those who were displaced and suffering under the industrialization of Britain, and he was extraordinarily successful. He devised a system of classes, circuits, and conferences that facilitated the growth of a stable movement in which people were known by face and name, and could receive assistance as they struggled to let their new faith shine in difficult circumstances. Here was liberty in a spiritual and social sense. He remained in the Church of England until his death, but shortly after that separate denominations known as "Methodist" began to appear among his followers.

It should be noted that about the same time a stream of Evangelicalism appeared among the Anglicans. It was stimulated by Methodism, and in places resembled it in many ways, but it resolutely remained in the structures of the mother church. An example of the clergy found in this stream was William Grimshaw (1708–63), who carried out an effective ministry in Haworth in west Yorkshire.

In the northern British colonies on the other side of the Atlantic, surprisingly similar conditions developed. After England had taken control of the French colony in what is now eastern Canada, the Church of England was granted special privileges. This position of power grew in the 1770s as Anglicans in large numbers began arriving from the war torn Thirteen Colonies to the south. These were the "United Empire Loyalists" who had refused to join the revolution led by Washington, Franklin, and the others.

At exactly the same time, other developments began to occur in Nova Scotia, one of the most easterly of Britain's North American colonies. In the 1760s "Yankees," as they called themselves, moved north to occupy farm land left vacant when French Catholic settlers were forcibly deported by the British. One of these who came with his parents was Henry Alline (1748–84). Shortly after a powerful conversion in 1770, he felt a strong call to preach, and he responded immediately. His approach was simple and direct but very effective. He travelled extensively in the colony with intermittent swings into neighboring New Brunswick. The revival that broke out under his ministry touched the whole area.[6]

5. See Tomkins, *John Wesley.*

6. Alline has been served by a considerable literature. His journal was reedited by

The upshot of all this activity was a kind of *Zeit Geist,* spirit of the age, felt in the eighteenth and early nineteenth century in areas around the north Atlantic. And there is more. At the same time slavery had become a major source of concern. Again, the practice was by no means new. It had gone on for millennia and probably wherever one people group had been able to dominant another. From at least the fifteenth century Europeans had purchased Africans from Africans, and before that they enslaved each other wherever possible. Alongside these practices the British conscience seems to have been growing in the eighteenth century. For example, many children who might have been abandoned on the streets of London were able to find refuge from 1739 on in the Foundling Hospital. This institution had been the passion of Captain Thomas Coram, supported by artist William Hogarth and musician George Frederick Handel.[7] At the same time there was a growing sense of pity, as offensive as that word may be to some, for black slaves and for others who had been brought to Britain as slaves and somehow found their freedom. Feeling seemed to crystallize in a court case that was heard in 1772.

The case was *Somerset vs. Stewart.* James Somerset was resisting attempts by his owner, James Stewart to carry him out of England by force. The decision by King's Bench judge Lord Chief Justice Mansfield was: "It [slavery] is so odious an evil, that nothing can be suffered to support it, but positive [specific or definite supporting] law. . . . I cannot say this case is allowed or approved by the law of England; and therefore the black must be discharged."[8] In other words, the judge was saying that since there was no actual law in England which permitted Stewart to claim Somerset as his property and drag him off, Somerset was free. While the ruling did not explicitly say that slavery was finished in the United Kingdom that was how it was widely understood. Mansfield's ruling increased sympathy for the poor blacks whom people saw begging on the streets of London and the large cities of the realm.

---

Beverley and Moody (*Life and Journal*); the late George Rawlyk explored his ministry carefully (*Nova Scotia's Massachusetts,* 249–51 and *Ravished by the Spirit,* 3–104 and elsewhere); and even William James included Alline in writing *The Varieties of Religious Experience,* 134 and 177.

7. Handel had been inspired by what he had seen August Hermann Francke doing in Halle, Germany, Handel's home town.

8. *Howell's State Trials,* 82.

It has been suggested that one of the factors that stimulated empathy for the blacks was the evangelical revival that Britain was experiencing. Certainly the Wesleys and Whitefield had extensive ministry among the poor. The impact of people like Grimshaw, and the Society of Friends, the Quakers, should be seen as part of the mix too. Among those who were feeling the responsibility most strongly to respond to the Africans' needs were Granville Sharp, William Wilberforce, Thomas Clarkson, and William Allen—evangelicals or Quakers all. Collectively they and those who worked with them came to be known as the "saints."

The idea Sharp had begun to promote was for a "Province of Freedom" to be established in Sierra Leone.[9] It was to be a carefully-organized, self-governing agricultural community with a strong religious and educational life which would foster warm, respectful relations with the chiefs of local tribes around them.[10] What developed could not have been further from what he had hoped and prayed for.

Sharp and his friends got a grant from the British government to proceed in 1787[11]. Four hundred and eleven prospective settlers, including a large number of white women who later claimed to have been married to black men under suspicious circumstances,[12] sailed in the spring of the same year. Arriving at Sierra Leone, a tract of land was purchased by the officer in command from a local chief. The relationship was haunted by the fact that the British and the local Africans had very different ideas about property ownership.[13] The British landed at the beginning of the rainy season which meant that it was impossible to plant crops even if they had wanted to. On top of that, the huts they had thrown up quickly provided no shelter at all. Disease struck, and people

9. However he credited Henry Smeathman, a botanist who had lived in Sierra Leone for four years, with the idea, [Sharp], *A Short Sketch*, 41.

10. [Sharp], *A Short Sketch*, 1, 2, 13 and 34.

11. Turner, "Limits," 326.

12. Falconbridge, *Two Voyages*, 64. This is reported by Anna Maria Falconbridge, the wife of Alexander Falconbridge, a British naval officer. She accompanied her husband to Sierra Leone to which he was sent by Sharp and others several years after the beginning of the settlement to try to reclaim something from the initial attempt. She provided an eye-witness account of events in Africa, and she must be taken seriously. However, her report came from someone who had had a very difficult time with her husband in Sierra Leone and who was quite likely treated badly by the committee that stood behind the resettlement venture. She ended up arguing for a position that gave very guarded support to slavery as she had seen it.

13. Wiggins, *Logs and Letters*, 112.

began to die. Local tribes who were uneasy with what the British were up to began to harass them. In the face of these circumstances, significant numbers of them abandoned the settlement for the relative security of working in the slave trade. Sharp, meanwhile, was pouring his own money into the venture in an attempt to stabilize it.

Alexander Falconbridge was sent to Sierra Leone in hopes of salvaging something from the first attempt at settlement. After considerable effort to locate the members of the original colony of freed slaves who had gone to live among the native population, he could gather only 46 men and women.[14] Having provided some support, he returned to Britain, and shortly after arrival he and his wife received a letter from Granville Sharp telling them that the St. George Company, under which the first attempt had been made, was now the Sierra Leone Company and asking them to travel to London as soon as possible.[15] The second phase of the Sierra Leone adventure was about to unfold, and the settlement, which had been called "Granville Town," would be known at "Freetown."[16]

As the American War of Independence dragged to an end in the early 1780's approximately 2,000 Africans—including slaves who had been given freedom in return for enlistment in the British army—their families and others, had been transported to Nova Scotia. Once there, they found the conditions they had to survive in intolerable, and they complained bitterly. These complaints were ringing in British government ears at the same time as it was becoming obvious that something significant had to be done to save the Sierra Leone settlement. Perhaps an infusion of a large number of former African slaves would be the answer. In 1791 John Clarkson arrived at the Nova Scotian camps and offered transportation to anyone who wished to go to Sierra Leone. Apparently he gave the fullest possible account of what had been happening there so that no one would be acting under false impressions.[17] Approximately 1200 people gathered, almost all of whom were active Methodists or Baptists.[18]

---

14. Falconbridge, *Two Voyages*, 63.

15. Falconbridge, *Two Voyages*, 123.

16. Turner, "Limits," 327.

17. Falconbridge had negotiated the repossession of land occupied earlier, but he was crushed when he discovered that Lt. John Clarkson was to be Superintendent of Freetown, not he, himself (Falconbridge, *Two Voyages*, 137).

18. Pybus, "'One Militant Saint,'" 3.

The story of one family will serve to put human faces on this. This family was made up of Mary and Caesar Perth, their baby Susan, Mary's daughters, Zilph and Hannah Savills, and another of her daughters, Patience Freeman. Patience had married, and her husband would follow them later. They were all freed slaves who had sailed out of New York in 1782.[19]

The flotilla Clarkson had assembled reached Sierra Leone in April 1792 and the prospective settlers waded ashore singing a Wesleyan hymn—"The day of Jubilee is come! Return ye, ransomed Sinners, home."[20] Anna Falconbridge liked the settlers,[21] noting on January 24, 1793,

> Among the Black Settlers are seven religious sects, and each sect has one or more preachers attached to it, who alternately preach throughout the whole night; indeed, I never met with, heard, or read of, any set of people observing the same appearance of godliness; for I do not remember since they first landed here, my ever awaking (and I have awoke at every hour of the night), without hearing preachings from some quarter or other.[22]

Again there were very severe difficulties. The company's largest ship, used to supply the colony, was destroyed by fire in 1793.[23] The following year, most of Freetown was razed by a French bombardment and whatever was left was plundered. A large part of the company's fleet was either captured or sunk in the attack. The company's loss was set at £400,000.[24] The French were back again in 1798–99, capturing four out of six ships that the company had sent out while another one was wrecked off the coast.[25] In addition to all that, slavery continued, if Falconbridge's account can be trusted. She claimed that 2,000 slaves had been shipped from Sierra Leone to the West Indies in 1792.[26] Settlers

19. Pybus, "'One Militant Saint,'" 3.

20. Anna Falconbridge thought the whole undertaking was hair-brained and scandalous—and there were grounds for her opinion (Falconbridge, *Two Voyages*, 125 and 148).

21. Falconbridge, *Two Voyages*, 139.

22. Falconbridge, *Two Voyages*, 201.

23. Misevich, "Sierra Leone," 3.

24. *Allgemeine Literatur*, 664.

25. Turner, "Limits," 328.

26. Falconbridge, *Two Voyages*, 193.

found these ongoing circumstances deeply disturbing to the extent that riots broke out in 1800.

1800 was the year another layer was added to the citizenry of Sierra Leone. Five hundred and thirty-eight "maroons" arrived from Nova Scotia. These were fugitive slaves who had escaped from plantations in Jamaica, organized communities in the mountains, and successfully fought the British. Deceived after a truce, they had been herded onto ships and sent to Nova Scotia. For 3½ years they pleaded with the authorities to rescue them from the unlivable climate, and finally they were hustled off to Sierra Leone. There they strengthened the population mix.[27]

The company persevered for several more years until British legislators stepped in, not least because it was thought important to preserve their foothold on the west coast of Africa during their wars with the French. In 1807 The Abolition Act, ending the slave trade was past.[28] Later that year a bill transferring the colony to the Crown was passed to come into law on January 1, 1808, and shortly after that a court representing the Vice-Admiralty Court was situated at Sierra Leone.[29] More trouble followed.

The first judge to occupy the bench was a fiery, very-determined Irishman, Robert Thorpe, Esq. Left to his own devices by London, he cobbled together a legal foundation to support the Royal Navy's orders to seize any slave ship it could reach. Armed with that, the sea dogs became remarkably effective. Tara Helfman pointed out that 1,991 slaves taken off seized ships were released at Sierra Leone between 1807 and 1811. The next year another 1,500 joined them. Prior to 1817 more than 200 ships from Spain alone had been captured, condemned as slavers, and had their human cargo freed at Sierra Leone.[30] Obviously the nations under whose flags these ships sailed were not happy with this action, but because of Britain's dominance on the seas there was no way

---

27. Lockett, "Deportation," 9–12.

28 William Wilberforce had been pushing for this since 1789 (Wiggins, *Logs and Letters*, 92). In 1807 the US also past an act prohibiting the importation of slaves. It was to come into effect on January 1, 1808 (Helfman, "Court of Vice Admiralty," 1134 n. 38).

29. *The Navy List*, p.130.

30. Helfman, "Court of Vice Admiralty," 1143–47. The slaves who were freed are known somewhat ironically as "recaptives." First, they were taken into slavery and then they were seized again and freed.

to stop it directly. The eventual result was that Britain and most of the other slaving nations had to sit down at the negotiating table and work out timetables for the ending of the international trade in human beings as it operated at that time. Judge Thorpe and the Royal Navy had played key roles in preserving the liberty of countless people.[31]

However important as these events were in Sierra Leone they were not top priority in London. The struggle with Napoleon held that spot. Second place may have been occupied by the war between the US and Britain being fought in North America. The war began on June 19, 1812 and ended with the Treaty of Ghent on December 23, 1814, but the shooting did not stop for sometime. In fact, the Battle of New Orleans took place on January 8, 1815[32]. Into this international uncertainty sailed Paul Cuffe—ship owner, captain, and person extraordinaire.

Paul Cuffe

## *EVENT*

Who was Paul Cuffe? There is a description of him at age 52—"His person is tall, well formed and athletic: his deportment conciliating, and yet dignified and serious."[33] He was also an African-American, and he was commemorated in a poem:

> Take for example, venerable Cuffe
>
> Had he delighted the vile stuff to sip
>
> He never had commanded a fine ship.
>
> It gives us pleasure to record his name
>
> And give one verse to celebrate his fame;

31. Helfman, "Court of Vice Admiralty," 1156. It is a story for another day, but Thorpe and the Royal Colony's first governor, the 25-year old Thomas Perronet Thompson, became thorns in the sides of the "Saints," who had stood behind the Sierra Leone adventure in the first place, forcing them to think very carefully about how free recaptives released into the colony actually were. (Thorpe, *Reply*, 26 and 107–109; Turner, "Limits of Abolition," 332, 346 and 340; [Sharp], *A Short Sketch*, 8, 21 and 27)

32. Remember the tune?—"We fired our guns and the British kept a comin," Jimmy Driftwood's song recorded by Johnny Horton in 1959.

33. "Memoirs," 284–92. The magazine carrying this description was published in Belfast, North Ireland and existed only from 1808 to 1814. The piece it carried on Cuffe demonstrated his international reputation.

Industrious, temperate, honest, just and true,

An able Sailor, and commander too:—

A pious Christian, by his God approv'd,

Justly esteem'd in life, he died belov'd. [34]

Cuffe was being held up as a moral example in this poem delivered before a congregation of sailors in a mission in New Bedford, MA, and it was being presented twenty years after his death. He was a man whose life and his vision of freedom both recommend him to our attention.

## Life

Born in 1759, Paul Cuffe was one of ten children in a unique family. His father, Kofi, was a freed slave from Africa, an Akan from Ghana. Having changed his name to Cuffe, Slocum Kofi married Ruth Moses, a native American from Martha's Vineyard in 1746. At age fourteen their son Paul launched a career on the sea, joining the crew of a whaling vessel on its way to South America.[35] He married Alice Pequit on February 25, 1783,[36] and shortly after they moved to a 140-acre farm on the banks of what is now the East Branch of the Westport River. As a sailor and a merchant, he never looked back. He and his brother built ships,[37] and soon he had them sailing back and forth across the south and north Atlantic to ports as far away as South Africa and Russia.

The crews Cuffe assembled merit note. Almost all members were African or Native-American. He related to them warmly, at least once calling them "our little family,"[38] but he maintained high standards on his ship. Crew members were expected not to swear, tattle, drink alcohol, or be quarrelsome. He promised to provide suitable provisions, but no liquor.[39] These crews captured some serious scrutiny. One observer wrote:

34. Enoch Mudge, *Temperance Address*, 10.

35. Wiggins, *Logs and Letters*, 46–48.

36. Marriage Certificate. Paul Cuffe Collection.

37. Their largest was the *Alpha*, which could carry 268 tons. It was launched in August 1806 from Westport (Wiggins, *Logs and Letters*, 94 n. 22).

38. Cuffe, Remarks, December 29, 1811. Wiggins, 178.

39. Cuffe to Thomas, April 12, 1815. Wiggins, 339.

During the time I have been at Liverpool, Paul Cuffee, a black man, owner and master of a vessel, has come into port, from Sierra Leone on the coast of Africa. He is a member of our society [Quakers], and resides in New England. The whole of his crew are black also. This, together with the cleanliness of his vessel, and the excellent order prevailing on board, has excited very general attention. It has, I believe, opened the minds of many in tender feelings towards the poor suffering Africans, who, they see, are men like themselves, capable of becoming, like Paul Cuffee, valuable and useful members both of civil and religious society.[40]

Marion Kilson noted that Cuffe built his career around his family and the other important dimension of his life, the Society of Friends, or Quakers.[41] Having joined the Friends in 1808, Cuffe's relationship with them quickly became deep and warm. In 1810–11, as he was planning one of his major undertakings, letters to, from, and about him flowed back and forth within and among Quaker circles on both sides of the Atlantic showing how widely-known and appreciated he had become. In return Cuffe clearly demonstrated his commitment to the interests of the Friends. Forty-seven percent of the cost of major work required on the Westport Meeting House in 1813 was underwritten by Cuffe.[42]

Westport Meeting House

40. *Memoirs, Stephen Grellet*, 1, 171.

41. Kilson, "Cuffe's Social Networks," 9.

42. Westport Meeting House. Paul Cuffe Collection.

When necessary these connections and his own personality could take him to some extraordinary places. In 1812 he was able to gain access to President Madison, Secretary of State Gallatin, and members of the US Congress when he was trying (successfully) to free a ship of his which had been impounded.[43]

Paul Cuffe was a man of deep and vital faith. We see it as he circulated among the residents of a colony in Africa,[44] but we see it even more clearly in his relationships with his own family.[45] The businessman had the heart of an evangelist. The same faith and warmth carried him into rich friendships during the months in 1811 when he stayed in London. In speaking of an evening at the home of prominent Quaker and pharmacologist, William Allen, he said "I believe I may say the presence of the precious Comforter was felt to be near."[46] He was staying with the Allens, and a month later he could refer to returning to their residence by saying I "came home."[47] A few days later, when he left London, Allen wrote in his journal, "Took leave of P. Cuffee (sic) with much nearness of spirit."[48] These men recognized the common concerns and faith they shared.

Much the same can be said for Cuffe and Thomas and Frances Thompson. Thomas was a pharmacist in Liverpool. Cuffe spent a good part of his visit to Britain in 1811 in their home. In 1814 Frances wrote saying she and her husband wanted him to regard their house as home.[49] Later he wrote saying, "When I am permitted to contemplate on my being adopted to your family, it brings a passage of the Scriptures to mind, I was a stranger."[50] quoting Mt 25:35 and 36.

We must be clear about what is happening here. These are not just Hallmark sentimental niceties. This is the early nineteenth century, and this is a black man who had been welcomed with great warmth into the homes of prominent, middle and upper-middle class whites. It is quite

43. Cuffe, *Transactions*, July 2, 1812, Wiggins, 212.

44. Cuffe, *Remarks*, March 19, 1811, Wiggins, 109; Cuffe, *Remarks*, November 24, 1811, Wiggins, 170; and Lockes to Cuffe, July 13, 1816, Wiggins, 421.

45. Cuffe, *Remarks*, December 18, 1811, Wiggins, 175; Cuffe, *Remarks*, December 22, 1811, Wiggins, 176; and Cuffe to Wainer, December 26, 1816, Wiggins, 486.

46. Cuffe, *Remarks*, July 28, 1811, Wiggins, 139.

47. Cuffe, *Remarks*, August 25, 1811, Wiggins, 148.

48. *Life of William Allen*, 1, 103.

49. Thompson to Cuffe, March 22, 1814, Paul Cuffe Collection.

50. Cuffe to Thompson, September 26, 1815, Library of Religious Society of Friends.

likely that Cuffe had never experienced anything like this before, and this reception may have influenced his own understanding of himself, or at least confirmed it.

Paul Cuffe's grave

Paul Cuffe died on August 27, 1817. Several years later Stephen Gould who had been in Westport that August wrote to Thomas Thompson to share more information regarding the death of his friend. Cuffe had asked Gould to visit him and bring a physician whom Gould had talked about. Gould did, but the doctor recognized that there was nothing he could do. A few days later Gould went back and sat with Cuffe. He said he found "a sweet quiet frame of mind." Once death had occurred, the funeral was held in the Westport Meeting House, complete with lively testimonies.[51] Interment followed behind the Meeting House, and both Paul's and Alice's graves may be visited there today.

In the light of the preoccupation with freedom on both sides of the north Atlantic, what was Cuffe's vision? As appeared in one of his earlier letters, it had two dimensions, and it remained the same throughout the rest of his life. Writing to two of his friends in 1809, John James and Alexander Wilson, he told them that he had been thinking about an exploratory trip to Sierra Leone for some years, and he confessed to "feeling a real desire that the inhabitants of Africa might become an enlightened

51. Gould to Thompson, May 20, 1822, Library of Religious Society of Friends.

people and be so favored as to give general satisfaction to those who are endeavouring to establish them in the true light of Christianity."[52] And in his mind, a critical part of that enlightenment was freedom for Africans: "I have been led to believe that the abolishing of the slave trade would prove a blessing to all nations, kindred and people who hath united in this institution."[53]

Here was a man in his fifties with a very wide experience of life. There were likely many conversations through which his ideas were formed, and he had no doubt absorbed much. Nevertheless, what he had seen and gathered for himself probably provided his basic ideas, and what he kept on experiencing sharpened his focus. He eventually saw Africa. People had been talking to him about civilization, and he saw that, too. He spent some time in what people thought was one of the most civilized places in the world, London. He visited the tourist sites, he saw a factory in production, and he was very impressed with what "civilization" could do.[54]

The plan he developed as a means to carrying out his vision was a trade triangle.[55] Goods, and even people, could be carried from the United States to Sierra Leone. Raw materials and products could be transported to London from there. Finally, the link could be closed by shipping goods from Britain to the US or to Sierra Leone, and if it were to the latter, then raw materials could be taken from there to the US. This network would "assist Africa in its civilization,"[56] and it would undercut slavery by making trade in goods more profitable than trade in people. It would open the door for the establishment of Christianity.

Consider the slavery component of this trading scheme. Here was an African American tacitly acknowledging that the white demand for slaves was beyond his control, so he decided to focus on the supply. He was going to try to get Africans in Africa to stop selling Africans. Throughout the rest of his life a great deal of time, energy, and money went into the effort to bring those plans into reality.

He made three trips to Sierra Leone: two from Westport and one from London. On the first he was there from March 1 to May 12, 1811.

52. Cuffe to James and Wilson, June 10, 1809. Wiggins, 80.

53. Cuffe to Bonthren, September 4, 1811, Paul Cuffe Collection.

54. Cuffe, Remarks, August 31, 1811, Wiggins, 150.

55. Cuffe to John Cuffe, August 8, 1811, Wiggins, 145.

56. Cuffe, Remarks, September 4, 1811, Wiggins, 151.

He knew all about the disasters the various groups of settlers has faced: attacks by local tribes and the French, riots, and the loss of ships,[57] but he threw himself into making things better, carrying on extensive conversations with the governor, the settlers, and the chiefs of local tribes. He helped draft a petition on behalf of the settlers, aimed at making them self-reliant. He reported on the colony to William Allen, telling him that the population then stood at 1,197, not counting another twenty-five percent living just beyond the settlement, mostly "recaptives" taken off slave ships brought into port. Cuffe added that there were six very active churches, 230 girls and boys in six schools, and many adults going to a night school program. There were problems—too much alcohol, not enough hard work, and too many young men running off to sea in the crews of foreign ships rather than staying in the colony to become businessmen and traders. In spite of that, Cuffe saw potential: "I see no reason why they may not become a nation to be numbered among the historians' nations of the world."[58]

Then he was off to London. The arrival of his ship created the stir Stephen Grellet mentioned, and among other things he saw the sights and created deep, lasting friendships. He also met with the committee of the African Institution. He gave the Chair, the Duke of Gloucester, an African robe, a letter box, and a dagger made in Africa, and he received warm statements of support from the committee.[59]

A month later he embarked for Sierra Leone again, and when he arrived, he stayed for a little over three months. He commented repeatedly on slave ships coming into port after being seized by the British navy. It must have troubled him deeply to see how robust the trade in human beings continued to be. His time was spent in selling his cargo and gathering another one to take to the US. He also talked at length with officials of the colony and settlers in efforts to move forward some of the initiatives begun when he was there previously. He conducted his own survey of the colony to determine what crops might grow and where mills might be built, and he bought a house and lot. He was so determined to see the colony prosper.

57. Cuffe to Gibbons, January 16, 1817, Wiggins, 495.

58. Cuffe to Allen, April 22, 1811, Wiggins, 118.

59. Committee of Directors of the African Institute, August 27, 1811, Paul Cuffe Collection and Cuffe, Remarks, August 27, 1811, Wiggins, 148.

Cuffe sailed for home and arrived safely only to discover that there was a war in progress between Britain and the US. The citizens of his part of the US, around New Bedford, Massachusettes, had voted unanimously against the war and refused all participation,[60] but that did not keep Cuffe from having his ship impounded and having to go to great length to get it back. The hostilities made it impossible for him to follow up on his vision, but he continued to get encouragement. Thomas Clarkson and William Allen wrote telling him of what they hoped to be able to arrange, no doubt on the basis of their excellent lobbying capacities. [61] In fact, a year and a half later they and several others were putting their money to work. They were raising capital to help underwrite the economic development of Sierra Leone, having pledged to seek no profit for themselves.[62]

While still in Westport and dealing with many commercial, personal, and philanthropic issues and carrying on an extensive correspondence, Cuffe responded to letters from several faculty members at the Theological Seminary at Andover. In 1815 he wrote Nathan Lord elaborating on his vision and his plans. He also pointed out that one of the main obstacles in the way of drying up the flow of slaves was the concern of the Africans who sell other Africans to whites. They were afraid that if they stopped they would quickly become impoverished.[63]

Cuffe did make one more trip to Sierra Leone. He left on his ship the *Traveller* early in 1816, taking 38 African Americans who had applied for passage and been approved. He also took all the iron needed to build a saw mill, a wagon, and a plough.[64] Remarkably, he paid not only the passengers' trip expenses out of his own pocket, but also the cost of providing for them there until they could fend for themselves. It was a huge financial burden.[65]

Mysteriously, there is no log book for the trip. He was in the colony from February 3 to April 5, 1816, but by comparison to his other visits, there is very little information about his movements. He must have been pleased that the settlers he had taken seemed satisfied with the land

60. *History of Bristol County, Massachusetts*, 116.

61. Clarkson and Allen to Cuffe, July 1, 1812, Paul Cuffe Collection.

62. *Life of William Allen*, 139.

63. Cuffe to Lord, April 19, 1815, Old Dartmouth Historical Society Library.

64. Cuffe to Allen, December 4, 1815, Paul Cuffe Collection.

65. Cuffe to Morse, August 10, 1816, Wiggins, 436.

grants they had received, and he saw signs of commercial development. In spite of it all, the slave trade was still going strong, and he saw the place of liquor as a major problem.[66] Cuffe's vision of social, political, and spiritual freedom, like many visions, was only being realized very, very slowly.

## DEVELOPMENTS

How did Sierra Leone fare subsequent to Cuffe's three visits? Cuffe never stopped being concerned with Africans and Sierra Leone. He saw the colony as an important place for blacks to demonstrate that they could govern themselves effectively,[67] and he could report that he had seen signs of progress.[68] In the second last letter he ever wrote, he said, " If the free people of colour would exert themselves more and more in industry and honesty, it would be a great help towards the liberating [of] those who still remain in bondage."[69] Cuffe's heartfelt commitment compelled him to talk about his Africa sisters and brothers and to talk freedom right to the end.

As the nineteenth century progressed, Sierra Leone did develop in some positive ways. Deveneaux had some glowing comments to make. Pointing to its population of around 60,000 in the 1840s, he said that "the settlement surmounted all obstacles.[70] He argued that the key to its success was the effectiveness with which the colonials manipulated the colonial system in their appeal to public opinion through their newspapers. Writing in 1976 he said , "What actually occurred was a curious blend of Western and African cultures, a blend taking place all over Africa today and widely welcomed as modernization."[71] Lockett suggested that Sierra Leone became a model for Liberia which was established later,[72] and Helfman thought that the Admiralty Court and Judge Robert Thorpe's work gave some shape to the international "Mixed Prize Commissions" which functioned from 1819 to 1871and which attempted to control the

---

66. Cuffe to Allen, April 4, 1816, Paul Cuffe Collection.
67. Cuffe to Harris, August 10, 1816, Wiggins, 437.
68. Cuffe to Brian, January 16, 1817, Wiggins, 497.
69. Cuffe to Forten, March 1, 1817, Wiggins, 509.
70. Deveneaux, "Public Opinion," 46.
71. Deveneaux, "Public Opinion," 50.
72. Lockett, "Deportation of Maroons," 12.

slave trade.[73] Finally, both Elizabeth Isichei[74] and Andrew Walls[75] have drawn attention to the significant roles in Christian missions in Africa played by people who were descendents of the multi-layered population of Sierra Leone.

## CONCLUSION

There were always good intentions behind the settlement in Sierra Leone. Regrettably, for those who dreamed the dream and those who lived it out, it staggered amidst bad planning, corruption, turmoil, despair, and violence on its way to eventual improvement. Looming large in the midst of it all was Paul Cuffe, encouraging his people to discover who and what they were, ignited by his vision of freedom. In that respect he was a person of his age, and he sailed with the winds of liberty that were blowing on both sides of the Atlantic. His presence adds nobility to the picture we are assembling.

73. Helfman, "Court of Vice Admiralty," 1152.

74. Isichei, *A History of Christianity in Africa*, 171–72.

75. Walls, *Missionary Movement*, 105.

# 11

# The Gospel in the Heart of China

## 1865 AD

### INTRODUCTION

T HE EXTRAORDINARY STORY OF the founding of Sierra Leone along with the role that Paul Cuffe played in supporting the colony carried us well into the nineteenth century. "Modernity" is one way to describe this time, but there is another way to view the period, and that is through the lens of revolution. A revolutionary era started around the middle of the seventeenth century in the western world—part of the thrust toward freedom—and it flows right into the present. I have nodded briefly at major developments in science, philosophy, and technology. The revolution that continues in some of those areas is accelerating daily. In other areas the revolution appears to have lost its steam and is possibly regressing. And what of the Christian story? Was it going from strength to strength or taking a different turn?

Certainly the evidence is ambiguous, and the focus of this chapter will line up witnesses that appear to be to the contrary, but in the western world the Christian community in the middle of the nineteenth century was beginning its slide into relative social impotence—or so it seems. There can be no question but that the impact Christians have on the west is dramatically less than it was a hundred and fifty years ago, but the decline had started even before then. By end of the nineteenth century German philosopher Friedrich Nietzsche thought he could proclaim, "God is dead! God remains dead! And we have killed him!", and he could point to churches as the tombs and monuments of God.[1]

Hans Urs von Balthasar had a different take on those events which had gathered momentum in the nineteenth century and continued to unfold through his lifetime. He suggested that as Christ poured himself into the lives of the needy with power flowing out from him (Mk 5:30 and Lk 6:19) leaving him weakened and in need of retreat to the Father, so the Church has poured itself into the world.[2] He mentions human rights to illustrate what he means, and to that I would add justice, compassion, education, health, and the place of women, all of which have blossomed where Christianity has had a major presence. Von Balthasar's proposal was that as Christians have had more and more of what they have uniquely offered taken up by the wider society, they have looked weaker and weaker. He then reminded us that Paul realized he had the greatest strength when he recognized his weakness most fully (1 Cor 4:10–13, to which I add 2 Cor 12:9 and 10) and encouraged us to rest in the love of the Father and from that draw strength—something to bear in mind as we move on into the story.

The nineteenth century was a time of declining influence of Christianity in parts of western culture, of revival among Christians, and dramatic outreach beyond the west. Here was an intensification of different views of reality, or the clashing of ontological assumptions.

## SETTING

Developments in science and technology in the nineteenth century were quite staggering by any standards. I do not wish to labor the obvious, so I will point to only two iconic events. One was Darwin's publication in 1859 of his *Origin of the Species*. It argued for evolution through natural selection and came to symbolize the transformative power of scientific discovery. The other was the patenting of electrical telegraphy in 1837 in both the UK and the US. It shrank the world, decontextualized information, and accelerated its transfer unimaginably. These discoveries and ideas were erupting out of scholars' studies and laboratories with each new insight demanding a reevaluation or a reconfiguration of reality.[3]

1. Nietzsche, *The Gay Science (The Joyful Wisdom)*, III, sec. 125.

2. Von Balthasar, *Razing the Bastions*, 65–69.

3. Postman, *Technopoly*, 18.

The expression of human ingenuity which had been a persistent stream throughout the ages, became a river, and then a tsunami.

The philosophers were busy, too. The names of three stand out. The first is the Scot, David Hume (1711–76). He was an empiricist who argued that our senses play a critical role in the substance of thought. The second is Immanuel Kant (1724–1804). His *Critique of Pure Reason* challenged us all with its phenomenal and noumenal realms and its *ding an sich* (thing in itself) which we can never reach. Last is Georg Hegel (1770–1831), one of the great German Idealists. He offered, among other ideas, both a picture of the history of civilization as the outworking of "the Absolute" or World-Spirit (*Geist*) and a system of dialectical reasoning featuring thesis—antithesis—synthesis. These are tiny caricatures of their work, but they are meant to stimulate some interest in their thought.

Philosophers and many others, along with the scientists I mentioned and many of their colleagues were part, unwittingly perhaps, of the process leading to *scientific objectivism*. This is an assumption that truth can only be found through the rational application of scientific principles. A very large segment of western elites accept this assumption, and, as a result, dismiss religion, including Christianity, as having any important place in understanding human experience. The process was well under way by the middle of the nineteenth century.

In different ways, these intellectual currents impacted theologians who were working at the time. Friedrich Daniel Ernest Schleiermacher (1768–1834) found the basis of religion in a feeling of "absolute dependence." Doctrines, he said, were subjective religious experiences arising from our own feelings and, as a result, were relative and secondary in value. According to Schleiermacher, theology is no longer a pursuit of timeless truths but the product of thought embedded in particular times and places. Consequently, it must continuously rewrite itself to accommodate new expressions. David Strauss (1808–74) was influenced by Schleiermacher and Hegel, and stood in the wake of Reimarus. In his *Life of Jesus* (1835), Strauss denied the historicity of all the supernatural parts of the Gospels. After running into difficulty in holding a teaching position at the university, he eventually rejected the Christian faith in favor of scientific naturalism.

While pulses in the scientific and philosophic worlds were moving towards a marginalization of Christianity, there were quite opposite events unfolding in different parts of the world in the early to mid-nine-teenth century . In fact, this was an era of the deepening of spirituality and of revivals within Christianity on both sides of the Atlantic. There were revivals early in the century in southern Germany and at about the same time *Le Réveil* (The Wakening) began in Switzerland and southern France. Both of these movements touched the spiritual lives of many, but they also had very practical effects. The establishment and/or growth of the YMCA, the Red Cross, and even kindergarten has been traced to participants. Elsewhere on the east side of the Atlantic, both Britain and north Ireland were touched by waves of deep spiritual earnestness.

On the other side of the Atlantic, what is now called the Second Great Awakening was sweeping New England, involving primarily Congregationalists and Baptists. Another dimension to this religious intensity was added in 1801 at Cane Ridge, Bourbon County, Kentucky. With revivals occurring in other places in the state, Presbyterian minister Barton Warren Stone called for an annual sacramental communion service to be held in early August. These services were well known in Presbyterian circles. They were held outdoors and could last for two or three days. Many more than expected came to this communion service, including people from other denominations. People camped around the Meeting House. Services ran more or less day and night with as many as four preachers, usually Presbyterians, Methodists, or Baptists, holding forth at the same time in different parts of the grounds. It is estimated that between 3,000 and 4,000 people found new faith in the highly emotional services. When food in the area for people and horses ran out, everyone packed up and left. Estimates of the total numbers attending ran as high as 30,000. This was frontier revivalism, and the "camp meeting," a practice which continues into the present, was born. Canada had its own version of this four years later when perhaps 3,000 people gathered near Hay Bay, Ontario in very similar conditions and with similar although smaller results.

On both sides of the Great Lakes, camp meetings and smaller, local series of revival meetings became a normal part of the religious scene, spawning patterns of worship, music, and religious expectations that have persisted into the present with modifications. Even Roman Catholics offered their version of this approach to faith, with priests who were known for captivating preaching and miraculous cures holding parish missions.[4]

This approach to religion institutionalized in a number of ways, and one who played a large role in that was Charles Grandison Finney (1792–1875). Finney was converted in 1821 and shortly thereafter felt himself led into revivalism. He developed what he called "new measures" by which a revival could be brought about. Naturally there should be prayer, but there were other steps that one could take to make sure that a revival occurred. Among other things he stipulated meetings at unusual times, long meetings, and use of the "anxious bench" at which those convicted of sin could kneel to repent. Finney did not just theorize about practical matters. He also focused on theology and became one of the leading theologians on the subject of revivalism. The Awakening continued until 1857–8, but in 1835 Finney moved to Oberlin, Ohio where he became pastor of the town's church and professor of theology at the college which had been founded in 1833. He held the presidency of the college from 1851 until 1866 and remained pastor of the church until 1872. He continued to lecture at the college occasionally until his death.

The atmosphere of revival in the western world stimulated another development. The nineteenth century also continued an era of global missions launched by Protestants. The first missionaries to India, Ziegenbalg and Plütschau, had gone there in 1706 under the auspices of the King of Denmark. Working with recently-founded Baptist Missionary Society, William Carey (1761–1834) also made his way to India. He left England with his family in July 1793. In spite of severe illness and deaths within his family, Carey carried out a pioneering ministry of translation and teaching and developed principles to guide missionary outreach. His ideas were quite similar to those Ziegenbalg had worked out, emphasizing language, culture, the Bible, and an indigenous church.

Protestants were catching the vision of establishing the Christian gospel in other parts of the world. The London Missionary Society was formed in 1795, and the Society for Missions to Africa and the East followed in 1799. Among the early members of the latter were William Wilberforce and Henry Thornton. It was renamed the Church Missionary Society for Africa and the East in 1812. Along with these, the Basel Mission was launched in Switzerland in 1815.

4. Grant, *Spires*, 182–85.

In this context, the name of Henry Venn (1796–1873) could be mentioned. Venn served as Secretary of the Church Missionary Society from 1841 to 1870. Among other things, he called for the "euthanasia of missions," meaning that as soon as possible after the establishment of Christianity in various parts of the world, the Church should be passed completely into the hands of local people. The ideal he proposed was churches which were self-governing, self-supporting, and self-propagating. Here are the ideas of Ziebenbalg and Carey appearing in yet another form, and we shall come across them again. Many of these goals and methods are exhibited precisely in the person and ministry on which I will focus now—James Hudson Taylor, founder of the China Inland Mission (now Overseas Missionary Fellowship).

### *EVENT*

Born in Barnsley, central England in 1832, Hudson Taylor grew up surrounded by deep Christian faith. His father, James, was a pharmacist and a Methodist lay preacher. Hudson experienced a profound conversion in 1849. We get a sense of the intensity of his faith from a letter he wrote to his beloved sister, Amelia, and the documents suggest a fascinating development.

The letter opens with a page and a quarter of biblical quotations, mostly from Paul, after which Taylor assures her that he is happy in God's love, but that he feels deeply unworthy. "I so often give way to temptation. I am so apt to be frothy and giddy, and I sometimes give way to my teasing disposition; pray for me, my dear Amelia, pray for me."[5] We hear echoes of Wesley and a hint of the coming Holiness Movement when he goes on to announce, "I am seeking for entire sanctification." What is intriguing is an insert which accompanies the letter: "He [Christ] has revealed himself to me in an overwhelming manner. He has cleansed me from all sin, from all my idols. He has given me a new heart. Glory, Glory, Glory to his ever-blessed name. I can't write for joy." The longing that he had just confessed had been fulfilled. He was ecstatic. It was the vividness of that spirituality which undergirded everything else that was going to happen in his life.

There was a particular focus of his walk with God which never left him—the country of China. Sometime later as he reflected on his con-

---

5. Taylor to Amelia Taylor, December 2, 1849.

version, Taylor said, "From that time to this, the conviction has never left me that I was called to China."[6] Back in 1849, immediately after his conversion, he had begun to read on China and study Chinese. In 1850 he wrote to Amelia, his mother,—"I have not the slightest idea *how* I shall go, but this I know, I *shall* go."[7] Here is a passion in the nineteen year old that would never fade.

His path to China turned out to be surprisingly direct. He spent just over a year studying medicine at the Royal London Opthalmic Hospital, Moorfields, "That I may be enabled to serve the Lord better,"[8] but on arrival in London he also quickly made contact with the Chinese Evangelisation Society to see if he might go out with them. They were interested, but we get a sense of his independent spirit when he was offended by their telling him they would need references before they could proceed. He wrote to his mother, "I shall thank the Committee for their kindness, & trouble them no further, as I do not see them consistent with my views."[9] He quickly backed down and provided the references (one of which was from his mother!).

The CES suggested that if he were prepared to interrupt his medical studies, they might be able to send him quite soon.[10] He agreed to that, a decision he regretted later.[11] We get another look at his twenty-one year old self-assurance here. He had to submit an extensive and candid application before the CES would make its final decision to send him. Believing that all Christians were equal, he stated in his application that there should be no distinction between clergy and laity and that all Christians had the right to preach, baptize and administer the Lord's Supper. He wrote to his mother saying "priestcraft has, in all ages, been the greatest curse to the church & the world,"[12] and he was sure he would be rejected because of his position. But in his next letter he wrote, "I have

6. Taylor to George Pearse, April 25, 1851.

7. Talyor to Amelia Taylor, November 11, 1850.

8. Taylor to Amelia Taylor (Mother), August 27, 1852.

9. Taylor to Amelia Taylor (Mother), October 11, 1852.

10. He discussed the decision with his mother in a letter, indicating that he would probably accept the offer. That made real to him the possibility of leaving his family soon and never seeing them again. There is real pain in the letter, and he has trouble bringing it to a close. Taylor to Amelia Taylor (Mother), June 5, 1853.

11. Taylor to James Taylor (Father), August 7, 1855—"I wish I had had a Medical Diploma before I left,—I ought to have had one at all costs."

12. Taylor to Amelia Taylor (Mother), June 19, 1853.

just received a note from Mr. Bird informing me that I am accepted by the committee, and that as soon as I can make arrangements for going out, they are prepared to send me."[13] Then the challenges began.

First, it was leaving behind his family and friends, perhaps never to see them again. Then it was departure on September 19, 1853 and a very difficult five-month voyage in a sailing ship to Shanghai. On arrival in China he discovered the country was in the midst of a civil war with the rebels holed up in the city and the Imperial army laying siege outside. Furthermore, none of the contacts whose names he had were there at the time. In fact, one had died and another had moved to the United States. He coped with this extraordinarily difficult situation by calling on his faith in God: "may we all, sure of Jesus' love, when everything else fails—seek to be more like Him & soon—soon we shall meet, where no sun can scorch nor cold chill—where all sorrow and trial shall be no more. Till then may we be willing to bear the cross, & not only to do, but to suffer His will."[14]

The difficulties only mounted. He saw and felt the horrors of war—bullets hitting his house, artillery shells landing nearby, prisoners tortured, severed heads hanging by their hair. He froze and sweltered as the seasons changed; he suffered through repeated bouts of diarrhea and fever; no mail from anyone; money running short; inability to speak the language; paralyzed with fear when jerked out of sleep by gun fire; struggling with language study and efforts to learn photography; and desperately lonely. In addition to all that, Taylor made his first mention of ". . . the curse of China," opium smoking.[15] Faced with it all, he wrote: ". . . may God raise up & send out many laborers into these parts of His Vineyard & sustain and bless those who are already out. No amount of romantic excitement can do that. There is so much that is repulsive to the flesh, that nothing but the power of God can fit and sustain His servants in such a sphere, and His blessing alone can give them success."[16] He was coming to learn very concretely one of the principles he and his mission would live by—God will provide what his servants need.

13. Taylor to Amelia Taylor (Mother), July 9, 1853.

14. Taylor to Pearse and Bird, Mar. 2 and 3, 1854.

15. Taylor, *Journal*, March, 1854. Stifling the opium trade became a major cause of his and of the CIM. See Taylor, "Opium and the Gospel: Strange Scene on a River Boat," 30 and Kessler, Review of *Crusaders Against Opium,* 1068–70.

16. Taylor to Pearse, April 22, 1854.

The challenges kept coming. His language skills improved and he started preaching in Chinese;[17] he began to move out among the Chinese, but he found himself hamstrung at every turn. Communication between China and Britain took the better part of a year, reducing decision making to an agonizing process. He and the CES had trouble agreeing on objectives. The mission often did not get money to their missionaries on time and their financial expectations were unclear. Then the bank in which they had their accounts collapsed. All this led to his resigning from the society—"I resign my connection with the society entirely, from this time forth."[18] In reality, it was not as harsh as that sentence sounds. Taylor resigned as fairly and as amicably as possible, and he remained on good terms with the Committee members.

The great joy of this period was Taylor's marriage to Maria Dyer, a missionaries' daughter. Her parents had died, leaving her and her sister in the care of other people.

Hudson and Maria Taylor

No doubt, given Taylor's priorities, his interest was stoked not only by the fact that she was an attractive young woman with a rich supply of

17. Taylor, *Journal*, September 19, 1854.
18. Taylor to Pearse, May 27, 1857.

suitors. She also had a broad and idiomatic grasp on one of the vernacular Chinese dialects, and she was putting this skill and her life experience to good use by teaching in a school operated by a friend. She was also engaging in evangelism on the side.[19] A few months after their wedding in 1858 Taylor was able to tell a friend how well Maria's school was growing,[20] with pleasure, no doubt. It was a match made in heaven.

The marriage was filled with love, respect, mutual support, and passion. Early in his marriage, Taylor wrote, "That I—who have so long been lonely & despised . . . been tried & wronged & persecuted, almost to despair should now be able to clasp to my bosom, *my own*, my precious, my tenderly affectionate wife—such a wife! –who loves me *so* much—I sometimes feel I must be in a dream."[21] And after years of marriage, Maria could close a letter to her husband saying,

> "O how I should like to lie in yr arms. Accept this fond love of
>
> Yr own devoted wifie,
>
> M. J. Taylor."[22]

However encouraging their relationship was, 1860 found them both exhausted and in poor health. Desperately in need of recuperation, they took their baby and headed for Britain. Home was precisely what they needed. As their strength grew, they began to deal with the problem of how they would get back to China. Hudson went back to school and completed medical work and in 1862 was admitted as a Member to the Royal College of Surgeons, licensed in midwifery.[23] In 1865 Taylor created the means of their return—the China Inland Mission. It was bold idea.

Taylor saw the mission as a means of carrying out his own call from God to China. That was basic. He had seen very clearly that he would not be able to do what he wanted to do by himself, so he was looking for "helpers." This was not a missionary society; the people who applied and whom he chose were not members, they were "helpers;" there was to be no committee leading it. There was just J. Hudson Taylor. He was the director of the mission and whatever he decided had to be done, had

---

19  Broomhall, *Shaping Modern China*, 1, 388.

20. Taylor to Pearse, November 18, 1858.

21. Taylor to Amelia Taylor (Mother), May, 13, 1858.

22. Maria Taylor to Hudson Taylor, July 4, 1867.

23. *Medical Register*, 1864, p. 398.

to be complied with. Furthermore, anyone who agreed to come with Taylor was entirely on his own before God in the same way Taylor was. The Principles were outlined and agreed to by the men who been chosen to go to China with Taylor at a meeting in February 2, 1866.[24]

CIM's first contingent of missionaries, the "Lammermuir Party"

Taylor enlarged on this saying, "For our future support we rest on the faithfulness of Him who has sent us to do His work—not *ours*—and we believe that if the work is done faithfully and well we shall have abundant support."[25] Money would be accounted for scrupulously and administration in Britain would be handled by a dear friend, William Berger, who would act for Taylor there.

The idea looked fairly simple. As designed, the burden of leadership fell on Taylor alone—and it almost crushed him. After less than a year on the field, he wrote to his mother saying, "Pray for me, for I much need God's help & guidance—so many look to me & on so many points."[26] He was only thirty-four, but he looked as though he was digging his own grave. The position brought disciplinary matters, and he seemed to handle them well. He did not rush ahead, but gathered information carefully, and then he spoke and acted firmly and gently.[27]

24. "Principles," May 10, 1867. John Sell was absent and none of the women were present—surprising in the light of how the mission developed.

25. Taylor to William Muirhead, December 3, 1866.

26. Taylor to Amelia Taylor (Mother), December 16, 1866.

27. An example would be Taylor to Reid, January 9, 1873.

The CIM grew, and this was demonstrated by the number of missionaries it had in the field. In 1888 the count stood at 332.[28] In two years that had risen to 409, and in 1895 the tally was 621.[29] With that kind of growth an adequate structure simply had to be developed, but it turned out to be rather difficult to do. A Home Council was created in 1872 "For the management of the Home Affairs of the C.I.M."[30] The China Council came in 1883, structuring the work there into districts to make the ministry as effective and efficient as possible,[31] and the Home Council agreed to the developments.[32] 1885 saw the addition of the Auxiliary Council of Ladies, the Auxiliary Council for Scotland, and the Council for North America. These steps for some time actually threatened to blow the Mission apart.[33]

The primary issue was the relative power of the China and the Home Councils. The original idea in the founding of the CIM was that leadership and control must remain in China, and this was a key idea based on Taylor's experience with the CES. However, the Home Council was gradually assuming more power. The issue was not finally resolved until 1893. The Home Council conceded that the China Council was in a better position to lead than it was, and it was assured that its representations would be given careful consideration and attention.[34]

It is clear that we are dealing with a highly creative person. The story of Taylor and the CIM demonstrates just what an innovator he was. I am going to highlight three particular decisions he carried forward which made him stand out among those engaged in missions at the time. They also got him into a lot of hot water.

First, he insisted that women, single or married, could serve actively along side men. There was an abundant supply of outstanding men who poured their lives out in service with the CIM. None caused a greater public stir than the appearance of seven extraordinary young men, six

28. Austin, *China's Millions*, 186.

29. Broomhall, *Shaping Modern China*, 2, 458.

30. "Home Council," Oct. 4, 1872. See also Broomhall, *Shaping Modern China*, 2, 186.

31. Taylor to Members of CIM, August, 1883.

32. Broomhall, *Shaping Modern China*, 2, 448.

33 Austin, *China's Millions*, 349.

34. "Draft," January, 1893 and Broomhall, *Shaping Modern China*, 2, 487.

of whom were associated with Cambridge University—the "Cambridge Seven."[35]

The "Cambridge Seven" in Chinese dress

They all came from the highest levels of British society. One was an aristocrat who would turn down a staggering inheritance so that he could stay in China, another was the star on England's cricket team, two were Church of England clergymen, and another, who had not been at Cambridge, was an officer in the Royal Artillery. These caught the imagination of the media and drew crowds of thousands as they explained why they were turning their backs on brilliant futures to go to China. The women, by contrast, caused an even deeper stir for different reasons.

Taylor had a healthy respect for his own wife, Maria, and he had seen what she could do. When he assembled the first group of eighteen "helpers," known as the "Lammermuir Party" from the name of the ship on which they sailed to China, there were eleven women among them, including nine who were single. He may have been influenced by something he had read of Charles Gutzlaff, a German missionary who had worked extensively in China just before Taylor arrived,[36] or perhaps it grew out of the admiration he had for his sisters and his mother, but wherever it came from, it was almost unique at the time. He had an

35. Stanley P. Smith to J. Hudson Taylor, October 22, 1884. The artillery officer was Dixon Hoste who would succeed Taylor as General Director of the CIM in 1903.

36. Broomhall, *Shaping Modern China*, 1, 146.

experience early in his work in China which might have been significant for the position he took regarding women in ministry.

A young man who had been converted and who had sought baptism had been betrothed for five years. When he went home to start arranging the wedding with his wife to be, he was determined to have a Christian marriage, free from the traditional practices involving the worship of ancient gods. The young woman's family flatly refused and furthermore, refused to release him from the betrothal, so he was caught. If he did not marry the woman in question, he could not marry at all, and if he did marry her, he would have to compromise his Christian faith. One of the assumptions that seems to have been shared among missionaries there at the time was that one could reach families by reaching the men. This experience showed Taylor that this approach certainly did not work all of the time, and it led him to the conclusion that it was essential to create an agency which could work among women.[37]

One of the young women in the Lammermuir party, Jennie Faulding, quickly demonstrated that Taylor's confidence was well placed. It had been difficult for her parents to see her go, but she studied Chinese diligently on the ship out and then eagerly began her work. Within a year of arriving, she wrote to her mother saying, "If I could have fifty lives, I would live them all for poor China in its terrible destitution,"[38] and then later she commented that up to sixty women were attending the Sunday afternoon she was involved with.[39] At the same time a service others were offering to men was drawing about twenty.

Taylor received much criticism for making place for women. One of the most vocal in opposition was G. E. Moule, a Church of England clergyman who would later become a bishop in China. No amount of care in living arrangements or comment by Maria Taylor could blunt the scandal Moule thought he saw in Hudson Taylor's having all these young women around him.[40] He urged young men to leave the mission, he spread his suspicions among associates in China, and when he returned to England on furlough, he did everything he could to discredit Taylor and the CIM. Those who knew Taylor well contradicted Moule's view both in China and at home, and Faulding received excellent coun-

37. Taylor to Pearse, November 6, 1855.
38. Faulding to Faulding (Mother), July 15, 1867.
39. Faulding to Faulding (Mother), October 18, 1867.
40. Faulding to Faulding (Mother), February 23, 1867.

sel from Mary Berger, who worked in the CIM office in Britain with her husband, William—be careful about how you conduct yourself and live the rumors down.[41]

Again and again the CIM women demonstrated their competence and courage. Maria Taylor showed remarkable bravery during a life-threatening riot that we will address later, and she also was Taylor primary confidant and advisor as his ministry developed.[42] In 1878, Jennie Faulding Taylor, whom Hudson had married after Maria's death in China, effectively led a major famine relief program into central China, and in doing so became the first western women to enter that region.[43] He himself remained in London tied up with administration and taking care of their family. A. J. Broomhall provided a summary, saying, "Without doubt in their own minds Hudson Taylor and Jennie believed that the will of God was for women to be at the forefront with the men—and even without them." [44] In 1883, the equality of women and men in seniority in the mission and in the management of affairs on mission stations became CIM policy.[45] Later they laid down their lives along with the men in the tragedy of the Boxer Rebellion—1898 to 1901.[46]

The second area of innovation I will mention is Taylor's insistence that the CIM would identify with the receiving culture, that is, the Chinese culture. He expressed his opinion clearly to candidates applying for acceptance by the CIM in an extended letter written in August, 1867.

The fundamental problem with missions in China, as he saw it, was that dress, behavior, and buildings of missionaries all screamed that Christianity was a foreign religion and that it would turn converts into foreigners. Taylor's response was

41. Berger to Faulding, June 24, 1867.

42. Taylor to Taylor, July 4, 1867.

43. Broomhall, *Shaping Modern China*, 2, 330–35.

44. Broomhall, *Shaping Modern China*, 2, 362.

45. Austin, *China's Millions*, 237.

46. In January, 1900, Empress Dowager Cixi issued an edict legitimizing self-defence societies (Boxers) and vowing to exterminate all secret societies (Protestant and Catholic Christianity). This was done in the context of western imperial incursion. Empress Cixi declared war on western powers on June 21, 1900. (Austin, *China's Millions*, 401). In the chaos that followed, CIM saw 58 of their adults, men and women, and 21 children murdered (JHT/CIM, Box 16, School of Oriental and African Studies, London, United Kingdom). Following the overthrow of the rebellion by military power the CIM submitted its statement of losses as instructed, but then refused to claim or accept any compensation (Broomhall, *Shaping China's Future*, 2, 730).

but why should such a foreign aspect be given to Christianity? The word of God does not require it, nor do I conceive would reason justify it. It is not their denationalization but their Christianization we seek. We wish to see Christian Chinamen and China-women, —true Christians, but withal true *Chinese* in every sense of the word. We wish to see churches and Christian Chinese presided over by pastors and officers of their own coun- trymen, worshipping the true God in the land of their fathers, in their own tongue wherein they were born, and in edifices of a thoroughly Chinese style of architecture.[47]

He argued that Chinese customs and habits had evolved over the cen- turies, growing out of a people's experience of life where they lived. Insisting that the Chinese and their culture must be respected and ac- cepted, he said in the same document, "let us in everything unsinful become Chinese."

This meant for Taylor learning the language, and his correspon- dence documents his struggle.[48] Along with eating and living like the Chinese, it meant dressing like the Chinese. Taylor did not find this easy,[49] and when he first started he wasn't sure if it would make any difference,[50] but he persevered, concluded that it was very helpful, and made it policy for the CIM. There was rebellion within and ridicule outside, but Taylor insisted and by 1870 it had become settled policy to proclaim the message as widely as they could "with a minimal intrusion of foreignness upon the Chinese."[51] The goal, after all, was a Chinese Church. The hope for Christianity in the culture was trained Chinese leadership of churches with the supporting missionary scaffolding being removed when it was no longer needed and taken somewhere else. In one of her letters, Jennie Faulding gave concrete expression to the abstract concept: "We have been forming a native church," she told her mother. "La-djun who reached here on Friday last has been appointed the pas-

---

47. Taylor, "Letter to Candidates," August, 1867. This is a twenty-one page, hand- written document which would later would be modified and published as the *Principles and Practice* of the CIM.

48. See Taylor to Pearse, July 14, 1854 and Taylor to Taylor, August, 7, 1855.

49. Taylor to Amelia Taylor (sister), August 6, 1855.

50. Taylor to Pearse, September 1, 1855.

51. Broomhall, *Shaping Modern China*, 2, 81.

tor," and three other men were elected as elders. Jennie saw it and loved it.[52]

The third example of Taylor's innovative spirit is perhaps the first he thought of—his mission would penetrate the interior of China. The *Treaty of Nanjing (Nanking)* seemed to open the door. The British had wrung it out of the Chinese in 1842, paralyzing their internal trade routes by positioning gunboats at intersections of rivers and canals. Article II of the treaty allowed British citizens to carry on business freely in five designated port cities, and it was in those that most western missionary work was being done. However, Article I also said that subjects of China and the UK "shall enjoy full security and protection for their persons and property within the Dominions of the other." [53] The *Treaty of Tien-Tsin* (1858) went even further. Article XXIX permitted both US citizens and Chinese converts to practice their Christianity without fear of harassment if they were discrete about it; Article XI granted US citizens carrying out their business the protection of the government, while Article XII cautioned people using the appropriate points of entry against going into the country to sell goods.[54] Granted the second treaty referred to US citizens, but for an "up-and-at-'em" kind of missionary like Taylor, this was encouraging.

In the early days, 1854, he still did not know the language, but he just had to get inland. He went in with a friend on June 12 and then in again on June 19. They gave out books and tracts, but he saw a lot of eye disease, and he even operated on one man.[55] Two ideas had begun to fuse: travel inland and medical care go well together. By the end of the year, he was bursting with ideas for ministry. He had made another trip inland, he had bought a furnished boat, and he had seen how much sense it would make to open a couple of schools and not only teach there, but provide medical care also. He even rolled out a plan to build a headquarters, a hospital and a school in Shanghai for about £1000,[56] but the Committee back home was not interested.[57] Then in March, 1855 he and newly-arrived missionary, Dr. William Parker, made an extensive sweep

---

52. Faulding to Faulding (Mother), July 9, 1867.

53. *Treaty of Nanjing*, Article I.

54. *Treaty of Tien-Tsin*, Articles XI, XII, and XXIX.

55. Taylor to Pearse, June 26, 1854.

56. Taylor to Pearse, December 28, 1854.

57. Taylor to Pearse, February 28, 1855.

inland. They visited three cities, three towns, and numerous villages. The trip illustrated the "scarcely-to-be-exaggerated value of medical aid as a help to missionary labour." It gave them access to "a class of respectable persons" who would not have stood at street meetings or struggled in crowds for books.[58] Then in May he made another tour by himself. This time he was away for twenty-eight days. He visited fifty-eight cities, fifty-one of which had never before been visited by a Protestant.[59] A pattern had been established.

When Taylor returned in 1866 as the General Director of CIM, that pattern still gripped him. Late in the year, writing to William Muirhead, he laid out his plan. There were then nineteen CIM agents in China. All but two were "residing away from the free ports,"[60] and he was intending to stay away from those locations and any others already occupied by other missionaries. He aim was "to place at least two missionaries with the same number of native helpers in each unoccupied province of China proper," and later, if no one else went, he would try to extend into "Chinese Tartary," as well as Tibet and Korea. That was his dream, and he never lost sight of it.

The passion remained strong through endless difficulties. Jennie Faulding wrote to her father, reporting how their medical practice got them into trouble occasionally. Rumors spread that they were poisoning children and adults in order to remove their organs and use them for something else. Taylor managed to get a local governmental official to squash the rumors.[61] In August, 1868, a group of CIM people were involved in a major riot in Yangzhou. The most gripping narrative of the events is found in scribbled pencil notes made by Maria Taylor. She was right in the middle of it and pregnant at the time. Acting heroically she saved people from serious injury on two occasions, and she and others had to leap from a second story window to escape from a mob and the flames as the compound burned. She and Henry Reid were injured, he more seriously than she, but they lost most of their belongings. The building they had rented was destroyed, and the incident touched off an international row.[62]

58. Taylor to Pearse, April 2, 1855.

59. Taylor, *Journal*, June 2, 1855.

60. Taylor to Muirhead, December 27, 1866.

61. Faulding to Faulding, March 30, 1867.

62. Maria S. Taylor, August, 1868, William Rudland, August, 1868, and George

The response to this brush with death? The next month Taylor wrote to his mother, saying, "Many of our number are much stirred to press into the interior, & our recent disasters . . . only make us more determined to go on, leaning on the almighty favour of our Captain. Pray for us."[63] A few months later Hudson Taylor and Josiah Jackson climbed a large hill and counted thirty-five towns, villages, and hamlets stretching out before them. Taylor exclaimed to Maria, "When will the gospel reach the dwellers in these places!"[64] It was that kind of concern which drove them forward.

Broomhall commented on CIM's well-developed itinerant approach, referring to the extraordinary distances both men and women travelled.[65] J. E Cardwell could be a prime example of the strategy when in 1871 he travelled widely visiting hundreds of towns and selling thousands of pieces of literature.[66] Broomhall also drew attention to favorable treatment CIM got in the 1881 report submitted by a British official, Consul Challoner Alabaster. Alabaster stated that CIM's constant travelling and keen sensitivity to local situations made it possible for their men and women to live and work in many places. In fact, he claimed that CIM had "shown the true way of spreading Christianity in China"[67]—high commendation and welcome justification.

Without doubt, James Hudson Taylor was an innovator, and he met opposition as innovators often do. In addition, many assumed he was a manipulative, controlling autocrat. As I met him in his letters and in the reflections of others, I really do not think he was. As a human being he made mistakes, of that we can be sure. He was a person with a vision he believed to be from God, and he wanted desperately to carry it through. And it was costly. The most pathetic document I saw among Taylor's papers was the tragic letter in which Taylor tells his three older children who are in Britain of the deaths of two of their brothers and informs them that they are "now motherless."[68] Maria had died in his arms. He buried her and three of their children in China.

---

Duncan, August, 1868.

63. Taylor to Amelia Taylor (Mother), Sept. 13, 1868.

64. Taylor to Maria Taylor, March 22, 1869.

65. Broomhall, *Shaping Modern China*, 2, 352.

66. Broomhall, *Shaping Modern China*, 2, 202.

67. Broomhall. *Shaping Modern China*, 2, 373.

68. Taylor to his children, August 1, 1870. With it is one half of Maria's light brown-

There was of course some degree of compensation. Taylor did marry again. The woman he married was Jennie Faulding, one of the Lammermuir party who had gone to China in 1866 with Hudson and Maria. She became very close to Maria and her family, and in her own ministry she showed she was a strong, intelligent, reliable person. In her Taylor found another wonderful companion, and his love for her grew deep as well. While travelling in North America in 1888, Taylor writhed under his separation from her. He wrote insisting he would not do it for anyone or anything other than Jesus, and he closed saying, "*All*, yes all,—my *best*, my *dearest*, my all, —all for Jesus. Amen! Unutterable love to *my* own, from *her* own."[69]

Some of Taylor's practices had been put into service by others before him and some appeared in the work of others after him. The list includes George Müller, Bartholomew Ziegenbalg, Heinrich Plütschau, Charles Gutzlaff, William Carey, and Henry Venn. Many of those practices and the ideas behind them are the staples of a good missionary program. Taylor's signature contribution was to bring them together and drive them into practice.

## DEVELOPMENTS

The currents to which I pointed earlier in the chapter continued to flow around, behind, and under what Taylor and his associates were doing. Missions persisted as a front-of-mind concern for a lot of Christians and emphases we have noted surfaced here and there. For example, Bishop A. R. Tucker of Uganda (in office from 1890 to 1908) addressed the relationship between the foreign mission and the local church, arguing that there should be genuine equality between the two.

The spiritual intensity we saw in the camp meetings and even in Taylor himself expressed itself as the century unfolded in the Holiness Movement. There were at least two branches. The first had an identifiable Wesleyan flavor related to some of the Methodist responses to the camp meeting. A key issue was achieving sanctification, which by some was understood to mean the complete eradication of the sinful nature. This was often seen to occur as an experience subsequent to conversion. The idea of a "third blessing" arose in the teaching of Benjamin

---

blonde hair which he had saved. He urges that it be treated with great care.

69. Taylor to Jennie Taylor, August 25, 1888.

Irwin (US) and Ralph C. Horner (Canada). It was a baptism for power, and a phrase also used to refer to sanctification, "baptism in/of the Holy Spirit," was also associated with it. It was in this context that Phoebe Palmer (1807–74) carried out her ministry, but she reached beyond the Holiness Movement to a broader audience. She welcomed evangelicals from all denominations.

The second branch of the movement was non-Wesleyan. Its primary home was the Keswick Conference in the Lake District of Britain. The emphasis here was more upon the suppression or overcoming of sinful desire rather than eradication.

Spiritual intensity also became linked to social consciousness. William Booth (1829–1912) moved to London from Wales in 1864. His focus of ministry was the destitute, the street people of his day. In 1880 he founded the Salvation Army. Its emphases were street evangelism and practical, down-to-earth philanthropy. The "Sally Ann" continues to play a key role in many parts of the world today.

Concurrent with this longing for spiritual depth and global missionary outreach, the most significant culture shapers of the twentieth and twenty-first centuries were hard at work. I refer to Marx, Freud, and Nietzsche. Karl Marx (1818–83) wrote *The Communist Manifesto* (with Engels) and *Das Kapital*. Fundamental to his thought is dialectical materialism, an economic theory that sees a determining relationship between modes of material production and the social structure of society. Differing modes of production lead to the stratification of society and to the struggle for dominance among the levels. According to Marx, the social tides of humanity would see feudalism followed by capitalism, which would give way to socialism, to be succeeded in turn by communism in an irresistible current.

There still are Marxists in various places, but the Marxian analysis ultimately failed. Marx expected socialism and then communism to follow capitalism in Britain, but they didn't. On the other hand, in Russia and China society skipped from feudalism to communism and now, perhaps more so in Russia, to capitalism. In the USSR and its satellites, Communism failed to provide for the economic needs of states, and the grand experiment of Russian dominance came to an end, illustrated most vividly by the falling of the Berlin wall. China too has moved from ideological Maoism toward modern capitalism, maintaining much of its socialism structures with the market becoming the new master.

Out of chronological order, but next I will comment on Sigmund Freud (1856–1939). He is famous as one of the chief originators of psychoanalysis. In his interpretation of the human being, mind is the theatre of psychic conflict involving the *Id* (instinct) and the *Superego* (values absorbed from society). The *Ego* regulates the conflict, determining how the desires from instinct can be safely fulfilled. One of the strongest sources of neuroses/psychoses is sexual desire. It is widely recognized that Freud's theories were based on a very small sample of disturbed middle-class Viennese who happened to be women. The general theory has been rejected by most of the psychiatric community, but the centrality of sexuality has continued unabated.

With a German Lutheran background, Friedrich Nietzsche (1844–1900) launched into philosophy and literature, beginning to teach at Basel in 1868. One of his characters, the Madman, proclaimed the death of God, meaning that we now exist in the universe entirely on our own. Nietzsche lived out of a kind of nihilism in which there is no rhyme or reason to human experience. We must become "Overcomers," "Supermen," *Übermenchen*, who recognize the lack of any kind of order in reality and get on with life.

Nietzsche has been called "The most notorious philosopher the world has known," and "A philosopher you can really get excited about." His thinking has gripped a great many others—Theodore Adorno, Henri Bergson, Martin Buber, J.-P. Sartre, Albert Camus. Max Weber, Martin Heidigger—and has been identified by some as the dominant philosophy of the western world today.[70]

## CONCLUSION

The nineteenth century was a truly momentous period of human experience. Science, philosophy, and religion were all erupting in the West together. It was a period of growing tension among ways of looking at reality, among ontological assumptions. On one hand, Christianity with its promise of a relationship with God captured many hearts in the western world and then reached intercontinentally as never before. On the other hand, the culture shapers whom I have mentioned and many of those intellectuals whom they have influenced moved in a very different direction. Standing in a line of thinkers that passes from the

70. "A philosopher you can get excited about," 29.

sixteenth century and through the enlightenment, they share a world view which shrinks reality to that which can be perceived by the human senses. Christianity, like all other religions, is seen as a human construct shaped by materialistic and socio-historical forces. This is the real battle of the Titans.

# 12

# Fire at Azusa

## 1906 AD

### INTRODUCTION

A s we step into the twentieth century and lean toward the twenty-first, there is no relief from the surge of change which both deepens in intensity and speed, training the human family to assume that this is the way we ought to live. The landmarks which once gave a sense of direction and place blur as we flash past them. In the midst of this directionless, super-heated revision of life Pentecostalism was born. For a brief few years the movement was drenched by public curiosity, and then it became one of those pieces that slipped off the table and was lost from sight. For at least one half of its first century the wider public was hardly aware that it existed. No more. It now occupies a growing place in the historical puzzle. Its global proliferation involving millions of members has caught the attention of serious scholarship and stimulated exacting attempts to understand it. This chapter will focus on William Joseph Seymour and his wife, Jennie Evans Seymour who were in the eye of the storm offering guidance as the group was taking its early steps.

### SETTING

It is a cliché to say that the twentieth century dawned with the West riding the crest of a wave of optimism, but it truly was. It is not clear how fully this was understood, but people were entering a world that to all appearances was changing and shrinking at a remarkable pace.

Those who were aware of it probably felt more than a little excitement and maybe even apprehension. Transportation had been revolutionized by the steam engine. Communications now featured the telegraph and the radio, bringing information from around the world with an unprecedented ease. All these inventions rested on the leaps forward that had been made by technology. Neil Postman's warning would have been as relevant then as now: "To be unaware that a technology comes equipped with a program for social change, to maintain that technology is neutral, to make the assumption that technology is always a friend to culture, is, at this late hour [1984], stupidity plain and simple."[1] Then as now, these modern creations were embraced with an astonishing lack of reflection on their possible implications. Humanity was being catapulted into the most intense conversation with itself ever.

It was an era of expanding western power. The UK, France, Germany, and Belgium had all had their tastes of empire, but the new century that was opening up would belong to the United States of America. The USA carved out a sphere of unprecedented international influence, becoming in the eyes of many the epitome of affluence and freedom. Optimism was palpable. The world was progressing, evolving; science and technology were carrying it forward. The work of two scientists among others, Albert Einstein and Ernest Rutherford, opened vistas that swung from the heart of the atom to the extremities of the universe. This was modernity, and it felt good. How merciful that the future was veiled, but it came.

War is what came—the War to End All Wars. It was hideous, and it did not end all wars. According to Norman Davies, 1914 opened a period which lasted until 1945. It was an ". . . era when Europe took leave of its senses."[2] More than 10,000,000 young men died.[3] And this was only the first act of the two act drama, according to Davies. More was coming.

A time of carefree partying followed the war only to be interrupted by the blow of another catastrophe—the Great Depression. Unemployment soared, fortunes were lost, men "rode the rails" from one part of the vast North American continent to another in hopes of finding work. Wild-eyed optimism was hanging on the ropes beaten and bloodied.

1. Postman, *Amusing*, 157.
2. Davies, *Europe*, 897.
3. Davies, *Europe*, 925.

Where was the Church in all this? The Church was alive and active, providing a stabilizing influence in these difficult times. 1910 saw a great international conference of Protestants gathered in Edinburgh. Using the new tools of communication and travel, church representatives had gathered to discuss missionary strategy. Their motto: "Global evangelization in this generation." Western missionaries were engaged in almost every region of the world.

As the twentieth century opened, a new Liberalism held sway in the institutionalized churches on both sides of the Atlantic. In North American, it was dominant in the US from the late nineteenth century, sweeping into Canada later. Liberalism found its most cogent expression in a Social Gospel that emphasized addressing human needs in the here and now. Its champion was Walter Rauchenbush, promising the Kingdom of God through social action.

Some comments by Prof. Douglas Hall are apt here. He quoted H. Richard Niebuhr who argued:

> The romantic conception of the kingdom of God involved no discontinuities, no crises, no tragedies, or sacrifices, no loss of all things, no cross and resurrection. . . . In religion it reconciled God and man by deifying the latter and humanizing the former. . . . Christ the Redeemer became Jesus the teacher or the spiritual genius in whom the religious capacities of mankind were fully developed. . . . Evolution, growth, development, the culture of the religious life, the nurture of the kindly sentiments, the extension of humanitarian ideals, and the progress of civilization took the place of the Christian revolutions. . . . a God without wrath brought men without sin into a kingdom without judgment through the ministrations of a Christ without a cross.[4]

From there, Hall went on to point out that before World War I in an attempt to make itself more acceptable Christianity laid aside words like sin, the demonic, spiritual death, divine wrath, and others, which meant that when the war struck the Church was left without a vocabulary to help the reeling population of Europe to think about what it was experiencing.[5] The death and destruction demonstrated "the sheer

---

4. Hall, "'The Great War,'" 8.
5. Hall, "'The Great War,'" 8.

inadequacy of a faith that had adapted itself too easily to the happy assumptions of modernity."[6]

That war prompted similar thoughts in a Swiss pastor, Karl Barth. As a consequence, he felt himself driven back to Scripture to listen more acutely in order to hear the voice of God again. He did hear, and the result was a new approach to theology known as Neo-orthodoxy.

In the same context Evangelicalism became increasingly self-conscious. Pietism persisted in Germany as did the Evangelical stream in the Church of England. In America, Christians who recognized evangelicalism in each other had begun to organize. As long ago as 1846 The Evangelical Alliance in the United States was formed. Then in the early twentieth century, the strength of Liberalism prompted a response in America. A series of essays known as "The Fundamentals" appeared. There were ninety essays in all, many written by widely-known scholars, which laid out what was believed to be the essentials of orthodox Protestant theology. Finally in 1942 The National Association of Evangelicals was formed. And then, something quite surprising emerged in the Christian story.

## EVENT

"This is a world-wide revival, the last Pentecostal revival to bring our Jesus. The church is taking her last march to meet her beloved."[7] That is an insider's view of one of the key moments in the beginning of a branch of Christianity now often gathered under the name Pentecostalism. A precise definition of Pentecostalism is problematic. I am using the word "Pentecostal" with a capital P to refer to a movement which was important in the appearance of denominations identifiable by that name. In 2000 Barratt and Johnson found 740 of them globally.[8] It is generally agreed that Pentecostals believe that the religious experience of speaking in tongues as found in Acts 2:4 extends through to the present. They believe that the "gifts of the Spirit" mentioned in 1 Cor. 12:6–8 are also to be understood as common Christian experiences, and they believe that God intervenes in human affairs to provide spiritual, emotional, and physical healing. There is much more to be said about these identifying

---

6. Hall, "'The Great War,'" 10.

7. *Apostolic Faith*, September, 1906, 4.

8. Barrett and Johnson, "Global Statistics," 286.

beliefs, but most Pentecostals also accept the primary doctrines of orthodox Christianity, and in many parts of the world, they are expanding into powerful spiritual and social forces.

Along side the capital "P" Pentecostals, there are many other pentecostals who belong to tiny, informal groups drawn together because members hold in common some or all of the above experiences. There are also many others who hold to much the same beliefs, but who are found in older Christian denominations. These are usually referred to as "charismatics." Then there are again those who share these beliefs and experiences, but who stand outside both Pentecostal denominations and the older Christian denominations. They have been called "neocharismatics." We must be cautious, however, in emphasizing these categories too strongly because that might introduce more precision into this stream within Christianity than actually exists. While all sub-groups of this branch would identify themselves with founding moments such as the Acts account, interrelations among them are remarkably complex and fluid.

It may be useful to look at some comments by scholars regarding this branch of Christianity. First, David Martin, an eminent British sociologist who has written extensively on Pentecostalism since 1990: "The most dramatic development of Christianity in the century recently completed has been Pentecostalism and its vast charismatic penumbra."[9] He went on to state that sheer numbers (250,000,000 conservatively) meant that Pentecostalism had "to be placed in the context of other massive religious mobilizations, notably those within Islam but also within Hinduism and Buddhism."[10] Second, historian Mark Noll said, "One of the most momentous developments in the twentieth-century history of Christianity must certainly be the emergence of Pentecostalism as a dynamic force around the world."[11] The third statement comes from Philip Jenkins, who is noted for his acute "big picture" presentations on several religious issues. His impression echoes Martin and Noll: "Since there were only a handful of Pentecostals in 1900, and several hundred million today, is it not reasonable to identify this as perhaps

9. Martin, *Pentecostalism*, 1. See also his "Undermining the Old Principles: Rescripting Pentecostal Accounts."

10. Martin, *Pentecostalism*, 1.

11. Noll, *Turning Points*, 299.

the most successful social movement of the past century?"[12] The last opinion comes from Diarmaid MacCulloch, one of the leading Church historians writing today. He has several significant volumes out on Reformation history, and he has just produced a massive work on the Church in general. MacCulloch wrote, "The rise of Pentecostalism and its Charismatic offshoots was one of the greatest surprises of twentieth-century Christianity—a century when most of the other surprises turned out to be unpleasant."[13] All of these scholars are acknowledging the multiplicity of sub-groups exhibiting a particular Pentecostal spirituality, and the momentousness of their numbers, unprecedented for a religious group in the modern era and beyond.

Using actual numbers and estimates of the various sub-groups involved, it was determined that in 2010 there were 613,010,000 Pentecostals/Charismatics/ Neocharismatics in the world.[14] Two of the researchers who compiled those statistics, Barrett and Johnson, had placed the total in 2000 at 532,767,390,[15] and in that year, the number of Pentecostals alone stood at 65,832,970.[16] There was no figure available for Pentecostals alone in 2010.

As we observe this flourishing stream in the Christian tradition, we see a very diverse and rapidly expanding development. The experiences of two people who were involved early on will help to guide us into the movement at a time predating the appearance of its various streams. They are William Joseph Seymour and his wife Jennie Evans Moore Seymour. William is fairly well known. He was an African American born on May 2, 1870 in Centerville, Louisiana to parents who had been slaves.[17] He died of a heart attack in Los Angeles on September 28, 1922, and at that time his death went largely unnoticed.[18] Very little is known of the details of Jennie's life, apart from the fact that she married William

---

12. Jenkins. *Next Christendom*, 8.

13. MacCulloch, *Christianity*, 914.

14. Johnson, Barrett, and Crossing, "Christianity 2010," 36.

15. Barrett and Johnson, "Global Statistics," 287.

16. Barrett and Johnson, "Global Statistics," 286.

17. Robeck, *Azusa Street*, 17. Many have written about Seymour and the Azusa Street mission, but the work done by Prof. Cecil M. Robeck, Jr. from Fuller Seminary is the definitive study so far. I will be relying heavily on his book.

18. Robeck, *Azusa Street*, 319.

in 1908 and died in Los Angeles in 1936.[19] Their experiences in early Pentecostalism are important in their own right, but they also provide a framework within which we can watch the formative early years of a movement which has become an international phenomenon. We will examine two periods that are sharply contrasted: 1900–6 and 1907–9.

First, we look at the early years, 1900 to 1906. They will take us from Topeka, Kansas to Los Angeles, California. In 1900, twenty-seven year old Charles Fox Parham opened a Bible school in Topeka—"Bro. Parham became convinced that there was no religious school that tallied up with the second chapter of Acts."[20] Early in 1901 extraordinary things began to happen. Under what they perceived to be the touch of God, students began to speak in tongues. Parham described his reaction after he got back to his school and saw what was happening:

> He said they seemed to pay no attention at all to him, and he knelt in one corner and said: 'O God, what does this mean?' The Lord said: 'Are you able to stand for the experience in the face of persecution and howling mobs?' He said: 'Yes, Lord, if you will give me the experience, for the laborer must first be partaker of the fruits.' Instantly the Lord took his vocal organs, and he was preaching the Word in another language.[21]

Here is the very center of the Pentecostal ethos: immediate and direct conversation between God and the believer, and tongues. For Parham this meant that God miraculously gave people the ability actually to speak in foreign languages. He interpreted this as a sign that God wanted the new tongue speakers to go abroad to preach the Gospel.[22] The Pentecostals moved away from this idea fairly soon, but it played an important role in the early days, and the experiences in Topeka gave Parham status. The very first issue of *The Apostolic Faith* named Parham as "God's leader in the Apostolic Faith movement."[23]

As that role was developing Parham travelled for several years, sharing his experiences and his insights. One of those who heard his message and accepted it was William J. Seymour, who had already established a career as a preacher in Holiness circles. Through a series of

19. Robeck, *Azusa Street*, 315.
20. *Apostolic Faith*, October, 1906, 1.
21. *Apostolic Faith*, October, 1906, 1.
22. Goff, "Parham, Charles Fox, " 955.
23. *Apostolic Faith*, September, 1906, 1.

events in April 1906, Seymour found himself in Los Angeles, but locked out of the church to which he had come to minister. He had come with an important set of assumptions that would shape his ministry in Los Angeles. Seymour was non-sectarian; he was convinced of racial equality and of the equality of women and men; he supported the holiness standards of personal behavior; and he taught that there were three ordinances (sacraments)—baptism (by immersion), the Lord's Supper, and foot washing.[24] However, he had accepted Parham's idea that baptism in the Holy Spirit was a third distinct experience after conversion and sanctification, and that it was intended to give a person power to serve Christ. The evidence of this third experience was speaking in tongues. It was tongues that created a predicament for Seymour.[25]

Seymour and some friends continued to meet for prayer. When their meetings got too large, they shifted to 214 (now 216) North Bonnie Brae Street. Both number and intensity increased there, and on April 9, 1906 speaking in tongues appeared, meaning to them that people had received special power from God for service. One of the first to receive was Jennie Evans Moore.[26] Interest in that area of Los Angeles skyrocketed, Seymour himself began to speak in tongues on April 12, 1906, and numbers swelled quickly forcing him and those attending to find a larger place to gather. 312 Azusa Street filled the bill.

Describing events, one commentator said, "The meetings are held in an old Methodist church that had been converted in part into a tenement house, leaving a large, unplastered, barn-like room on the ground floor."[27] The description seems to have been apt. The lower floor had been the stable which had housed the horses of the worshippers who had met upstairs when the building had served as an African Methodist Episcopal Church. It had only an eight or nine foot ceiling.[28] The place was cleaned out, sawdust and straw were spread on the floor, planks were laid across nail kegs and backless chairs and arranged in a square.

24. Robeck, *Azusa Street*, 30. The last of these sounds a little unusual to many, but the practice of foot washing is observed in the Greek Orthodox, Roman Catholic, Anglican, and other Christian bodies on the Thursday of Holy Week (Maundy Thursday). It is celebrated as an ordinance by the Church of God, Cleveland, Tennessee and other Protestant groups.

25. Robeck, *Azusa Street*, 63.

26. Robeck, *Azusa Street*, 68.

27. *Apostolic Faith*, September, 1906, 1.

28. Robeck, *Azusa Street*, 71.

A wooden altar was hurriedly assembled,[29] and a pulpit for Seymour was created by spreading a cotton cloth over a large wooden packing crate used for shipping shoes. A space on the second floor was designated to be a prayer room, and an apartment for Seymour was set up. Everything was ready.[30]

Services started on April 15, 1906, Easter Sunday,[31] and by mid-July between 500 and 700 people were attending services.[32] One observer/ participant, Rev. T. G. Attebury, pastor of People's Church, Los Angeles, and editor/publisher of the paper *The Evangelist*, wrote, "Perhaps no religious movement in the history of this coast has proved of greater interest to the Christian world than that begun and carried on by the Azusa Street Mission of this city under the leadership of Rev. W. J. Seymour." [33] What happened at Azusa has echoed throughout Pentecostalism and its offshoots from that day to this. Joe Creech offered an explanation. He insisted that "Azusa became the central mythic event for early pentecostalism"[34] because, as he explained later, "To pentecostals Azusa signaled, with all the telltale signs, the full outpouring of God's Latter Rain."[35]

"The full outpouring of God's Latter Rain"—in emphasizing this, Creech has caught one of the significant ideas of early Pentecostalism. The concept of a "Latter Rain" as an important feature of events leading to the end of the world appears to have had a rather convoluted history. It wends through the writing of a Chilean Jesuit, Manuel Lacunza, through the ministry of Edward Irving, a Scottish Presbyterian whose ministry electrified many in London in the 1830s, on to John Nelson Darby, a key figure in the Plymouth Brethren, and resurfaces in Charles Fox Parham. In the Acts 2 account of the first Christian Pentecost, Parham and his associates found reference to the outpouring of the Spirit at the end of time in a quotation of Jl 2:28–9, which also says that this will occur in connection with the former and latter rains, or autumn and spring rains, the showers at the beginning and the end of the rainy season (Jl 2:23). Either on their own or with the help of others, Pentecostals came to the

---

29. Robeck, *Azusa Street*, 140.

30. Robeck, *Azusa Street*, 73.

31. Robeck, *Azusa Street*, 75.

32. Robeck, *Azusa Street*, 81.

33. T. G. Attebury, *Apostolic Faith*, November, 1906, 3.

34. Creech, "Visions of Glory," 407.

35. Creech, "Visions of Glory," 421.

conclusion that the first Christian Pentecost was the "Former Rain" and that what they were experiencing was the "Latter Rain." The important conclusion drawn from this was that with the outpouring of the Spirit that they were now experiencing, the stage was now set for the events of the end of the world to begin.

These experiences were hard to describe and even harder to understand. There were charges of fanaticism that hung over the reports of tongues, foreign languages being spoken, prophecies, healings, people lying prostrate for hours, services lasting day and night, amazing conversions, people leaving for mission fields within hours of their "receiving a new language" in Spirit baptism.[36] There is no question but that the meetings were raucous. People believed they were meeting with God in a profound manner, and they were responding spiritually, emotionally, and bodily. One may be pleased or embarrassed, but in and amongst everything that was going on there, perceptions of God and patterns of worship were being forged that encircle the globe today.

The fact of the matter is that religious experiences that overwhelm rational understanding have been with humanity as far back as knowledge extends. Consider Jacob wrestling with the angel and Moses among the clouds, lightening, and thunder on the mountain. These experiences are also found in the New Testament,[37] repeatedly in the Early Church, among the Desert Fathers and Mothers, in Hildegard of Bingen, in St. Teresa of Avila, in John Wesley's meetings, in the massive St. Joseph's Oratory in Montreal, and that list is fragmentary at best. These people at Azusa, including those ranging from the most unpretentious seasonal worker to George Studd, a member of a wealthy, aristocratic British family, felt themselves confronted starkly by the holiness and the love of God.

The second time segment we will consider moves beyond the early years, past 1906. Services continued in much the same manner from

36. *Apostolic Faith*, November, 1906, 2. Robeck reported that approximately two dozen missionaries left during the first year of the revival (Robeck, *Azusa Street*, 241), and he also commented on the tragedies (Robeck, *Azusa Street*, 267–70). Coupled with frequent street meetings held in all conditions (*Apostolic Faith*, October, 1906, 4) this zeal to evangelize in foreign countries embedded a "missional" orientation in Pentecostals that has survived to the present. See Robbins, "Globalization," 117–43.

37. Luke Timothy Johnson offered a perceptive study which shows how much difficulty New Testament scholarship has had with the religious experiences which permeate the New Testament—*Religious Experience in Earliest Christianity*.

1906 until early 1909. What was that short period three-year period like and how has all this been understood since?

The mission's leadership centered around Seymour. *The Apostolic Faith* described him as "simply a humble pastor of the flock over which the Holy Spirit has made him overseer, according to Acts 20:28."[38] It was his voice which was heard most frequently in the mission as he exhorted and encouraged those present, and he was the author of most of the signed and unsigned longer teachings which were published in *The Apostolic Faith.* That meant he was providing for those who came and went the first interpretation of what they were seeing and experiencing.

He was also the one who guided the meetings, preserving whatever order there was. Remember he had never been in anything like this before, and it is quite likely that no one else there had either. He was learning as he taught. He corrected and guided people gently,[39] counseling people to "Keep your eyes on Jesus and not on the manifestations, not seeking to get some great thing more than somebody else."[40] Seymour's strength was in his humility. He prayed for long periods, he affirmed the equality of all who attended, and he gave everyone room to participate.[41]

From about July, 1906 until early 1907, Seymour had surrounded himself with an interracial staff of very capable men and women who planned and carried forward the development of Azusa's ministry.[42] He demonstrated enough ego strength to share leadership, giving these who worked with him space to expand their visions. When most of these moved onto other places in the United States to spread the word of what was happening in Los Angeles, Seymour was left with two African-American women, Sister Prince and his future wife, Jennie Moore; plus two whites, Hiram Smith, a former Methodist and Seymour's closest confidante, and Seymour's secretary and editor of *The Apostolic Faith,* Clara Lum.[43]

---

38. *Apostolic Faith*, December, 1906, 1.

39. Robeck, *Azusa Street*, 111.

40. *Apostolic Faith*, October-January, 1908, 4.

41. Robeck, *Azusa Street*, 90.

42. Robeck, *Azusa Street*, 90.

43. Robeck, *Azusa Street*, 107.

Early leadership team at Azusa St. Mission

Experience seemed to be reinforcing some of the assumptions Seymour had brought to Los Angeles with him. Their paper proclaimed, "One token of the Lord's coming is that He is melting all races and nations together, and they are filled with the power and glory of God."[44] It also contained a long piece in which Seymour argued for the validity of women's ministry—

> It is contrary to the Scriptures that woman should not have her part in the salvation work to which God has called her. We have no right to lay a straw in her way, but to be men of holiness, purity and virtue, to hold up the standard and encourage the woman in her work, and God will honor and bless us as never before. It is the same Holy Spirit in the woman as in the man.[45]

Regrettably, these ideals were not to last for long. Many early Pentecostals opposed them, and they soon came under pressure.[46]

The first three years of the Azusa Street Mission's life must have been filled with both joy and disappointment. Along with the exhilarating services, there was a sense of unity—"The sweetest thing of all is the loving harmony,"[47] and that sentiment was echoed a few months later referring

44. *Apostolic Faith*, February-March, 1907, 7.

45. *Apostolic Faith*, January, 1908, 2.

46. Creech, "Visions of Glory," 410.

47. *Apostolic Faith*, November, 1906,1.

not only to the mission, itself, but several other places of ministry also. The editor said, "We stand as assemblies and missions all in perfect harmony. Azusa Mission stands for the unity of God's people everywhere."[48]

By the time the editor spoke, the bliss had already come under attack, and that was only the beginning of new concerns. Charles Parham had arrived in November 1906 and was shocked at what was going on at the mission. He was appalled with the full racial integration, the role Seymour was playing, and the way they ministered to those who were praying. He attempted to take over the mission, but was thwarted.[49] Things calmed down, but then a year and a half later trusted secretary Clara Lum suddenly took *The Apostolic Faith* and the mission's mailing lists without authorization and left. She went to Portland, Oregon where she joined another of Seymour's former staff members who had established a mission there independently of Azusa Street.[50] In 1912 yet another takeover was attempted by another white preacher, also one who had earlier been baptized in the Spirit at Azusa. W. H. Durham of Chicago came close to succeeding, but Seymour turned aside that attempt also. The sweet harmony of the Spirit had been torn apart by ministerial, personal, and doctrinal struggles.

In the years that followed, Seymour carried on his ministry, but he saw it continually shrinking. When he died on September 28, 1922, Jennie Evans Seymour, whom he had married in 1908, took over the leadership of the mission. Under her ministry the decline in attendance continued. In 1930 yet another takeover was launched, this time by seventy-eight-year old Ruthford D. Griffith. The courts eventually found in favor of Jennie Seymour, but by that time the building on Azusa Street had been torn down and Seymour had taken her small group back to Bonnie Brae Street.[51] Jennie Seymour died on July 2, 1936.

The revival on Azusa Street blazed into existence, electrified innumerable lives, and then over time sputtered and went out. With other "moves of the Spirit" occurring at around the same time elsewhere, it left behind it a movement that in places continues to thrive and grow. The historians and sociologists quoted earlier make that clear. In other places the movement has institutionalized and seen its growth rate decline. In

48. *Apostolic Faith*, January, 1907, 1.

49. Robeck, *Azusa Street*, 127.

50. Robeck, *Azusa Street*, 302–10.

51. Robeck. *Azusa Street*, 320.

some respects Azusa was ahead of its time, particularly in its inclusive views on race and gender.

William and Jennie Seymour

## DEVELOPMENTS

What would soon become a global phenomenon, Pentecostalism, was well underway by 1910. The world it entered and in which its early expansion occurred was dangerous and was also rapidly shrinking by virtue of commercial innovation. As we moved toward the middle of the twentieth century, the general improvement of everything that the earlier optimism had assumed just did not happen. The second half of that European drama to which Norman Davies referred broke out in

1939—World War II. Accompanying the usual horrors of death and destruction in modern warfare were the nightmares of the Nazi concentration camps and the unleashing of the so far ultimate Weapon of Mass Destruction in the Asian theatre. In that and in the scores of internal, factional wars that have followed, chief among them the war which brought Mao se Tung to power in China in 1949 and the Korean War which followed shortly after, the human family had demonstrated repeatedly its skill in ruinous disruption and mass extermination.

Layered with the military and political upheavals came widespread social change. Starting in the late nineteenth century new art forms flourished—"beat" poetry, abstract art, cubism, and atonal music moved into coffee houses and concert halls as the twentieth century gained momentum. Existentialism and Nietzsche radiated from France. In the fifties the marketing world created a new category of human beings— "teenagers." Their musical longings quickly found an outlet in rock and roll and ELVIS. Co-dependent industries, music and communications, erupted featuring records, "45s," "78s," and "LPs," TV, and pop stars. A decade later another wave of music crossed the Atlantic, the Beatles. Coinciding with these sea changes was the beginning of the "baby boom," that bulge of people that began to work its way through the culture. We did not know it in the West, but we were sitting on a volcano. Modernity was feeling the heat. All across Africa, the Caribbean, and elsewhere independence was in the air, bringing a harvest of ideas heavy with the ripe fruit of freedom. With varying degrees of ease and success colonies shook off the hold of their European masters.

The 1960s brought its own special brand of unprecedented change, much of it driven by technology. In China Chairman Mao released the "Cultural Revolution." There was no overlooking the volcano China felt. In absolute contrast to what was happening there, individual rights flew to the top of the agenda in the West. Commenting on an understanding of life that dominated American culture, Robert Bellah and associates painted this picture: "Its center is the autonomous individual, presumed able to choose the roles he [sic] will play and the commitments he [sic] will make, not on the basis of higher truths but according to the criterion of life effectiveness as the individual judges it,"[52] and Bellah referred to American elites as portraying "the devastating

52. Bellah, *Habits of the Heart*, 47.

cultural and psychological narcissism of our current overclass."[53] The fact of the matter is that this is a challenge not only for the Americans, but for the whole of the west.

A further presence exerting its influence was globalization, or rather a merging of westernization and globalization. It is not only western manufacturing jobs and call and service centers that are shifting south and east, but so are western values and assumptions about life. While immigration from the south and the east flocks into the west, there is every indication that the absorption of western lifestyles will accelerate, too. Salaries, ideas, moral expectations, and people are enmeshed in ongoing intercontinental transference. The Davos World Economic Forum was called into existence thirty-eight years ago to watch over these global shifts. It "is an independent international organization committed to improving the state of the world by engaging leaders in partnerships to shape global, regional and industry agendas."[54]

Uncertainty seems to lurk on every hand. Books dealing with "big" subjects continue to roll off the press. I think of those by Thomas Homer-Dixon,[55] who has addressed the Davos Forum on several occasions, and Laurence C. Smith.[56] Along with many others they have given us a sense of the complexities and challenges of our world. In the *Upside of Down*, Homer-Dixon identifies population, energy, environment, climate, and the economy as factors threatening widescale social breakdown.[57] He calls these "tectonic stresses," borrowing a phrase from geology. Smith talks about "four global forces that have been busily shaping our 2050 world for tens to hundreds of years."[58] They are demography, natural resources, climate change, and globalization. These challenges Homer-Dixon and Smith point to are ample causes for anxiety, without having included September 11, 2001 and the potential clash of cultures of which it could be a foretaste.

One certainty in our world is the presence and vitality of religion— much to the surprise of commentators throughout the first half of the

53. Bellah, *Habits of the Heart*, xxxi.

54. On line: http://www.weforum.org/en/about/History%20and%20Achievements/index.htm.

55. *The Ingenuity Gap* and *The Upside of Down*.

56. *The World in 2050*.

57. Homer-Dixon, *The Upside of Down*, 102.

58. Smith, *The World in 2050*, 9.

twentieth century who assured us that its funeral was imminent. The position they argued for was known as the "secularization theory." One of those who maintained that stance but who has since modified his thinking is Peter Berger. In 1999 he said bluntly, "The assumption that we live in a secularized world is false."[59] The weakness of the earlier argument is now widely recognized.

Where is Christianity in the midst of this global uncertainty and the strength of secularizing tendencies? If you look to the South and the East Christianity is erupting, while in the north it is lagging. Comparing the number of Christians in various global regions in 2000 and then in 2010 is informative. The numbers are: Africa—361,649,000 and 470,601,000, a 30.2% increase; Asia—274,626,000 and 347,964,000, a 26.7% increase; Latin America—478,537,000 and 543,150,000, a 13.5% increase; Oceania—21,070,000 and 23,471,000, an 11.4% increase; North America—210,098,000 and 226,885,000, an 8% increase, and Europe—549,529,000 and 560,860,000, a 2% increase.[60] We could spend a long time teasing out explanations and the significance of those numbers, but they are pretty arresting just as they stand. They certainly help to explain the argument of one of Philip Jenkins' books—*The Next Christendom: The Coming of Global Christianity*. In it Jenkins discusses the possibility of Christians on both sides of the south Atlantic, that is, Africa and Latin America, recognizing each other and making some kind of a connection.[61] His point is that they could then become the most significant bloc in global Christianity, a position once occupied by Europe.

That leaves Christians of the North/West something to think about, and of course, the picture is not easy to interpret. In the United States, very useful work is being done by Rodney Stark and the Institute for Studies of Religion at Baylor. They present results showing that in the United States attendance at church by Christians has held steady at 36% since 1973,[62] but simultaneously the number of members per thousand persons in the overall population has fallen for some denominations and risen for others. For example, for the Christian Church (Disciples) between 1960 and 2000 there was a decline of 71% in their number of

59. Berger. "Desecularization," 2.

60. The statistics on which these calculations were made are found in Johnson, "Christianity 2010," 36.

61. Jenkins, *The Next Christendom*, throughout.

62. Stark, "Introduction," 9.

members per thousand of population, but an increase during the same period of 786% for the same period for the Church of God in Christ.[63] Stark observed a not very subtle pattern: conservative churches grow while liberal church decline.[64]

In offering an explanation for that difference in performance, Stark said conservatives do better than liberal churches "Because they work much harder at attracting and holding members. How do they do that? By inspiring their members to witness to others."[65] Another of the Baylor group's studies carried the explanation further. Christopher Bader's work showed that "strict" churches (identical to conservative churches) grow because they make more demands on people, both with reference to what they believe and how they live. The fact that many willingly accept those demands prompts others to conclude that the groups must be offering very satisfying experiences with God.[66] Summarizing, Bader said, "Strict churches are strong because groups that ask more from their members get more from them,"[67] and that benefits the churches in every way.

Some of the work of well-known Canadian sociologist, Reg Bibby, carried this further. The survey research published in one of his recent books showed that a large proportion of Canadian teenagers, he called them the "emerging millennials," could be interested in greater involvement with a religious group if they "found it to be worthwhile." [68] And what would make it worthwhile? Bibby had determined that in earlier work. To be attractive the religious groups have to address the whole of life, the spiritual, the personal, and the social.[69] In fact, the groups that are doing this are the groups that are growing.

Under a commission from the Anglican Church, the late Pierre Berton, well-known in Canada as a journalist and a television personality,

63. Stark, "Church Growth," 22. The Church of God in Christ is the largest African-American Pentecostal denomination in North America.

64. Stark, "Church Growth," 24. He had made similar observations and explained what he meant by "conservative" and "liberal" in an earlier study, Rodney Stark and Charles Y. Glock, *American Piety: The Nature of Religious Commitment* .Berkeley: University of California Press, 1968. See Stark, "Introduction," 1–6.

65. Stark, "Church Growth," 25.

66. Bader, "Strict Churches," 32–35.

67. Bader, "Strict Churches," 36.

68. Bibby, *Emerging Millennials*, 181.

69. Bibby, *Restless Gods*, 187.

published *The Comfortable Pew* in 1965. It was intended to be a provocative and critical book, and in some respects it was. One thought stood out for me. Berton stated that in the second half of the twentieth century "The Church stands in danger of forgetting exactly what [its] message is."[70] Whatever exactly Berton meant by those words, a very similar idea was raised by Robert Bellah, pondering religious conditions in America: "To what extent are the religious communities in America . . . still sufficiently strong as communities to understand the condensed code of their own traditions, or to what extent has the world in which we live so invaded and eviscerated those communities that they have difficulty understanding their own core meanings?" [71] Do they really know who they are or why they exist? If we value the religious life that has been most prominent in North America for the past four hundred years, these questions are troubling.

Harvey Cox has offered a different perspective on these changes. In a paper in which he started off as though he were going to discuss secularization, he shifted the focus to concentrate on religion itself. He noted that religion has not died as some early in the twentieth century were convinced it would. However, he raised the idea that the resurgence of religion might be evidence of something else. He mused that this religious re-emergence, "could . . . mark the beginning of a long and fundamental reordering of worldviews, one in which cultural patterns that have endured since the Enlightenment would be markedly altered or even replaced."[72] He went on, "My own work on this topic has led me to the tentative conclusion that what we are witnessing is *neither* secularization *nor* its opposite ("resacralization"). Rather, it is a *transformation of religion*, a creative series of self-adaptations by religions to the new conditions created by the modernity that some of them helped to spawn."[73]

I see evidence of this subtle self-transformation from most points on the western Christian spectrum. As everywhere, there is tremendous pressure in western culture to conform. This pressure is not new, but technological advances are making it possible for cultural values to be disseminated with an efficiency never before possible. When

70. Berton, *Comfortable Pew*, 98.

71. Bellah, "History of Habit," 215.

72. Cox, "Myth of the Twentieth Century," 139.

73. Cox, "Myth of the Twentieth Century," 139.

Christianity conforms it is rarely, if ever, safe for the Gospel. Cox's suspicions are troubling.

## CONCLUSION

Given the rapid flow of change, the twenty-first century requires Christians like everybody else to be nimble. Yet it will have to be negotiated as all centuries before it were. But it is not enough just to be light on our feet. That is only half the trick. Christians need to learn how to be light *and* deeply informed of their past

# Bibliography

Afonsa. "Selected Letters."*Monumenta Missionaria Africa. Africa Occidental.* Edited by Antonio Brasio Lisboa: Agencia Geral do Ultramar, 1952. 9 vols.

Aguiar, Rui. To King Manuel, May 25, 1516. "Selected Letters." *Monuenta Missionaria Africa. Africa Occiddental.* Lisboa: Agencia Gerl do Ultramar, 1952. 9 vols.

Aigle, Denise. "The Letters of Eijigidei, Hülegü, and Abaqa: Mongol Overtures or Christian Ventriloquism?" *Inner Asia.* 7 (2005) 143–62.

*Allgemeine Literatur-Zeitung.* 187 (June 17, 1796) 658–64. Online: http://zs.thulb .uni-jena.de/servlets/MCRIViewServlet/jportal_derivate_0043276/ALZ_1796_ Bd.1+2_375_A2.tif.?mode=generalLayout&XSL.MCR.Module-iview.move=reset.

*The Apostolic Faith.* In *Like as of Fire.* A reprint of the old Azusa Street papers. Collected by Fred T. Corum. Wilmington, MS, 1981.

Argula von Grumbach. "Letters," *Argula von Grumbach: A Woman's Voice in the Reformation.* Edited by Peter Matheson. Edinburgh: T & T Clark, 1995.

Athanasius. *The Life of Antony and the Letter to Marcellinus.* Translated by Robert C. Gregg. Mahwah, NJ: Paulist, 1980.

Austin, Alvyn. *China's Millions: The China Inland Mission and Late Qing Society, 1832–1905.* Grand Rapids: William B. Eerdmans, 2007.

Ayres, Lewis. "Athanasius' Initial Defense of the Term 'Ομοούσιος: Rereading the *De Decretis.*" *Journal of Early Christian Studies.* 12 (2004) 337–59.

———. "Nicaea and Its Legacy: An Introduction." *Harvard Theological Review.* 100 (2007) 141–44.

Bader, Christopher. "Strict Churches: The Reasons for Their Popularity. In *What Americans Really believe: New Findings from the Baylor Surveys of Religion,* 29–36. Waco: Baylor University Press, 2008.

Balthasar, Hans Urs von. *Razing the Bastions: On the Church in This Age.* Forward Bishop Christoph Schonborn, OP. Translated by Brian McNeill, CRV. San Francisco: Ignatius Press, 1993.

Bardaisan. *The Book of the Laws of Countries Nations.* Edited and Translated by H. J. W. Drijvers. New Introduction by Jan Willem Drijvers. Piscataway, NJ: Gorgias, 2007.

Barrett, D. B. and T. M. Johnson. "Global Statistics." In *The New International Dictionary of Pentecostal and Charismatic Movements: Revised and Expanded* Edition, 284–302. Edited by Stanley M. Burgess and Eduard M. van der Maas. Grand Rapids: Zondervan, 2002.

Bartlett, W. B. *God Wills It! An Illustrated History of the Crusades.* Phoenix Mill: Sutton Publishing, 1999.

Bates, T. R. "Gramsci and the Theory of Hegemony," *Journal of the History of Ideas*. 36 (1975) 351–66.

Bauckham, Richard. "Apocryphal and Pseudepigraphical Literature." *Dictionary of the Later New Testament and Its Developments*, 68–73. Edited by R. P. Martin and P. H. Davids. Downers Grove: InterVarsity Press, 1997.

———. "For What Offence Was James Put to Death?" *James the Just and Christian Origins*, 199–32. Edited by Bruce Chilton and Craig A. Evans. *Supplements to Novum Testamentum*, 98. Leiden, Boston, Köln: Brill, 1999.

———."James and the Gentiles." *History, Literature, and Society in Acts*, 154–84. Edited by Ben Withington, III. Cambridge: Cambridge University Press, 1996.

———."James and the Jerusalem Church." *The Book of Acts in Its Palestinian Setting*, 415–80. Vol. 4, *The Book of Acts in Its First Century Setting*. Grand Rapids: Eerdmans, 1995.

———. "James and Jesus." *The Brother of Jesus: James the Just and His Mission*, 100–37. Edited by Bruce Chilton and Jacob Neuser. Louisville, London: Westminster John Knox Press, 2001.

———. *James: Wisdom of James, Disciple of Jesus the Sage*. London and New York: Routledge, 1999.

———. *Jesus and the Eye Witnesses: The Gospels as Eyewitness Testimony*. Grand Rapids: Eerdmans, 2007.

———. *Jude and the Relatives of Jesus in the Early Church*. Edinburgh: T & T. Clark, 1990;

Baum, Wilhelm and Dietmar W. Winkler, *The Church of the East: A Concise History*. London and New York: Routledge Curzon, 2000.

Baumer, Christoph. *The Church of the East: An Illustrated History of Assyrian Christianity*. Translated by Miranda G. Henry. New York and London: I. B. Tauris, 2006.

———. "Survey of Nestorianism and of Ancient Nestorian Architectural Relics in the Iranian Realm." *Jingjiao: The Church of the East in China and Central Asia*, 445–74. Edited by Roman Malek and Peter Hofrichter in *Collectanea Serica*. Sankt Augustin: Institut Monumenta Serica, 2006.

Bautz, Friedrich Wilhelm. "Francke, August Hermann." *Biographisch-Bibliographisches Kirchenlexikon*, Band II (1990) col. 85–90. No pages. Online: http://www.kirchenlexikon.de/f/francke_a_h.html.

Beck, Hans-Georg. "The Byzantine Church from 886 to 1054." *The Church in the Age of Feudalism*. Translated by Anselm Biggs. Vol.3, *Handbook of Church History*. Edited by Hubert Jedin and John Dolan, 404–25. New York: Herder and Herder, 1969.

———. "The Greek Church in the Epoch of Iconoclasm." *The Church in the Age of Feudalism*. Translated by Anselm Biggs. Vol.3, *Handbook of Church History*. Edited by Hubert Jedin and John Dolan, 26–102. New York: Herder and Herder, 1969.

Bellah, Robert N., Richard Madsen, William M. Sullivan, Ann Swidler, and Steven M. Tipton. *Habits of the Heart: Individualism and Commitment in American Life*. updated ed., Berkley: University of California Press, 1996.

Bellah, Robert N. "History of Habit." In *The Robert Bellah Reader*, 203–20. Edited by Robert N. Bellah and Steven M. Tipton. Durham and London: Duke University Press, 2006.

Berger, Mary to Jennie Faulding, June 24, 1867. CIM/JHT, School of Oriental and African Studies, London, United Kingdom .

Berger, Peter L. "The Desecularization of the World: A Global Overview." *The Desecularization of the World: Resurgent Religion and World Politics*, 1–18. Edited by Peter L. Berger. Grand Rapids: Eerdmans, 1999.

Beverley, James and Barry Moody, Editors. *The Life and Journal of The Rev. Mr. Henry Alline*. Hantsport, NS: Lancelot Press, 1982.

Bibby, Reginald W. with Sarah Russell and Ron Rolheiser. *The Emerging Millennials:How Canada's Newest Generation Is Responding to Change & Choice*. Lethbridge: A Project Canada Book, 2009.

————. *Restless Gods: The Renaissance of Religion in Canada*. Toronto: Stoddart, 2002.

Bidawid, Raphael J. *Les Lettres du Patriarche Nestorien Timothée I*. Vol. 187, *Studi Testi*. Vatican City: Biblioteca Apostolica Vaticana, 1956.

"Biography of Pastor Aaron." In Vol.3, *Halle and the Beginnings of Protestant Christianity in India*, 1401–16. Edited by Andreas Gross, Y. Vincent Kumaradoss, and Heike Liebau. Halle: Frankische Stiftungen, 2006

Bizhen, Xie. "The History of Quanzhou Nestorianism." *Jingjiao: The Church of the East in China and Central Asia*, 257–76. Edited by Roman Malek and Peter Hofrichter in *Collectanea Serica*. Sankt Augustin: Institut Monumenta Serica, 2006.

Blumhofer, Edith L. "Revisiting Azusa Street: A Centennial Retrospect." *International Bulletin of Missionary Research*. 30 (2006) 59–64.

Boehrer, George C. A. "The Franciscans and Portuguese Colonization in Africa and the Atlantic Islands, 1415–99." *The Americas*. 11 (1955) 389–403.

*The Book of Margery Kempe*. Translated by B. A. Windeatt. London: Penguin, 1994.

Bornstein, Daniel E. "Living Christianity." Medieval Christianity, 1-25. Edited by Daniel E. Bornstein. Vol. 4, *A People's History of Christianity*. Edited by Denis R. Janz. Minneapolis: Fortress Press, 2009.

Bossy, John. "The Counter-Reformation and the People of Central Europe." *The Counter-Reformation: the Essential Readings*, 86–104. Edited by David M Luebke. Oxford: Blackwell, 1999.

Boucharlat, Rémy. "Marie-Joseph Steve, *L'île de Khārg, une page de l'histoire du Golfe Persique et du monaschisme oriental*." No pages. Online: http://abstractairanica. revues.org/document3026.html.

Boyarin, Daniel. "Rethinking Jewish Christianity: An Argument for Dismantling a Dubious Category (to which is appended a Correction of my Border Lines)." *Jewish Quarterly Review*. 99 (2009) 7–36.

Brock, Sebastian. "The 'Nestorian' Church: A Lamentable Misnomer." *Bulletin of John Rylands University Library of Manchester*. 78 (1996) 23–35.

Broomhall, A. J. *The Shaping of Modern China: Hudson Taylor's Life and Legacy*. 2 vols. Pasadena, CA: Piquant Editions, 2005. 2 Volumes.

Brown, Peter. *Augustine of Hippo*. 2nd ed. Berkeley: University of California Press, 2000.

————. *The Body and Society: Men, Women and Sexual Renunciation in Early Christianity*. New York: Columbia University Prss, 1988.

Brunner, Daniel L. *Halle Pietists in England—Anthony William Boehm and the Society for Promoting Christian Knowledge*. Göttingen. 1993.

Burstein, Stanley M. "When Greek Was an African Language: The Role of Greek culture in Ancient and Medieval Nubia." *Journal of World Hiastory*. 19 (2008) 41–61.

Chen, Huaiyu. "The Connection Between *Jingjiao* and Buddhist Texts in Late Tang China." *Jingjiao: The Church of the East in China and Central Asia*, 93–113. Edited by Roman Malek and Peter Hofrichter in *Collectanea Serica*. Sankt Augustin: Institut Monumenta Serica, 2006.

Chilton, Bruce. "Epilogue." *The Brother of Jesus: James the Just and His Mission*, 185–6. Edited by Bruce Chilton and Jacob Neuser. Louisville, London: Westminster John Knox Press, 2001.

Chupungco, Anscar J., OSB. "History of the Liturgy Until the Fourth Century." *Introduction to the Liturgy*, 95–113. Vol 1, *Handbook for Liturgical Studies*, the Pontifical Liturgical Institute. Collegeville, Minnesota: Liturgical Press, 1997.

*The Chronicle of Zuqnīn: Parts III and IV, A.D. 488–775.* Translated by Amir Harrak. Vol 36, *Mediaeval Sources in Translation*. Toronto: Pontifical Institute of Mediaeval Studies, 1999.

Clarke, G. W, "Religio Licita," *Anchor Bible Dictionary.* New York: Doubleday, 1992. 5: 665–67.

Clarkson, Thomas and William Allen to Paul Cuffe, July 1, 1812. Paul Cuffee Collection, New Bedford Free Public Library, Box 1.

*The Cloud of Unknowing.* Edited with introduction by James Walsh, S.J. Preface by Simon Tugwell, O.P. *The Classics of Western Spirituality.* Mahwah, N.J.: Paulist Press, 1981.

Codex Theodosianus XVI.1.2. *Creeds, Councils and Controversies: Documents illustrating the history of the Church, Ad 337–461*, 150. Edited by J. Stevenson and revised by W. H. C. Frend. London: SPCK, 1989.

Cohn, Samuel K., Jr. "The Black Death and the Burning of the Jews." *Past and Present.* 196 (2007) 3–36.

Comneno, Maria Adelaide Lola. "Nestorianism in Central Asia During trhe First Millennium:Archaeological Evidence." *Journal of the Assyrian Academic Society.* 11 (1997) 20–67.

Committee of Directors of the African Institute, Aug. 27, 1811. Paul Cuffee Collection, New Bedford Free Public Library, Box 3.

"Constitutions, Fourth Lateran Council—1215," sec. 68. In *Decrees of the Ecumenical Couincils, Volume One*, Nicaea I to Lateran V, 266. Ed. Norman P. Tanner. Washington, D.C.: Georgetown University Press, 1990.

Cowdrey, H. E. J. "Introduction." *The Register of Pope Gregory VII: An English Translation*, 11-16.Trans. H. E. J. Cowdrey. Oxford:Oxford Univeristy Press, 2002.

Cox, Harvey. "The Myth of the Twentieth Century: The Rise and Fall of 'Secularization.'" In *The Twentieth Century: A Theological Overview*, 135–43. Edited by Gregory Baum. Ottawa: Novalis, 1999.

Creech, Joe. "Visions of Glory: The Place of the Azusa Street Revival in Pentecostal History." *Church History.* 65 (1996) 405–24.

Cuffe, Paul. Remarks, Mar. 19, 1811. Rosalind Cobb Wiggins. *Captain Paul Cuffe's Logs and Letters, 1808–1817: A Black Quaker's "Voice from Within the Veil."* Washington, D.C.: Howard University Press, 1996.

———. Remarks, Aug. 27, 1811. Rosalind Cobb Wiggins. *Captain Paul Cuffe's Logs and Letters, 1808–1817: A Black Quaker's "Voice from Within the Veil."* Washington, D.C.: Howard University Press, 1996.

———. Remarks, Aug, 31, 1811. Rosalind Cobb Wiggins. *Captain Paul Cuffe's Logs and Letters, 1808–1817: A Black Quaker's "Voice from Within the Veil."* Washington, D.C.: Howard University Press, 1996.

——— Remarks, Sept. 4, 1811. Rosalind Cobb Wiggins. *Captain Paul Cuffe's Logs and Letters, 1808–1817: A Black Quaker's "Voice from Within the Veil."* Washington, D.C.: Howard University Press, 1996.

————. Remarks, Nov. 24, 1811. Rosalind Cobb Wiggins. *Captain Paul Cuffe's Logs and Letters, 1808–1817: A Black Quaker's "Voice from Within the Veil."* Washington, D.C.: Howard University Press, 1996.

————. Remarks, Dec. 18, 1811. Rosalind Cobb Wiggins. *Captain Paul Cuffe's Logs and Letters, 1808–1817: A Black Quaker's "Voice from Within the Veil."* Washington, D.C.: Howard University Press, 1996

————. Remarks, Dec. 22, 1811. Rosalind Cobb Wiggins. *Captain Paul Cuffe's Logs and Letters, 1808–1817: A Black Quaker's "Voice from Within the Veil."* Washington, D.C.: Howard University Press, 1996

————. Remarks, Dec. 29, 1811. Rosalind Cobb Wiggins. *Captain Paul Cuffe's Logs and Letters, 1808–1817: A Black Quaker's "Voice from Within the Veil."* Washington, D.C.: Howard University Press, 1996.

————to John James and Alexander Wilson, June 10, 1809. Rosalind Cobb Wiggins. *Captain Paul Cuffe's Logs and Letters, 1808–1817: A Black Quaker's "Voice from Within the Veil."* Washington, D.C.: Howard University Press, 1996.

————to William Allen, April 22, 1811. Rosalind Cobb Wiggins. *Captain Paul Cuffe's Logs and Letters, 1808–1817: A Black Quaker's "Voice from Within the Veil."* Washington, D.C.: Howard University Press, 1996.

————to John Cuffe, Aug. 8, 1811. Rosalind Cobb Wiggins. *Captain Paul Cuffe's Logs and Letters, 1808–1817: A Black Quaker's "Voice from Within the Veil."* Washington, D.C.: Howard University Press, 1996.

————to Ann Bonthren, Sept. 4, 1811. Paul Cuffee Collection, New Bedford Free Public Library, Box 1.

————to Augustus Thomas, April 12, 1815. Rosalind Cobb Wiggins. *Captain Paul Cuffe's Logs and Letters, 1808–1817: A Black Quaker's "Voice from Within the Veil."* Washington, D.C.: Howard University Press, 1996.

————to Nathan Lord, April 19, 1815. Old Dartmouth Historical Society Library, Mss.10, Box 1.

————to Thomas and Frances Thompson, Sept. 26, 1815. MS Vol 334, Library of the Religious Society of Friends, London, UK.

————to William Allen, Dec. 4, 1815. Paul Cuffee Collection, New Bedford Free Public Library, Box 1.

————to William Allen, April 4, 1816. Paul Cuffee Collection, New Bedford Free Public Library, Box 3.

————to Jedediah Morse, Aug. 10, 1816. Rosalind Cobb Wiggins. *Captain Paul Cuffe's Logs and Letters, 1808–1817: A Black Quaker's "Voice from Within the Veil."* Washington, D.C.: Howard University Press, 1996.

————to Thomas Wainer, Dec. 26, 1816. Rosalind Cobb Wiggins. *Captain Paul Cuffe's Logs and Letters, 1808–1817: A Black Quaker's "Voice from Within the Veil."* Washington, D.C.: Howard University Press, 1996.

————to William Gibbons, Jan. 16, 1817. Rosalind Cobb Wiggins. *Captain Paul Cuffe's Logs and Letters, 1808–1817: A Black Quaker's "Voice from Within the Veil."* Washington, D.C.: Howard University Press, 1996.

————to James Forten, Mar. 1, 1817. Rosalind Cobb Wiggins. *Captain Paul Cuffe's Logs and Letters, 1808–1817: A Black Quaker's "Voice from Within the Veil."* Washington, D.C.: Howard University Press, 1996.

————.Transactions, July 2, 1812. Rosalind Cobb Wiggins. *Captain Paul Cuffe's Logs and Letters, 1808–1817: A Black Quaker's "Voice from Within the Veil."* Washington, D.C.: Howard University Press, 1996.

Davids, Peter H. "Palestinian Traditions in the Epistle of James." *James the Just and Christian Origins*, 33–57. Edited by Bruce Chilton and Craig A. Evans. *Supplements to Novum Testamentum*, XCVIII. Leiden, Boston, Köln: Brill, 1999.

Davies, Norman. *Europe: A History.* London: Pimlico, 1997.

Dawson, Christopher. "Introduction." *The Mongol Mission: Narrative and Letters of the Franciscan Missionaries in Mongolia and China in the Thirteenth and Fourteenth Centuries*, 7-35. Edited with Introduction by Christopher Dawson. Translated by a Nun of Stanbrook Abbey. *The Makers of Christendom.* London and New York: Sheed and Ward, 1955.

*Decrees of the Ecumenical Councils. Volume One Nicaea I to Lateran V.* Edited by Norman P. Tanner S.J. London and Washington, D.C.: Sheed & Ward and Georgetown University Press, 1990.

*The Deeds of Pope Innocent III by an Anonymous Author.* Translated with introduction and notes by James. M. Powell. Washington, D.C.: Catholic University of America Press, 2004.

Deveneaux, Gustan Kashope. "Public Opinion and Colonial Policy in Nineteenth-Century Sierra Leone. "*The International Journal of African Historical Studies.* 9 (1976) 46–67.

Dickens, Mark. "Syriac Gravestones in the Tashkent History Museum." In *Hidden Treasures and Intercultural Encounters: Studies on East Syriac Christianity in China and Central Asia*, Editors Dietmar W. Winkler and Li Tang, 13–49. Berlin: Lit, 2009.

Dio Cassius, "Epitome of Book LXVII, 14." *Roman History, Books LXI-LXX.* Translated by Earnest Cary. *Loeb Classical Library*, 176. Cambridge, MA and London: Harvary University Press, 2000 (1925).

Doran, Susan and Christopher Durston. *Princes, Pastors and People: the Church and Religion in England, 1500–1700.* 2nd ed. London: Routledge, 2003.

"Draft re. Severance of Missionaries," January, 1893. CIM/JHT, School of Oriental and African Studies, London, United Kingdom.

Duffy, Eamon. *The Stripping of the Altars: Traditional Religion in England c.1400-c.1580.* New Haven and London: Yale University Press, 1992.

————.*The Voices of Morebath: Reformation and Rebellion in an English Village.* New Haven and London: Yale University Press, 2001.

Duncan, George. August, 1868. CIM/JHT, School of Oriental and African Studies, London, United Kingdom .

Dyer, Thomas Henry. *The History of Modern Europe: from the Fall of Constantinople in 1453 to the War in Crimea in 1857.* Vol 2, London: John Murray, 1861.

Erasmus. To the Elector Frederick of Saxony, April 14, 1519." *The Correspondence of Erasmus, Letters 842–992, 1518 to 1519. Collected Works of Erasmus*, 6. Translated by R. A. B. Mynors and D. F. S. Thomson. Annotated by Peter G. Bietenhholz. Toronto & Buffalo: University of Toronto Press, 1982.

Eskilden, Stephen. "Parallel themes in Chinese Nestorianism and Medieval Daoist Religion." *Jingjiao: The Church of the East in China and Central Asia*, 57–91. Edited by Roman Malek and Peter Hofrichter in *Collectanea Serica*. Sankt Augustin: Institut Monumenta Serica, 2006.

Eusebius, *Ecclesiastical History*. *Loeb Classical Llibrary*. 2 Vols. London: Heinneman, 1955.

Ewig, Eugen. "The Western Church from the Death of Louis the Pious to the End of the Carolingian Period." Translated by Anselm Biggs. Vol. 3, *Handbook of Church History*. Edited by Hubert Jedin and John Dolan, 126–73. New York: Herder and Herder, 1969.

Falconbridge, Anna Maria. *Two Voyages to Sierra Leon during the Years 1791–2-3*. London: n.p., 1794. Online:www.archive.org/stream/twovoyagestosieoothorgoog#page/n11/mode/1up.

Faulding, Jennie to Faulding (Mother) February 23, 1867. CIM/JHT, School of Oriental and African Studies, London, United Kingdom .

———. To William Faulding, March 30, 1867. CIM/JHT, School of Oriental and African Studies, London, United Kingdom .

———. To Faulding (Mother), July 9, 1867. CIM/JHT, School of Oriental and African Studies, London, United Kingdom .

———. To Faulding (Mother), July 15, 1867. CIM/JHT, School of Oriental and African Studies, London, United Kingdom .

———. To Faulding (Mother), Oct. 18, 1867. CIM/JHT, School of Oriental and African Studies, London, United Kingdom .

Fiensey, David A. "The Composition of the Jerusalem Church." *The Book of Acts in Its Palestinian Setting*, 213- 36. Vol. 4, *The Book of Acts in Its First Century Setting*. Grand Rapids: Eerdmans, 1995.

Finucane, Ronald C. *Soldiers of the Faith: Crusaders and Moslems at War*. London: Phoenix, 2004.

Frazee, Charles A. "The Origins of Clertical Celibacy in the Western Church." *Church History*. 57 (2005) 108–26.

Frend, W. H. C. *Martyrdom and Persecution in the Early Church: a Study of a Conflict from the Maccabees to Donatus*, 1965. Reprint, Grand Rapids: Baker, 1981.

———. "Pagans, Christians, and 'the Barbarian Conspiracy' of A.D. 367 in Roman Britain." *Britannia*. 23(1992) 121–31.

———. *Rabbinic Judaism and Early Christianity* with *Tradition and Transmission in Early Christianity*. Grand Rapids: Eerdmans, 1998.

Gensichen, Hans-Werner. "Dänish-Hallische Mission." Band VII, *Theologische Realenzyklopädie*. Berlin, New York: Walter de Gruyter, 1981.

———. "Imitating the Wisdom of the Almighty: Ziegenbalg's Progam of Evangelism." *Concordia Theological Monthly*. 28 (1957) 835–43.

Gerhardsson, Birger. *Memory and Manuscript: Oral Tradition and Written Transmission in Rabbinic Judaism and Early Christianity* with *Tradition and Transmission in Early Christianity*. Grand Rapids: Eerdmans, 1998.

———. *Reliability and the Gospel Tradition*. Peabody: Hendrickson, 2001.

———. "The Secret of the Transmission of the Unwritten Jesus Tradition." *New Testament Studies*. 51 (2005) 1–18.

Germann, W. *Ziegenbalg und Plütschau. Die Gründungsjahre der Tranksbarschen Mission. Ein Beitrag zur Geschichte des Pietismus nach handschriftlichen Quellen und ältesten Drucken*. Erlangen: Andreas Diechert, 1868.

Glebe-Møller, Jens. "The Realm of Grace Presupposes the Realm of Power. The Danish Debate about the Theological Legitimacy of Mission." Vol. I, *Halle and the*

*Beginnings of Protestant Christianity in India*, 89–106. Edited by Andreas Gross, Y. Vincent Kumaradoss and Heike Liebau. Halle: Frankische Stiftungen, 2006.

Goff, J. R., Jr. "Parham, Charles Fox (1873–1929)." *The New International Dictionary of Pentecostal and Charismatic Movements: Revised and Expanded Edition*, 955–57. Edited by Stanley M. Burgess and Eduard M. van der Maas, Grand Rapids: Zondervan, 2002.

González, Justo L. *The Changing Shape of Church History*. St.Louis, MI: Chalice Press, 2002.

Gould, Stephen to Thomas Thompson, May 20, 1822. MSS Portfolio 29, 38, 5–7, Library of the Religious Society of Friends, London, UK.

Grant, John Webster. *A Profusion of Spires: Religion in Nineteen-Century Ontario*. Toronto: University of Toronto Press, 1988.

Gray, Richard. "A Kongo Princess, The Kongo Ambassadors and the Papacy." *Journal of Religion in Africa*. 29 (1999) 140–54.

Grebel, Conrad. To Zwingli, July 31, 1518. *The Sources of Swiss Anabaptism: the Grebel Letters and Related Documents*, 63–4. Edited by Leland Harder. Kitchener, ON: Herald Press, 1985.

Gröschl, Jürgen. "Missionaries of the Danish-Halle and English-Halle Missions in India." Translated by Rekha Kamath Rajan. Vol. 3, *Halle and the Beginnings of Protestant Christianity in India*, 1497–1527. Edited by Andreas Gross, Y. Vincent Kumaradoss and Heike Liebau. Halle: Frankische Stiftungen, 2006.

Grzymski, Krzysztof. "Landscape Archaeology of Nubia and Central Sudan." *The African Archaeological Review*. 21 (2004) 7–30.

Hadjar, Abdallah. *The Church of St. Simeon the Stylite and Other Archaeological Sites in the Mountains of Simeon and Halaqa*. Translated Paul J. Amash. Damascus, Syria: Sidawi, n.d.

Hall, Douglas John. "'The Great War' and the Theologians." *The Twentieth Century: A Theological Overview*, 3–13. Edited by Gergory Baum. Ottawa: Novalis, 1999.

Harrak, Amir. "Trade Routes and the Christianization of the Near East." *Journal of the Canadian Society for Syriac Studies*. 2 (2002) 46–61.

Helfman, Tara. "The Court of Vice Admiralty at Sierra Leone and the Abolition of the West African Slave Trade." *The Yale Law Journal*. 115 (2006) 1122–56.

Hengel, Martin. *Acts and the History of Earliest Christianity*. Philadelphia: Fortress,1979.

Herbers, Klaus. "Formosus." *Dictionary of Popes and the Papacy*, 37–8. Edited by Bruns Steimer and Michael G. Parker. Translated Brian McNeil and Peter Heinigg. New York: Crossroad Publishing, 2001.

*Historia Do Congo, Obra Posthuma Do Visconde de Paiva Manso, Documentos*.Lisboa: Typographia de Academia, 1877. Online: http://ia311013.us.archive.org/2/items/ historicdocongodoojorduoft/historiadocongodoojorduoft,pdf.

*History of Bristol County, Massachusetts, with Biographical Sketches of Many of Its Pioneers and Prominent Men*. Compiler: D. Hamilton Hurd. Philadelphia: J. W. Lewis & C., 1883. Online: http://books.google.ca/books/download/history_of_bristol_county_ massachusetts.pdf.

Hollenweger, Walter J. *The Pentecostals*. Translated by R. A. Wilson. London: SCM, 1972.

Homer-Dixon, Thomas. *The Ingenuity Gap*. New York, Toronto: Alfred A. Knopf, 2000.

————. *The Upside of Down: Catastrophe, Creativity, and the Renewal of Civilization.* Toronto: Alfred A. Knopf, 2006.

"Home Council," October 4, 1872. CIM/JHT, School of Oriental and African Studies, London, United Kingdom.

*Howell's State Trials,* vol. 20, 82. Online: http://medicolegal.tripod.com/somersetvsteward .htm#decision.

Hunter, Erica. C. D. "The Church of the East in Central Asia." *Bulletin of the John Rylands University Library.* 78 (1996) 129–42.

Irschick, Eugene F. "Conversations in Tarangambadi: Caring for the Self in Early Eighteenth Century South India." *Comparative Studies of South Asia, Africa and the Middle East.* 23 (2003) 254–70.

James, William. *Varieties of Religious Experience.* New York: Mentor, 1958.

Jayaraman, Lalitha. "Tranquebar Mission's Contribution to Printing & Publishing." No pages. Online: www.gltc.edu/tricentenary/programmes/papers/Lalitha.doc.

Jenkins, Paul. Review of *A German Exploration of Indian Society: Ziegenbalg's "Malarbarian Heathenism* by Daniel Jeyaraj. *International Bulletin of Missionary Research.* 31 (2007) 217.

Jenkins, Philip. *God's Continent: Christianity, Islam, and Eurpoe's Religious Crisis.* Oxford: University Press, 2007.

————. *The Lost History of Christianity: The Thousand-Year Golden Age of the Church in the Middle East, Africa, and Asia—and How It Died.* New York: HarperCollins, 2008.

————. *The Next Christendom: The Coming Global Christianity.* Oxford: Oxford University Press, 2002.

Jeyaraj, Daniel. *Inkulturation in Tranquebar:Die Beitrag der frühen dänisch-halleischen Mission zum Werden einer indisch-einheimischen Kirche (1706–1730).* Erlangen: Verlag der Ev.-Luth., 1996.

Johnson, Luke Timothy. *Religious Experience in Earliest Christianity: A Missing Dimension in New Testament Studies.* Minneapolis: Fortress Press, 1998.

Johnson, Todd M., David B. Barrett, and Peter F. Crossing. "Christianity 2010: A View from the New Atlas of Global Christianity." *International Bulletin of Missionary Research.* 34 (2010) 29–36.

Kelly, J. N. D. *The Oxford Dictionary of Popes.* Oxford: Oxford University Press, 1986.

Kessler, Lawrence. Review of *Crusaders Against Opium: Protestant Missionaries in China, 1874–1917,* by Kathleen D. Lodwick. *The Journal of Asian Studies* 56 (1997) 1068–70.

Kempf, Friedrich. " Changes within the Christian West During the Gregorian Reform." *The Church in the Age of Feudalism,* Translated by Anselm Biggs. Vol.3, *Handbook of Church History.* Edited by Hubert Jedin and John Dolan, 426–72. New York: Herder and Herder, 1969.

————. "The Church and the Western Kingdoms from 900 to 1046." *The Church in the Age of Feudalism,* Translated by Anselm Biggs. Vol.3, Handbook of Church History. Edited by Hubert Jedin and John Dolan, 194–257. New York: Herder and Herder, 1969.

————. "The Gregorian Reform." *The Church in the Age of Feudalism,* Translated by Anselm Biggs. Vol.3, Handbook of Church History. Edited by Hubert Jedin and John Dolan, 355–403. New York: Herder and Herder, 1969.

Kilpatrick, Hilary. "Monasteries through Muslim Eyes: the Diyārāt Books." In *Christians at the Heart of Islamic Rule*, 19–37. Edited by David Thomas. Leiden, Boston: Brill, 2003.

Kilson, Marion. "Cuffe's Social Networks and Entrepreneurial Success." *Exploring Paul Cuffe: The Man and His Legacy, A Public Symposium, Saturday October 3, 2009.* New Bedford, MA, 8–17. Online:www.westporthistory.com/news/archives/000464 .html.

Kinzig, Wolfram. 'Non-Separation': Closeness and Co-operation between Jews and Christians in the Fourth Century." *Vigiliae Christianae*. 45 (1991) 27–53.

Klauser, Theodor. *A Short History of the Western Liturgy: An Account and Some Reflections.* Translated by John Halliburton. 2nd ed. Oxford: Oxford University Press, 1979.

Krodel, Gottfried G. *Letters I, Luther's Works, Vol. 48,* 48 and 205 n. 6. Edited and Translated by Gottfried G. Krodel. Philadelphia: Fortress Press, 1963.

————. *Letters II, Luther's Works, Vol. 49,* 313 n. 11. Edited and Translated by Gottfried G. Krodel. Philadelphia: Fortress Press, 1963.

Kydd, Ronald A. N. *Healing through the Centuries: Models for Understanding.* Peabody, MA: Hendrickson, 1998.

Lamb, H. H. *Climate, History and the Modern World.* 2nd ed. New York: routledge, 1995.

Laue, Theodore H. von. *The World Revolution of Westernization: The Twentieth Century in Global Perspective.* New York: Oxford University Press, 1987.

Le Goff, Jacques. *The Birth of Purgatory.* Translated by Arthur Goldhammer. Chicago: University of Chicago Press, 1981.

Lehmann, D. Arno. *It Began at Tranquebar: The Story of the Tranquebar Mission and the Beginnings of Protestant Christianity in India Published to Celebrate the 250th. Anniversary of the Landing of the First Protestant Missionaries at Tranquebar in 1706.* Translated by M. J. Lutz. Madras: Federation of Evangelical Lutheran Churches in India, 1956.

*The Letters of Hildegard of Bingen, Vol 2.* Translated by Joseph L Baird and Radd K. Ehrman. New York Oxford: Oxford University Press, 1998.

"The Letters of John of Monte Corvino." *The Mongol Mission: Narrative and Letters of the Franciscan Missionaries in Mongolia and China in the Thirteenth and Fourteenth Centuries,* 224–28. Edited with Introduction by Christopher Dawson. Translated by a Nun of Stanbrook Abbey. The Makers of Christendom. London and New York: Sheed and Ward, 1955.

*Les Lettres de 1289 and 1305 des ilkan Argun et Öljëit ü ä Philippe le Bel.* Harvard – Yenching Institute, *Scripta Mongolica*, Monograph Series I. London: Oxford University Press, 1962.

Lieu, Samuel N. C. "Nestorian Remains from Zaitun (Quanzhou), South China." In *Jingjiao: The Church of the East in China and Central Asia,* 277–91. Edited by Roman Malek and Peter Hofrichter. *Collectanea Serica*. Sankt Augustin: Institut Monumenta Serica, 2006.

*Life of William Allen with Selections from His Correspondence in Two Volumes.* Philadelphia: Longstreth, 1847. 2 vols.

Lock, Peter. *The Routledge Companion to the Crusades.* London and New York: Routledge, 2006.

Lockett, James D. "The Deportation of the Maroons of Trelawny Town to Nova Scotia, then Back to Africa." *Journal of Black Studies.* 30 (1999) 5–14.

Lockes, Perry to Paul Cuffe. July 13, 1816. Rosalind Cobb Wiggins. *Captain Paul Cuffe's Logs and Letters, 1808–1817: A Black Quaker's 'Voice from Within the Veil.'"* Washington, D.C.: Howard University Press, 1996.

Luebke, David M. "Introduction," *The Counter-Reformation: The Essential Readings*, 1–16. Oxford: Blackwell, 1999.

Luther, Martin. "Between June 12 and July 12, 1532, No. 1654." *Table Talk, Luther's Works, vol. 54,* 160. Ed. And Trans. Theodore G. Tappert. Philadelphia: Fortress Press, 1967.

————. "The Freedom of a Christian." *Martin Luther:Selections from His Writings*, 52–85. Edited with Introduction John Dillenberger.New York: Anchor Books, 1962.

————.To Frederick the Wise, January 5 or 6, 1519. *Letters I, Luther's Works, Vol. 48,* 96–100 . Edited and Translated by Gottfried G. Krodel. Philadelphia: Fortress Press, 1963.

————. To John von Staupitz, February 20, 1519. *Letters I, Luther's Works, Vol. 48,* 108. Edited and Translated Gottfried G. Krodel. Philadelphia: Fortress Press, 1963.

————. To George Spalatin, October 12, 1520. *Letters I, Luther's Works, Vol. 48,* 181. Edited and Translated Gottfried G. Krodel. Philadelphia: Fortress Press, 1963.

————. To Katie, June 5, 1530. *Letters II, Luther's Works*, Vol. 49, 312. Edited and Translated Gottfried G. Krodel. Philadelphia: Fortress Press, 1972.

MacCulloch, Diarmaid. *Thomas Cranmer: A Life.* New Haven & London: Yale University Press, 1996.

————. *Christianity: The First Three Thousand Years.* New York: Viking, 2010.

————. *Reformation: Europe's House Divided, 1490–1700.* London: Allan Lane, 2003.

Magnússon, Sigurdur Gylfi. "The Singularization of History: Social History and Microhistory within the Postmodern State of Knowledge." *Journal of Social History.* 36 (2007) 1–35.

Markham, Paul. "The Battle of Manzikert: Military Disaster or Political Failure?" No pages. Online: http://www.deremilitari.org/resources/articles/markham.htm.

Marriage Certificate, Paul Cuffee Collection, New Bedford Free Public Library, Box 3.

Martin, David. *Pentecostalism: The World Is Their Parish.* Oxford: Blackwell Publishing, 2002.

————. "Undermining the Old Principles: Rescripting Pentecostal Accounts." *PentecoStudies.* 5 (2006) 18–38. Online: http://www.glopent.net/pretecostudies/2006/dmartin2006. pdf.view.

The Martyrdom of Saints Perpetua and Felicitas. In *The Acts of the Christian Martyrs,* 107-31. Translated by Herbert Musurillo. Oxford: Clarendon Press 1972.

Matheson, Peter, Editor. *Argula von Grumbach: A Woman's Voice in the Reformation.* Edinburgh: T and T. Clark, 1995.

————. "Language of the Common Folk." *Reformation Christianity,* 259–83. Edited by Peter Matheson.Vol. 5, *A People's History of Christianity.* Minneapolis: Fortress, 2007.

————. "Martin Luther and Argula von Grumbach (1492–1556/7)." *Lutheran Quarterly.* 22 (2008) 1–15.

Matthew of Paris. *Matthew Paris's English History from the Year 1235–1273.* Translated by J. A. Giles. London: george Bell & Sons, 1889. Vol. 2.

McKnight, Scot. "A Parting within the Way: Jesus and James on Israel and Purity." *James the Just and Christian Origins,* 83-129. Edited by Bruce Chilton and Craig A. Evans. *Supplements to Novum Testamentum,* 98. Leiden, Boston, Köln: Brill, 1999.

McVeigh, Malcolm J. "The Early Congo Mission." *Missiology: An International Review.* 3 (1975) 501–18.

*The Medical Register.* London, 1864.

*Memoirs of the Life and Gospel Labours of Stephen Grellet.* Edited by Benjamin Seebohm. Philadelphia: Henry Longstreth, 1867. 2 vols. Online: www.archive.org/strteam/memoirsligeandgooseebgoog#page/n10/mode/1up.

"Memoirs of the Life of Paul Cuffee (sic), the Interesting Negro Navigator. *The Belfast Monthly Magazine* 7, 39 (Oct 31, 1811) 284–92. Online: http://www.jstor.org/stable/30074388.

Minns, Denis and Paul Parvis. *Justin, Philosopher and Martyr: Apologies.* Oxford: Oxford University Press, 2009.

Misevich, Philip. "The Sierra Leone Hinterland and the Provisioning of Early Freetown, 1792–1803." *Journal of Colonialism and Colonial History.* 9 (2008) 1–8. Online: Http://muse.jhu.edu/journals/journal_of_colonialism_and_colonial_history/v009/9.3.miseviche.html.

Mitchell, Margaret M. "From Jerusalem to the Ends of the Earth." In *Origins of Christianity,* Edited by Margaret Mary Mitchell and Frances Margaret Young, 295–301. *The Cambridge History of Christianity.* Cambridge: Cambridge University Press, 2006.

Moffett, Samuel H. *A History of Christianity in Asia, Volume I: Beginnings to 1500.* Maryknoll, N.Y.: Orbis Books, 1998.

Myllykoski, Matti. "James the Just in History and Tradition: Perspectives on Past and Present Scholarship (part I)." *Currents in Biblical Research.* 5 (2006) 73–122.

*The Navy List, Corrected to The End of December, 1814.* (By Authority of the Admiralty-Office) London: John Murray, 1815. http://books.google.ca/books?id=OxYYAAA MAAJ8&pg=PA130&lpg=PA130&dq=judge+robert+thorpe&source=bl&sts=r4d zWpGWt6&sig=073ukSmzx2bM7WrK6NLx-17pyRg&hl=pn&€

Nestingen, James A. "Gnesio-Lutherans" The Oxford Encyclopedia of the Reformation. Edited by Hans J. Hillerbrand. Oxford University Press,1996. http://www.oxfordreference.com/views/ENTRY.html?subview=Main&entry=t172.e0582.

*Njal's Saga.* Translated by Magnus Magnusson and Hermann Pálsson. Harmondsworth, UK: Penguin Books, 1960.

Nicolini-Zani, Matteo. "Past and Current Research on Tang *Jingiao* Documents: A Summary." *Jingjiao: The Church of the East in China and Central Asia,* 23–44.. Edited by Roman Malek and Peter Hofrichter in *Collectanea Serica.* Sankt Augustin: Institut Monumenta Serica, 2006.

Nietzsche, Friedrich. *The Gay Science (The Joyful Wisdom).* No pages. Online: http://ebooks.adelaide.edu.au/n/nietzsche/friedrich/n67j/book 3.html#section169.

Noll, Mark A. *Turning Points: Decisive Moments in the History of Christianity.* 2nd ed. Grand Rapids: Baker Academic, 2000.

Nørgaard, Anders. "The Mission's Relationship to the Danes." *It Began in Copehhagen: Junctions in 300 Years of Indian-Danish Relations in Christian Mission,* 43–100. Edited by George Oommen and Hans Raun Iversen.Delhi: ISPCK, 2005.

Oberman, Heiko A. *Luther: Man between God and the Devil.* New York: Doubleday (Image), 1992.

O'Donnell, James J. *Augustine: A New Biography.* New York: CCCO, 2005.

Pabst, Erika. "The Wives of Missionaries: Their Experiences in India." Translated by Rekha Kamath Rajan. Vol.2, *Halle and the Beginnings of Protestant Christianity in India*, 685–704. Edited by Andreas Gross, Y. Vincent Kumaradoss and Heike Liebau. Halle: Frankische Stiftungen, 2006.

Painter, John. "Who Was James? Footprints as a Means of Identification." *The Brother of Jesus: James the Just and His Mission*, 10–65. Edited by Bruce Chilton and Jacob Neusner. Louisville, London: Westminster John Knox Press, 2001.

Palmer, Martin, *et al. The Jesus Sutras: Rediscovering the Lost Scrolls of Taoist Christianity*. New York: Balantine Wellspring, The Random House Publishing Group, 2001.

Parry, Ken. "The Art of the Church of the East." *Jingjiao: The Church of the East in China and Central Asia*, 321–33. Edited by Roman Malek and Peter Hofrichter in *Collectanea Serica*. Sankt Augustin: Institut Monumenta Serica, 2006.

Pedersen, Johannes. *De forste sammenstod mellem ordhodoksi og pietisme*. Band V in Danske Kirkes Histoire. n.p., 1951.

Pelikan, Jaroslav. *The Emergence of the Catholic Tradition (100–600). The Christian Tradition: A History of the Development of Doctrine*, Vol 1. Chicago and London: The University of Chicago Press, 1971.

———. *The Growth of Medieval Theology (600–1300). The Christian Tradition: A History of the Development of Doctrine*, Vol 3. Chicago and London: The University of Chicago Press, 1978.

Phillips, David. "Comparative Historical Studies in Education: Problems of Periodisation Reconsidered." *British Journal of Educational Studies*. 50 (2002) 363–77.

"A philosopher you can get excited about." Advertisement, *The New York Times Book Review*. October 8, 2006, 29

Pope Urban II. *The Collection Britannica, and the Council of Melfi (1089)*. Robert Somerville in collaboration with Stephan Kuttner. Oxford: Clarendon Press, 1996.

Postman, Neil. *Amusing Ourselves to Death: Public Discourse in the Age of Show Business*. New York: Penguin, 1985.

———. *Technopoly: The Surrender of Culture to Technology*. New York: Alfred A. Knopf, 1992.

Potts, D.T. "Kharg Island." No pages. Online: http://www.iranica.com/articles.ot_grp5/ot_khrag_20040224.html.

*Principles*, May 10, 1867. CIM/JHT, School of Oriental and African Studies, London, United Kingdom.

Pybus, Cassandra. "'One Militant Saint': the Much Travelled Life of Mary Perth." *Journal of Colonialism and Colonial History*. 9 (2008) 1–7." http://muse.jhu.edu/journals/journal_colonialism_and_colonial_history/v009/9.3.pybus.html.

Rajak, Tessa. "Was There a Roman Charter for the Jews? *The Journal of Roman Studies*, 74 (1984), 107–23.

Rajan, Rekha Kamath. "Cultural Delimitations: The Letters and Reports of Bartholomäus Ziegenbalg." Vol. 3, *Halle and the Beginnings of Protestant Christianity in India*, 1221–39. Edited by Andreas Gross, Y. Vincent Kumaradoss and Heike Liebau. Halle: Frankische Stiftungen, 2006.

Rawlyk, George A. *Nova Scotia's Massachusetts: A Study of Massachusetts-Nova Scotia Relations, 1630–1784*. Montreal and London:McGill-Queen's University Press, 1973.

———.*Ravished by the Spirit: Religious Revivals, Baptists, and Henry Alline*. Kingston and Montreal: McGill-Queen's University Press, 1984.

*The Register of Pope Gregory VII: An English Translation*. Translated by H. E. J. Cowdrey. Oxford: Oxford University Press, 2002.

Reinhardt, Wolfgang. "The Population Size of Jerusalem and the Numerical Growth of the Jerusalem Church." *The Book of Acts in Its Palestinian Setting*, 237–63. Vol. 4, *The Book of Acts in Its First Century Setting*. Grand Rapids: Eerdmans, 1995.

Reynolds, Gabriel Said. "A Medieval Islamic Polemic Against Certain Practices and Doctrines of the East Syrian Church: Introduction, Excerpts and Commentary." *Christians at the Heart of Islamic Rule*, 215–30. Edited by David Thomas. Leiden, Boston: Brill, 2003.

Reynolds, Rosalind Jaeger. "Reading Matilda: The Self-Fashioning Duchess." *Essays in Medieval Studies*. 19 (2002) 1–13.

Riley-Smith, Jonathan. "The Crusades, 1095–1198." *The New Cambridge Medieval History, Volume 4, Part 1, c. 1024–1198*, 534–63. Edited by David Luscombe and Jonathan Riley-Smith. Cambridge: Cambridge University Press, 2004. 17 May 2010 DOI:101017/CHOL9780521414104.015.

Robbins, Joel. "The Globalization of Pentecostal and Charismatic Christianity." *Annual Review of Anthropology*. 33 (2004) 117–43,

Robeck, Cecil M., Jr. *The Azusa Street Mission and Revival: The Birth of the Global Pentecostal Movement*. Nashvill, TN: Thomas Nelson, 2006.

"Royal Appointment and Instructions to the First Missionaries." Vol. 3, *Halle and the Beginnings of Protestant Christianity in India*, 1337–9. Edited by Andreas Gross, Y. Vincent Kumaradoss and Heike Liebau. Halle: Frankische Stiftungen, 2006.

Rubenson, Samuel. *The Letters of St. Antony: Monasticism and the Making of a Saint*. Edited and Translated by Samuel Rubenson. Minneapolis: Fortress Press, 1990.

Rubenstein, Jay, "Cannibals and Crusaders." *French Historical Studies*. 31 (2008) 435–552.

Rudland, William. August,1868. CIM/JHT, School of Oriental and African Studies, London, United Kingdom .

Saqaf, Syed Muthahar. "Tercentenary of Tranquebar Mission." *The Hindu*, July 6, 2006. No pages. Online: http://www.google.ca/Imgres?ingurl=http://www.hindu.com/2006/07/06.

Schneemelcher, Wilhelm, Editor. *New Testament Apocrypha*. English translation edited by R. McL. Wilson. Cambridge: James Clarke, 1991 and 1992. 2 vols.

Scholz, Sebastian. " Christopher." *Dictionary of Popes and Papacy*, 20. Edited by Brono Steimer and Michael G. Parker. Trans. Brian McNeill and Peter Heinigg. New York: Crossroads Publishings, 2001.

Séjourné, P. "Reliques, "*Dictionnaire de théologie catholique*. Edited by A. Valcant *et al.* Paris: Letouzey and Ané, 1939. Vo. 52.

[Sharp, Granville]. *A Short Sketch of Temporary Regulations (Until Better Shall Be Proposed) for the Intended Settlement on the Grain Coast of Africa, Near Sierra Leona*. 2nd ed, London: H. Baldwin, 1786. Online: archive.org/stream/shortsketchtempooshargoog#page/n182/mode/1up.

Singh, Brijraj. "'One Soul tho' not one Soyl'? International Protestantism and Ecumenism at the Beginning of the Eighteenth Century." *Studies in Eighteenth Century Culture* 31 (2002) 61–84.

Smith, Stanley P. to J. Hudson Taylor, October 22, 1884. CIM/JHT, School of Oriental and African Studies, London, United Kingdom.

Smith, Laurence C. *The World in 2050: Four Forces Shaping Civilization's Northern Future*. New York: Dutton, 2010.

Southern, R. W. *Western Society and the Church in the Middle Ages.* Grand Rapids: Eerdmans, 1970.

Socrates Scholasticus. "The Ecclesiastical History." Revised A. C. Zenos. *A Select Library of Nicene and Post-Nicene Fathers of the Christian Church, Second Series,* Vol. 2, 1–178. Edited by Philip Schall and Henry Wace. Grand Rapids: Eerdmans, 1957.

Sozomen. "The Ecclesiastical History." Revised by Chester D. Hartranft. . *A Select Library of Nicene and Post-Nicene Fathers of the Christian Church, Second Series,* Vol. 2, 233–437. Edited by Philip Schall and Henry Wace. Grand Rapids: Eerdmans, 1957.

Spalatinus, Georgius. "To Erasmus, December 11, 1516." *The Correspondence of Erasmus, Letters 446–593, 1516–1517. Collected Works of Erasmus,* 4. Translated by R. A. B. Mynors and D. F. S. Thomason, Annotated by Peter G. Bietenholz. Toronto and Buffalo: University of Toronto Press, 1977.

Spaulding, Jay. "Medieval Christian Nubia and the Islamic World: A Reconsideration of the Baqt Treaty." *The International Journal of African Historical Studies.* 28 (1995) 577–94.

Stark, Rodney. "Church Growth: Competing for Members." *What Americans Really Believe: New Findings from the Baylor Surveys of Religion,* 21–28. Waco: Baylor University Press, 2008.

———. "Introduction: The Stability and Diversity of American Faith." *What Americans Really Believe: New Findings from the Baylor Surveys of Religion,* 1–14. Waco: Baylor University Press, 2008.

———. "Religious Effects: In Praise of 'Idealistic Humbug.'" *Review of Religious Research* 41 (2000) 289–310.

Stofferahn, Steven. "Staying the Royal Sword: Alcuin and the Conversion Dilemma in Early Medieval Europe." *Historian.* 71 (2009 461–80.

Strauss, Gerald. "The Religious Policies of Dukes Wilhelm and Ludwig of Bavaria in the First Decade of the Protestant Era." *Church History.* 28 (1959) 350–73.

Tabbernee, William. *Montanist Inscriptions and Testimonia: Epigraphic Sources Illustrating the History of Montanism.* Vol. 16, *North American Patristic Society Patristic Monograph Series.* Macon: Mercer University Press, 1997.

Tacitus, *Annals,* XV.44.2–8 J. Stevenson, Editor. *A New Eusebius: Documents Illustrating the History of the Church to AD 337,* revised by W. H. C. Frend. London: SPCK, 1987. 2–3.

Tamcke, Martin. "Heinrich Plütschau: The Man in Ziegenbalg's Shadow." Vol. 2, *Halle and the Beginnings of Protestant Christianity in India,* 547–66. Edited by Andreas Gross, Y. Vincent Kumaradoss and Heike Liebau. Halle: Frankische Stiftungen, 2006.

Tang, Li. "A Preliminary Study on the *Jingjiao* Inscription of Luoyang: Text Analysis, Commentary and English Translation." *Hidden Treeasures and Intercultural Encounters: Studies on East Syriac Christianity in China and Central Asia,* 109–33. Edited by Dietmar W. Winkler and Li Tang. Berlin: Lit, 2009.

———. "Sorkaktani Beki: A Prominent Nestorian Woman at the Mongol Court." *Jingjiao: The Church of the East in China and Central Asia.* 349–55. Edited by Roman Malek and Peter Hofrichter in *Collectanea Serica.* Sankt Augustin: Institut Monumenta Serica, 2006.

———. *A Study of the History of Nestorian Christianity in China and its Literature in Chinese: Together with a New Englaish Translation of the Dun huang Nestorian*

*Documents.* 2nd. Revised edition. Vol. 87, *Series XXVII Asian and African Studies of European University Studies.* Frankfurt am Main: Peter Lang, 2004.

Taylor, J. Hudson. *Journal.* CIM/JHT, School of Oriental and African Studies, London, United Kingdom.

———. Letter to Candidates, August, 1867. CIM/JHT, School of Oriental and African Studies, London, United Kingdom.

———. "Opium and the Gospel in China: Strange Scene on a River Boat." *Britain's Crime against China: A Short History of the Opium Traffic.* Edited by Maurice Gregory, 30. London: Dyer Brothers, 1892.

———. To Amelia Taylor, (Mother) December 2, 1849. CIM/JHT, School of Oriental and African Studies, London, United Kingdom.

———. To Amelia Taylor, (Mother) November 11, 1850. CIM/JHT, School of Oriental and African Studies, London, United Kingdom.

———. To George Pearse, April 25, 1851. CIM/JHT, School of Oriental and African Studies, London, United Kingdom.

———. To Amelia Taylor (Mother), August 27, 1852. CIM/JHT, School of Oriental and African Studies, London, United Kingdom.

———. To Amelia Taylor (Mother), October 11, 1852. CIM/JHT, School of Oriental and African Studies, London, United Kingdom.

———. To Amelia Taylor (Mother), June 5, 1853. CIM/JHT, School of Oriental and African Studies, London, United Kingdom

———. To Amelia Taylor (Mother), June 19, 1853. CIM/JHT, School of Oriental and African Studies, London, United Kingdom.

———. To Amelia Taylor (Mother), July 9, 1853. CIM/JHT, School of Oriental and African Studies, London, United Kingdom.

———. To George Pearse and Charles Bird, March 2 and 3, 1854. CIM/JHT, School of Oriental and African Studies, London, United Kingdom.

———. To George Pearse, April 22, 1854. CIM/JHT, School of Oriental and African Studies, London, United Kingdom.

———. To George Pearse, June 26, 1854. CIM/JHT, School of Oriental and African Studies, London, United Kingdom.

———. To George Pearse, July 14, 1854. CIM/JHT, School of Oriental and African Studies, London, United Kingdom

———. To George Pearse, December 28, 1854. CIM/JHT, School of Oriental and African Studies, London, United Kingdom.

———. To George Pearse, February 28, 1855. CIM/JHT, School of Oriental and African Studies, London, United Kingdom.

———. To George Pearse, April 2,1855. CIM/JHT, School of Oriental and African Studies, London, United Kingdom.

———. To Amilia Taylor (Sister) August 6, 1855. CIM/JHT, School of Oriental and African Studies, London, United Kingdom

———. To James Taylor (Father), August 7, 1855. CIM/JHT, School of Oriental and African Studies, London, United Kingdom.

———. To George Pearse, September 1, 1855. CIM/JHT, School of Oriental and African Studies, London, United Kingdom.

———. To George Pearse, November 6, 1855. CIM/JHT, School of Oriental and African Studies, London, United Kingdom.

———. To George Pearse, May 27, 1857. CIM/JHT, School of Oriental and African Studies, London, United Kingdom.

———. To Amelia Taylor (Mother), May 13, 1858. CIM/JHT, School of Oriental and African Studies, London, United Kingdom.

———. To George Pearse, November 18, 1858. CIM/JHT, School of Oriental and African Studies, London, United Kingdom.

———. To William Muirhead, December 3, 1866. CIM/JHT, School of Oriental and African Studies, London, United Kingdom.

———. To Amelia Taylor (Mother), December 16, 1866. CIM/JHT, School of Oriental and African Studies, London, United Kingdom .

———. To William Muirhead, December 27,1866. CIM/JHT, School of Oriental and African Studies, London, United Kingdom.

———. To Amelia Taylor (Mother), September 13, 1868. CIM/JHT, School of Oriental and African Studies, London, United Kingdom .

———. To Maria Taylor, March 22, 1869. CIM/JHT, School of Oriental and African Studies, London, United Kingdom .

———. To His Children in London, August 1, 1870. CIM/JHT, School of Oriental and African Studies, London, United Kingdom .

———. To Henry Reid, January 9, 1873. CIM/JHT, School of Oriental and African Studies, London, United Kingdom.

———. To Members of the CIM, August 24, 1883. CIM/JHT, School of Oriental and African Studies, London, United Kingdom.

———. To Jennie Taylor, August 25, 1888. CIM/JHT, School of Oriental and African Studies, London, United Kingdom.

Taylor, Maria S. August, 1868. CIM/JHT, School of Oriental and African Studies, London, United Kingdom .

———. To Hudson Taylor, July 4, 1867. CIM/JHT, School of Oriental and African Studies, London, United Kingdom.

Tertullian, *A Treatise on the Soul.* Edited by J. H. Waszink. Amsterdam: J. M. Meulenhoff, 1947.

Thomas, David. "Introduction." *Christians at the Heart of Islamic Rule,* vii–xiv. Edited by David Thomas. Leiden, Boston: Brill, 2003.

Thompson, Frances to Paul Cuffe, March 22, 1814. Paul Cuffee Collection, New Bedford Free Public Library, Box 2.

Thompson, Glen L. "Was Alopen a 'Missionary'"? *Hidden Treasures and Intercultural Encounters: Studies on East Syriac Christianity in China and Central Asia,* Editors Dietmar W. Winkler and Li Tang, 267–78. Berlin: Lit, 2009.

Thornton, John. "African Political Ethics and the Slave Trade." No pages. Online: www. millersville,edu/~winthorp/Thornton.html.

———. "The Development of an African Catholic Church in the Kingdom of Kongo, 1491–1750." *The Journal of African History.* 25 (1984) 146–67.

———. "Early Kongo-Portuguese Relations: A New Interpretation." *History in Africa.* 8 (1981) 183–204.

———. "Origins and Early History of the Kingdom of the Kongo, c. 1350–1550." *The International Journal of Arican Historical Studies.* 34 (2001) 89–120.

———. *Warfare in Atlantic Africa, 1500–1800.* London: Uniferisty College London Press, 1999.

Thorpe, Robert, Esq. *A Reply "Point by Point" to the Special report of the Directors of the African Institution.* London: F.C. & J. Rivington, 1815. Online: www.archive.org. details/areplypintbypooothorgoog.

Timothy I. "The Apology of Timothy the Patriarch before the Caliph Madhi." Trans. A. Mingana in Woodbrooke Studies, in *Bulletin of the John Rylands Library.* 12 (1928) 137–298.

———. "Eiusdem ad Monachos Monasteri Mār Māronis," *Les Lettres du Patriarche Nestorien Timothée I: Étude Critique.* Edited and Translated by Raphael J. Bidawid, 91–125. Vol. 187, *Studi Testi.* Vatican City: Biblioteca Apostolica Vaticana, 1956.

———. *Les Lettres du Patriarche Nestorien Timothée I: Étude Critique.* Raphael J. Bidawid. Vol. 187, *Studi Testi.* Vatican City: Biblioteca Apostolica Vaticana, 1956.

Tomkins, Stephen. *John Wesley: A Biography.* Grand Rapids: Eerdmans, 2003.

Torjesen, Karen Jo. *When Women Were Priests: Women's Leadership in the Early Church and the Scandal of Their Subordination in the Rise of Christianity.* SanFrancisco: Harper, 1995.

*Treaty of Ninjing (Nanking),* 1842. Online: www.international.ucla.edu/eas/documents/ nanjing.htm. No pages.

*Treaty of Tien-Tsin,* June 18, 1858. Online: http:/web.jjay.cuny.edu/~jobrien/reference/ ob27.html. No pages.

Trevett, Christine. *Montanism: Gender, Authority and the New Prophecy.* Cambridge: University Press, 1996.

Trobisch, David. *The First Edition of the New Testament.* Oxford: University Press, 2000.

Turner, Michael J. "The Limits of Abolition: Government, Saints and the 'African Question,' c.1780–1820." *The Englsih Historical Review.* 112 (1997) 319–57.

Vermander, S.J., Benoit. "The Impact of Nestorianism on Contemporary Chinese Theology." *Jingjiao: The Church of the East in China and Central Asia,* 180–94. Edited by Roman Malek and Peter Hofrichter in *Collectanea Serica.* Sankt Augustin: Institut Monumenta Serica, 2006.

Vööbus, Arthur. "The Origin of Monasticism in Mesopotamia." *Church History.* 20 (1951) 27–37.

Wallace, Peter G. *The Long European Reformation: Religion, Political Conflict, and the Search for Conformity, 1350–1750.* New York:Palgrave Maxmillan, 2004.

Walls, Andrew F. "Mission, VI Von der Reformationzei bis zur Gegenwart." Band XXIII, *Theologische Realenzykopädie,* 40–47. Berlin, New York: Walter de Gruyter, 1994.

———. *The Missionary Movement in Christian History: Studies in the Transmission of Faith.* Maryknoll, New York: Orbis Books, 1996.

Wang, Ding. "Remnants of Christianity from Chinese Central Asia in Medieval Ages." *Jingjiao: The Church of the East in China and Central Asia,* 149–62. Editors Roman Malek and Peter Hofrichter, in *Collectanea Serica.* Sankt Augustin: Institut Monumenta Serica, 2006.

Westport Meeting House; Cost to Build, 1813. Paul Cuffee Collection, New Bedford Free Public Library, Box 3.

Whalen, Brett. "Rethinking the Schism of 1054: Authority, Heresy, and the Latin Rite." *Traditio.* 62 (2007) 1–24.

Wiggins, Rosalind Cobb. *Captain Paul Cuffe's Logs and Letters, 1808–1817: A Black Quaker's "Voice from Within the Veil."* Washington, D.C.: Howard University Press, 1996.

William of Rubruck. "The Journey of William Rubruck." *The Mongol Mission: Narrative and Letters of the Franciscan Missionaries in Mongolia and China in the Thirteenth and Fourteenth Centuries*, 89–220. Edited with Introduction by Christopher Dawson. Translated by a Nun of Stanbrook Abbey. *The Makers of Christendom*. London and New York: Sheed and Ward, 1955.

Williams, Rowan. *On Christian Theology*. Oxford: Blackwell Publishers, 2000.

Williams, William A. *The Tragedy of American Diplomacy*. Cleveland & New York: World, 1959.

Wood, Gordon S. *The Purpose of the Past: Reflections on the Uses of History*. New York: The Penguin Press, 2008.

Wright, N. T. *The Resurrection of the Son of God*. Vol. 3, *Christian Origins and the Question of God*. Minneapolis: Fortress Press, 2003.

Yuanyuan, Wang. "Doubt on the Viewpoint of Extinction of Nestorianism After the Tang Dynasty." Paper read at the Third International conference on the Church of the East in China and Central Asia, Salzburg, Austria, June 4–9, 2009.

Zeigenbalg, Bartholomäus. Bartholomäus Ziegenbalg to Linde, September 5, 1706. *Alte Briefe aus Indien: Unveröffentliche Briefe von Bartholomäus Ziegenbalg, 1701–1719*. Edited by D. Arno Lehmann. Berlin: Evangelische Verlagsanstalt, 1957.

———. Bartholomäus Ziegenbalg to Friends, September 5, 1706. *Alte Briefe aus Indien: Unveröffentliche Briefe von Bartholomäus Ziegenbalg, 1701–1719*. Edited by D. Arno Lehmann. Berlin: Evangelische Verlagsanstalt, 1957

———. To Friends, September 18, 1706. *Alte Briefe aus Indien: Unveröffentliche Briefe von Bartholomäus Ziegenbalg, 1701-1719*. Edited by D. Arno Lehmann. Berlin: Evangelische Verlagsanstalt, 1957.

———. Bartholomäus Ziegenbalg to ? September 25, 1706. *Alte Briefe aus Indien: Unveröffentliche Briefe von Bartholomäus Ziegenbalg, 1701–1719*. Edited by D. Arno Lehmann. Berlin: Evangelische Verlagsanstalt, 1957.

———. Bartholomäus Ziegenbalg to A. H. Francke, October 1, 1706. *Alte Briefe aus Indien: Unveröffentliche Briefe von Bartholomäus Ziegenbalg, 1701–1719*. Edited by D. Arno Lehmann. Berlin: Evangelische Verlagsanstalt, 1957.

———. Bartholomäus Ziegenbalg to Frederick IV, September 19, 1707. *Alte Briefe aus Indien: Unveröffentliche Briefe von Bartholomäus Ziegenbalg, 1701–1719*. Edited by D. Arno Lehmann. Berlin: Evangelische Verlagsanstalt, 1957.

———. Bartholomäus Ziegenbalg to D. Joachim Breithaupt, D. Paul Antonius and A. H. Francke, September 22, 1707. *Alte Briefe aus Indien: Unveröffentliche Briefe von Bartholomäus Ziegenbalg, 1701–1719*. Edited by D. Arno Lehmann. Berlin: Evangelische Verlagsanstalt, 1957.

———. Bartholomäus Ziegenbalg to F. J. Lütkens, August 22, 1708. *Alte Briefe aus Indien: Unveröffentliche Briefe von Bartholomäus Ziegenbalg, 1701–1719*. Edited by D. Arno Lehmann. Berlin: Evangelische Verlagsanstalt, 1957.

———. Bartholomäus Ziegenbalg to D. Joachim Breithaupt, D. Paul Antonius and A. H. Francke, October 1, 1708. *Alte Briefe aus Indien: Unveröffentliche Briefe von Bartholomäus Ziegenbalg, 1701–1719*. Edited by D. Arno Lehmann. Berlin: Evangelische Verlagsanstalt, 1957.

———. Bartholomäus Ziegenbalg to J. Lange, August 19, 1709. *Alte Briefe aus Indien: Unveröffentliche Briefe von Bartholomäus Ziegenbalg, 1701–1719*. Edited by D. Arno Lehmann. Berlin: Evangelische Verlagsanstalt, 1957.

————. Bartholomäus Ziegenbalg to A. H. Francke, October 1, 1709. *Alte Briefe aus Indien: Unveröffentliche Briefe von Bartholomäus Ziegenbalg, 1701–1719.* Edited by D. Arno Lehmann. Berlin: Evangelische Verlagsanstalt, 1957

————. Bartholomäus Ziegenbalg to J. Lange, October 7, 1709. *Alte Briefe aus Indien: Unveröffentliche Briefe von Bartholomäus Ziegenbalg, 1701–1719.* Edited by D. Arno Lehmann. Berlin: Evangelische Verlagsanstalt, 1957.

————. Bartholomäus Ziegenbalg to Rektor Weitzmann, October 7, 1709. *Alte Briefe aus Indien: Unveröffentliche Briefe von Bartholomäus Ziegenbalg, 1701–1719.* Edited by D. Arno Lehmann. Berlin: Evangelische Verlagsanstalt, 1957.

————. Bartholomäus Ziegenbalg to Lange, October, 23, 1709. *Alte Briefe aus Indien: Unveröffentliche Briefe von Bartholomäus Ziegenbalg, 1701–1719.* Edited by D. Arno Lehmann. Berlin: Evangelische Verlagsanstalt, 1957.

————. Bartholomäus Ziegenbalg to Frederick IV, December 28 , 1713. *Alte Briefe aus Indien: Unveröffentliche Briefe von Bartholomäus Ziegenbalg, 1701–1719.* Edited by D. Arno Lehmann. Berlin: Evangelische Verlagsanstalt, 1957.

————. *Thirty-Four Conferences between the Danish Missionaries and the Malabarian Bramans (or Heathen Priests)in the East Indies, Concerning the Truth of the Christian Religion: Together with some LETTERS Written by the Heathens to the Said Missionaries.* Trans. Mr. Philipps. London: W. Fleetwood, 1719.

# Index